the
digital
divide

*Arguments for and
Against Facebook, Google,
Texting, and the
Age of Social Networking*

the
digital
divide

EDITED AND INTRODUCED BY
Mark Bauerlein

>>>

JEREMY P. TARCHER/PENGUIN

a member of Penguin Group (USA) Inc.
New York

JEREMY P. TARCHER/PENGUIN
Published by the Penguin Group
Penguin Group (USA) Inc., 375 Hudson Street, New York, New York 10014, USA · Penguin Group (Canada), 90 Eglinton Avenue East, Suite 700, Toronto, Ontario M4P 2Y3, Canada (a division of Pearson Penguin Canada Inc.) · Penguin Books Ltd, 80 Strand, London WC2R 0RL, England · Penguin Ireland, 25 St Stephen's Green, Dublin 2, Ireland (a division of Penguin Books Ltd) · Penguin Group (Australia), 250 Camberwell Road, Camberwell, Victoria 3124, Australia (a division of Pearson Australia Group Pty Ltd) · Penguin Books India Pvt Ltd, 11 Community Centre, Panchsheel Park, New Delhi–110 017, India · Penguin Group (NZ), 67 Apollo Drive, Rosedale, North Shore 0632, New Zealand (a division of Pearson New Zealand Ltd) · Penguin Books (South Africa) (Pty) Ltd, 24 Sturdee Avenue, Rosebank, Johannesburg 2196, South Africa

Penguin Books Ltd, Registered Offices: 80 Strand, London WC2R 0RL, England

Most Tarcher/Penguin books are available at special quantity discounts for bulk purchase for sales promotions, premiums, fund-raising, and educational needs. Special books or book excerpts also can be created to fit specific needs. For details, write Penguin Group (USA) Inc. Special Markets, 375 Hudson Street, New York, NY 10014.

Library of Congress Cataloging-in-Publication Data

The digital divide: arguments for and against Facebook, Google, texting, and the age of social networking/edited and introduced by Mark Bauerlein.
    p.   cm.
Includes bibliographical references and index.
ISBN 978-1-58542-886-1
1. Digital divide. 2. Technological innovations—Social aspects. 3. Social networks. I. Bauerlein, Mark.
HM851.D524   2011   2011019688
303.48'33—dc23

Printed in the United States of America
10 9 8 7 6 5

Book design by Lucy Albanese

contents

section two: social life, personal life, school

section three: the fate of culture

<Mark Bauerlein>

introduction

MARK BAUERLEIN is a professor of English at Emory University. His books include *Literary Criticism: An Autopsy* (1997) and *Negrophobia: A Race Riot in Atlanta, 1906* (2001). His essays have appeared in *PMLA*, *Partisan Review*, *Wilson Quarterly*, and *Yale Review*, and his commentaries and reviews have appeared in *The Wall Street Journal*, *The Washington Post*, *The Weekly Standard*, *Reason* magazine, and elsewhere. More information can be found at www.dumbestgeneration.com.

IN EARLY 2011, *The Wall Street Journal* published an excerpt from a book called *Battle Hymn of the Tiger Mother*, a treatise on the superiority of "Chinese mothers" over "Western mothers," written by Yale law professor Amy Chua. The book excerpt was clearly intended to court controversy, but the exact way that that controversy played out illustrated well the new ways we communicate.

Within hours, it seemed, the article had exploded in op-eds, blogs, and follow-up stories from *The New Yorker* to NPR to *Newsweek* to angryasianman.com, with reactions ranging from enraged to regretful to cheering. The author's eldest daughter defended her mother in an effusive testimonial in the *New York Post*. I just Googled "Amy Chua" and 544,000 results came up. Most amazing of all, perhaps, was the response of readers—not the content, but the quantity. At the present moment, fully 6,901 comments have piled up on the website beneath the excerpt. And of course, as all this unfolded, the hardcover edition of *Tiger Mother* climbed to #4 on Amazon. The book had only been available for a week.

For all the hoopla, however, we may be certain that in a few more days, attention will shift elsewhere to other affairs. That's the pace of news in the digital era. The ups and downs of current events run steeper and faster, as if a roller coaster were squeezed into a smaller space. Ballyhooed controversies happened before the Web came along, but they didn't arise, expand, and deflate so quickly and voluminously, and with so many participants in the process. In the days of print-only, the excerpt would have taken days or weeks to circulate to other journalists, and reader responses would have amounted to several dozen letters to the editor, three of them selected for publication in a later edition. By comparison, today's communication travels at light speed, and any edgy, comic, or otherwise quirky story or video can "go viral." Everybody can weigh in and say almost anything they want.

What does it mean? How are we to understand the change—or, perhaps more important, *what* is it that we are supposed to understand? What stands out in this case is that sublime number on the comments ledger: 6,901. It signifies the provocative nature of the excerpt and a watchful, interactive audience. The process sounds unequivocally positive, especially given the conditions the *The Wall Street Journal* sets for comments. "Community Rules" disallow anonymity, and "You must demonstrate appropriate respect" (no vulgarity). Violators are banned. As a result, comments there are thoughtful and critical.

Still, one has to wonder about the purpose of so many people writing so many things about a 2,500-word newspaper piece. It's a new phenomenon, unique to the Digital Age, and it calls for examination. Some of the contributors to this volume would maintain that this is democracy in action, meritoriously so. That ordinary people have the chance to speak back and have their opinions published at one of the nation's leading newspapers can only enhance civic life. Others, however, question what *Journal* readers think when they encounter 4,383 comments to a news story and believe that post #4,384 really matters. Is this democratic participation or fruitless vanity?

The writings in this anthology address that and many other questions. They present a range of judgments about the Digital Age and digital tools and behaviors that have enveloped our waking hours. Indeed, whenever people consider the marvelous and unprecedented ways that the Digital Age has transformed our lives, they should keep that curious fact in mind. However sweeping and abrupt the changes are, most individuals have absorbed them with dispatch. The flood of digital tools was and is mighty and abrupt, but adults and youths generally behave as if it has always been thus. Calmly and expertly, they wield devices and form habits that were inconceivable only ten or twenty years ago.

And it has happened so quickly. Cell phones, e-mail, the Web, YouTube, and the rest have speeded up communications, shopping, photographing, and studying, and they have also quickened the conversion of each new and desirable invention into a regular part of life. At a clip that would stun a pre-1980 person, novelties promptly become customs. One or another of them may mark a fabulous breakthrough, but they don't stand out for long as striking advances in the march of technology. Soon enough they settle into one more utility, one more tool or practice in the mundane course of job and leisure. How many decades passed between the invention of the telephone and its daily use by 90 percent of the population? Today, the path from private creation to pandemic consumption is measured in months.

Consider the Facebook phenomenon. The network dates back to 2004, but seems to have been around forever. In six years it has ballooned from a clubby undergraduate service at Harvard into a worldwide enterprise with more than 500 million users. It already has acquired a "biography," chronicled in the hit film *The Social Network* and books *The Facebook Effect: The Inside Story of the Company That Is Connecting the World* and *The Accidental Billionaires: The Founding of Facebook—A Tale of Sex, Money, Genius, and Betrayal.* Co-founder Marc Zuckerberg garnered *Time* magazine's 2010 Person of the Year award. A 2010 Harris Interactive poll of eighteen- to twenty-four-year-olds ranked Facebook #2 for brand familiarity and quality (Google came in first). In the month of April 2003, Americans spent zero minutes on Facebook. In April 2009, they logged 13,872,640,000 minutes.

Or think about the rise of texting among the young. In September 2008, Nielsen reported that thirteen- to seventeen-year-olds with a mobile device averaged 1,742 text messages per month. A few months later, Nielsen raised the total to 2,272 texts per month, and by mid-2009 teens passed the 2,500 marker. In October 2010, Nielsen set the monthly amount at 3,339. At that pace, consumer behavior signals a lot more than convenience or trendiness.

Note, too, yet another sign of mass adoption: the astounding dominance of Wikipedia, the online encyclopedia. It opened shop only ten years ago, but now contains some seventeen million entries (according to the Wikipedia entry on Wikipedia). In 2008, educator Michael Petrilli tested Wikipedia's popularity by choosing one hundred terms from U.S. and world history (The Mayflower Compact, Anwar Sadat, etc.) and typing them into Google. A Wikipedia entry came up first for eighty-seven (!) of them, second for twelve of them, and third once. Since the top spot in any Google search attracts 42 percent of all "click-throughs" (as AOL reported in a data release a few years back), Wikipedia's first-choice status is clear. What didn't exist in 2000 is now the towering source in civic and historical matters.

The popularity of these sites and actions has a paradoxical side effect. They appear altogether ordinary. People use them too much to register for very long their wondrous arrival. The content of a YouTube video or a text message may amuse or assist or shock a user, but YouTube itself and texting per se do not. Digital tools have proven so efficient and compelling and helpful that it now requires a leap of imagination to recall what life was like before their advent. It takes extreme, headline-grabbing cases to provoke popular recognition of the general impact, positive and negative, of Web tools on individuals and society. When in September 2010, for instance, two Rutgers University students secretly live-streamed a classmate in a sexual act with another man, prompting him to jump to his death off the George Washington Bridge, the episode became a vehicle for scrupulous discussions of harassment and privacy in the Digital Age for weeks. During the 2009 elections in Iran when individuals in the country used Twitter and Facebook as instruments of protest, organizing dissent online, spreading news past the firewalls of the state, and displaying vivid and hideous images of police crackdown, some observers christened it the Twitter Revolution.

Such episodes, newsworthy though they are, don't inspire balanced judgments of various benefits and pitfalls of the Web. When anonymous users turn message boards at *The New York Times* or Sarah Palin's Facebook page into playgrounds of rage and resentment, or when an offbeat, bullied high school kid goes online and finds far-off voices of sympathy, it is easy to render a verdict. When the 2009 U.S. National Texting Championship goes to a fifteen-year-old Iowan who honed her craft by averaging 14,000 texts per month, one might laugh or nod in dismay. It is harder to appreciate the Digital Age in its less dramatic occasions.

Of course, skepticism about the benefits of digital technology has but a limited field of application. The miraculous advances in medicine, finance, communications, logistics, travel, and dozens of other professions and industries render the overarching question "What is the significance of digital technology—is it good or bad?" ridiculous. Only in areas in which values and norms come into play does the debate, cast in such stark terms, have any substance. The deep assumptions and fundamental dispositions—how we think, what we expect, how we relate to others, and where we stand in the universe—are where we may usefully evaluate the Digital Age.

They are best approached through ordinary behaviors. If you walk into a coffee shop, order a latte, and sit down for an hour with the newspaper, you may find one of them right beside you. A twenty-year-old woman has a coffee in hand, too, but she's gazing at the screen of her laptop. Nothing unusual about that, but the common appearance shouldn't blind you to the phenomenal destiny she represents.

First of all, her activity is unknown. Everyone knows what you are doing—you can't read the paper and do anything else. Her tool, though, allows her to do a dozen different things, including reading what you're reading. She looks the same whether she reads a book, buys a book, or checks Facebook. This reclusiveness in public spaces is an important feature of digital conduct. It explains the frequent and annoying phenomenon of people in public handling private matters, for instance, an intimate cell phone call carried out in a doctor's waiting room and overheard by everyone there. One shouldn't blame the users too much for it, however (I've been guilty myself). The tool encourages it. Others can see and hear the user, but they don't know what flashes on the screen or sounds through the speaker. In the middle of a crowd, the user enjoys a semi-private relationship with things beyond.

There is an ominous corollary to this mode of withdrawal. It allows her to sip her coffee, enjoy the mild music in the room, and smile at passersby, all the while viewing and committing uncivil acts online, if she so chooses. Her real appearance may be prim and genteel, but her online focus might fall on the juvenile and uncouth. Perhaps she frequents sites such as collegeabc.com, the college gossip site filled with entries such as this one relating to my home institution: "Who is the shittiest person at emory?" Or she ends a courteous exchange with a busboy by turning to Lady Gaga on

YouTube moaning, "I want your ugly, I want your disease . . ." ("Bad Romance," with more than 335 million page views).

Nobody can tell, and that precise shelter removes one of the long-standing curbs on vicious conduct, namely, exposure. For the bare truth is that young people act well not so much from virtuous motives within as from social judgments without. The disapproving looks of others keep their lesser intentions in check. Not anymore. She can go anonymous in the virtual sphere and join the cyber-bullying, mobbing, and swearing, all the while appearing entirely decorous in the public sphere of the coffeehouse. The sites she enjoys have no gatekeepers, but that's not all. With the screen disengaging her from the surroundings, others nearby have no gatekeeping power.

These are just a few speculations about screen experience, and none of them are decisive. Neither do they establish whether each development is a good or bad one. We are called to do so, however, to judge the significance of it all, if only because we have otherwise assimilated digital tools so readily. That is the primary purpose of this assembly of writings. The selections range across the spectrum of appraisal, supporters of digital culture contrasted with critics, their conflicts applying to social networking, evolving ways of thought and inquiry, and the classroom. Some of the writings already enjoy canonical status. Tim O'Reilly's "What Is Web 2.0" (2005), for instance, helped solidify a fundamental recognition of the Web as a dynamic, collaborative application, not just a source of information and a desktop tool. Marc Prensky's "Digital Natives, Digital Immigrants," published 2001, coined terms that have had a tactical and widespread use among educators. Nicholas Carr's *Atlantic Monthly* essay "Is Google Making Us Stupid?" (2008) was one of the most discussed essays of the year.

Taken together, the selections form a far-reaching body of opinion about a rushing cataclysm that has upset centuries of social and intellectual practice. We do well to retain it. One of the dangers of the Digital Age is that technology changes so rapidly that it clouds our memory of things as they existed but a few years past. We forget the experiences of 1998 as soon as we acclimate to the tools of 2008. And if that's true, then the outlook we adopt now, even at the cutting edge of technology, may have little bearing upon ordinary experience ten years hence.

If we let the human realities that accompanied those older tools fall into oblivion, if the arrival and actual or potential disappearance of e-mail, laptops, and so on become just a set of distant facts, then we lose a part of our humanity, a historical sense of our recent selves. We have witnessed stunning transformations of society, politics, communication, and even selfhood. New identities have emerged or been fabulously empowered—the angry citizen with a video camera handy, the hyper–social networking teenager, the blog "troll," avatars. To understand them, to judge them well, we need steady and penetrating reminders of the changes they have wrought. The writers included here provide just that.

section one

the brain,
the senses

>>>

<Marc Prensky>

digital natives, digital immigrants

Originally published in *On the Horizon* (October 2001).

MARC PRENSKY is a writer, consultant, and inventor in the areas of education and learning. He is the author of *Digital Game-Based Learning* (2001) and *"Don't Bother Me Mom—I'm Learning"* (2005). He has designed more than one hundred software games, including multiuser games and simulations that run on all platforms. He has master's degrees from Yale University, Middlebury College, and Harvard Business School. His website is www.marcprensky.com.

IT IS AMAZING to me how in all the hoopla and debate these days about the decline of education in the U.S. we ignore the most fundamental of its causes. *Our students have changed radically. Today's students are no longer the people our educational system was designed to teach.*

Today's students have not just changed *incrementally* from those of the past, nor simply changed their slang, clothes, body adornments, or styles, as has happened between generations previously. A really big *discontinuity* has taken place. One might even call it a "singularity"—an event which changes things so fundamentally that there is absolutely no going back. This so-called "singularity" is the arrival and rapid dissemination of digital technology in the last decades of the twentieth century.

Today's students—K through college—represent the first generations to grow up with this new technology. They have spent their entire lives surrounded by and using computers, video games, digital music players, video cams, cell phones, and all the other toys and tools of the digital age. Today's average college grads have spent less than 5,000 hours of their lives reading, but over 10,000 hours playing video games (not to mention 20,000 hours watching TV). Computer games, e-mail, the Internet, cell phones and instant messaging are integral parts of their lives.

It is now clear that as a result of this ubiquitous environment and the sheer volume of their interaction with it, today's students *think and process information fundamentally differently* from their predecessors. These differences go far further and deeper than most educators suspect or realize. "Different kinds of experiences lead to different brain structures," says Dr. Bruce D. Perry of Baylor College of Medicine. As we shall see in the next installment, it is very likely that *our students' brains have physically changed*— and are different from ours—as a result of how they grew up. But whether or not this is *literally* true, we can say with certainty that their *thinking patterns* have changed. I will get to *how* they have changed in a minute.

What should we call these "new" students of today? Some refer to them as the N-[for Net]-gen or D-[for digital]-gen. But the most useful designation I have found for them is *Digital Natives*. Our students today are all "native speakers" of the digital language of computers, video games and the Internet.

So what does that make the rest of us? Those of us who were not born into the digital world but have, at some later point in our lives, become fascinated by and adopted many or most aspects of the new technology are, and always will be compared to them, *Digital Immigrants*.

The importance of the distinction is this: As Digital Immigrants learn—like all immigrants, some better than others—to adapt to their environment, they always retain, to some degree, their "accent," that is, their foot in the past. The "digital immigrant accent" can be seen in such things as turning to the Internet for information second rather than first, or in reading the manual for a program rather than assuming that the program itself will teach us to use it. Today's older folk were "socialized" differently from their kids, and are now in the process of learning a new language. And a language learned later in life, scientists tell us, goes into a different part of the brain.

There are hundreds of examples of the Digital Immigrant accent. They include printing out your e-mail (or having your secretary print it out for you—an even "thicker" accent); needing to print out a document written on the computer in order to edit it (rather than just editing on the screen); and bringing people physically into your office to see an interesting website (rather than just sending them the URL). I'm sure you can think of one or two examples of your own without much effort. My own favorite example is the "Did you get my e-mail?" phone call. Those of us who are Digital Immigrants can, and should, laugh at ourselves and our "accent."

But this is not just a joke. It's very serious, because the single biggest problem facing education today is that *our Digital Immigrant instructors, who speak an outdated language (that of the pre-digital age), are struggling to teach a population that speaks an entirely new language.*

This is obvious to the Digital Natives—school often feels pretty much as if we've brought in a population of heavily accented, unintelligible foreigners to lecture them. They often can't understand what the Immigrants are saying. What does "dial" a number mean, anyway?

Lest this perspective appear radical, rather than just descriptive, let me highlight some of the issues. Digital Natives are used to receiving information really fast. They like to parallel-process and multitask. They prefer their graphics *before* their text rather than the opposite. They prefer random access (like hypertext). They function best when networked. They thrive on instant gratification and frequent rewards. They prefer games to "serious" work. (Does any of this sound familiar?)

But Digital Immigrants typically have very little appreciation for these new skills that the Natives have acquired and perfected through years of interaction and practice. These skills are almost totally foreign to the Immigrants, who themselves learned—and so choose to teach—slowly, step-by-step, one thing at a time, individually, and above all, seriously. "My students just don't ____ like they used to," Digital Immigrant educators grouse. "I can't get them to _____ or to _____. They have no appreciation for _____ or _____." (Fill in the blanks; there are a wide variety of choices.)

Digital Immigrants don't believe their students can learn successfully while watching TV or listening to music, because they (the Immigrants) can't. Of course not—they didn't practice this skill constantly for all of their formative years. Digital Immigrants think learning can't (or shouldn't) be fun. Why should they—they didn't spend their formative years learning with *Sesame Street*.

Unfortunately for our Digital Immigrant teachers, the people sitting in their classes grew up on the "twitch speed" of video games and MTV. They are used to the instantaneity of hypertext, downloaded music, phones in their pockets, a library on their laptops, beamed messages and instant messaging. They've been networked most or all of their lives. They have little patience for lectures, step-by-step logic, and "tell-test" instruction.

Digital Immigrant teachers assume that learners are the same as they have always been, and that the same methods that worked for the teachers when they were students will work for their students now. *But that assumption is no longer valid.* Today's learners are *different*. "Www.hungry.com," said a kindergarten student recently at lunchtime. "Every time I go to school I have to power down," complains a high-school student. Is it that Digital Natives *can't* pay attention, or that they *choose not to*? Often from the Natives' point of view their Digital Immigrant instructors make their education *not worth* paying attention to compared to everything else they experience—and then they blame them for not paying attention!

And, more and more, they won't take it. "I went to a highly ranked college where all the professors came from MIT," says a former student. "But all they did was read from their textbooks. I quit." In the giddy Internet bubble of only a short while ago—when jobs were plentiful, especially in the areas where school offered little help—this was a real possibility. But the dot-com dropouts are now returning to school. They will have to confront once again the Immigrant/Native divide, and have even more trouble given their recent experiences. And that will make it even harder to teach them—and all the Digital Natives already in the system—in the traditional fashion.

So what should happen? Should the Digital Native students learn the old ways, or should their Digital Immigrant educators learn the new? Unfortunately, no matter how much the Immigrants may wish it, it is highly unlikely the Digital Natives will go backward. In the first place, it may be impossible—their brains may already be different. It also flies in the face of everything we know about cultural migration. Kids born into any new culture learn the new language easily, and forcefully resist using the old. Smart adult immigrants *accept* that they don't know about their new world and take advantage of their kids to help them learn and integrate. Not-so-smart (or not-so-flexible) immigrants spend most of their time grousing about how good things were in the "old country."

So unless we want to just forget about educating Digital Natives until they grow up and do it themselves, we had better confront this issue. And in so doing we need to reconsider both our methodology and our content.

First, our methodology. Today's teachers have to learn to communicate in the language and style of their students. This *doesn't* mean changing the meaning of what is important, or of good thinking skills. But it *does* mean going faster, less step-by-step, more in parallel, with more random access, among other things. Educators might ask "But how do we teach logic in this fashion?" While it's not immediately clear, we do need to figure it out.

Second, our content. It seems to me that after the digital "singularity" there are now *two kinds* of content: "Legacy" content (to borrow the computer term for old systems) and "Future" content.

"Legacy" content includes reading, writing, arithmetic, logical thinking, understanding the writings and ideas of the past, etc.—all of our "traditional" curriculum. It is of course still important, but it is from a different era. Some of it (such as logical thinking) will continue to be important, but some (perhaps like Euclidean geometry) will become less so, as did Latin and Greek.

"Future" content is to a large extent, not surprisingly, digital and technological. But while it includes software, hardware, robotics, nanotechnology, genomics, etc., *it also includes the ethics, politics, sociology, languages and other things that go with them.* This "Future" content is extremely interesting to today's students. But how many Digital Immigrants are prepared to teach it? Someone once suggested to me that kids should only be allowed to use computers in school that they have built themselves. It's a brilliant idea that is very doable from the point of view of the students' capabilities. But who could teach it?

As educators, we need to be thinking about how to teach *both* Legacy and Future content in the language of the Digital Natives. The first involves a major translation and change of methodology; the second involves all that PLUS new content and thinking. It's not actually clear to me which is harder—"learning new stuff" or "learning new ways to do old stuff." I suspect it's the latter.

So we have to invent, but not necessarily from scratch. Adapting materials to the language of Digital Natives has already been done successfully. My own preference for teaching Digital Natives is to invent computer games to do the job, even for the most serious content. After all, it's an idiom with which most of them are totally familiar.

Not long ago a group of professors showed up at my company with new computer-aided design (CAD) software they had developed for mechanical engineers. Their creation was so much better than what people were currently using that they had assumed the entire engineering world would quickly adopt it. But instead they encountered a lot of resistance, due in large part to the product's extremely steep learning curve—the software contained hundreds of new buttons, options and approaches to master.

Their marketers, however, had a brilliant idea. Observing that the users of CAD software were almost exclusively male engineers between twenty and thirty, they said, "Why not make the learning into a video game!" So we invented and created for them a computer game in the "first person shooter" style of the consumer games *Doom* and *Quake*, called *The Monkey Wrench Conspiracy*. Its player becomes an intergalactic secret agent who has to save a space station from an attack by the evil Dr. Monkey Wrench. The only way to defeat him is to use the CAD software, which the learner must employ to build tools, fix weapons, and defeat booby traps. There is one hour of game time, plus thirty "tasks," which can take from fifteen minutes to several hours. depending on one's experience level.

Monkey Wrench has been phenomenally successful in getting young people interested in learning the software. It is widely used by engineering students around the world, with over one million copies of the game in print in several languages. But while the game was easy for my Digital Native staff to invent, creating the content turned out to be more difficult for the professors, who were used to teaching courses that started with "Lesson 1—the Interface." We asked them instead to create a series of graded tasks into which the skills to be learned were embedded. The professors had made five- to ten-minute movies to illustrate key concepts; we asked them to cut them to under thirty seconds. The professors insisted that the learners do all the tasks in order; we asked them to allow random access. They wanted a slow academic pace; we wanted speed and urgency (we hired a Hollywood scriptwriter to provide this). They wanted written instructions; we wanted computer movies. They wanted the traditional pedagogical language of "learning objectives," "mastery," etc. (e.g., "in this exercise you will learn . . ."); our goal was to completely eliminate any language that even *smacked* of education.

In the end the professors and their staff came through brilliantly, but because of the large mind-shift required it took them twice as long as we had expected. As they saw the approach working, though, the new "Digital Native" methodology became their model for more and more teaching—both in and out of games—and their development speed increased dramatically.

Similar rethinking needs to be applied to all subjects at all levels. Although most attempts at "edutainment" to date have essentially failed from both the education and entertainment perspectives, we can—and will, I predict—do much better.

In math, for example, the debate must no longer be about *whether* to use calculators and computers—they are a part of the Digital Natives' world—but rather *how* to use them to instill the things that are useful to have internalized, from key skills and concepts to the multiplication tables. We should be focusing on "future math"—approximation, statistics, binary thinking.

In geography—which is all but ignored these days—there is no reason that a generation that can memorize over 100 Pokémon characters with all their characteristics, history, and evolution can't learn the names, populations, capitals, and relationships of all the 101 nations in the world. It just depends on how it is presented.

We need to invent Digital Native methodologies for *all* subjects, at *all* levels, using our students to guide us. The process has already begun—I know college professors inventing games for teaching subjects ranging from math to engineering to the Spanish Inquisition. We need to find ways of publicizing and spreading their successes.

A frequent objection I hear from Digital Immigrant educators is "this approach is great for *facts*, but it wouldn't work for 'my subject.'" Nonsense. This is just rationalization and lack of imagination. In my talks I now include "thought experiments" where I invite professors and teachers to suggest a subject or topic, and I attempt—on the spot—to invent a game or other Digital Native method for learning it. *Classical philosophy?* Create a game in which the philosophers debate and the learners have to pick out what each would say. *The Holocaust?* Create a simulation where students role-play the meeting at Wannsee, or one where they can experience the *true* horror of the camps, as opposed to the films like *Schindler's List*. It's just dumb (and lazy) of educators—not to mention ineffective—to presume that (despite their traditions) the Digital Immigrant way is the *only* way to teach, and that the Digital Natives' "language" is not as capable as their own of encompassing any and every idea.

So if Digital Immigrant educators *really* want to reach Digital Natives—i.e., all their students—they will have to change. It's high time for them to stop their grousing, and as the Nike motto of the Digital Native generation says, "Just do it!" They *will* succeed in the long run—and their successes will come that much sooner if their administrators support them.

<Marc Prensky>

do they really *think* differently?

Originally published in *On the Horizon*
(December 2001).

*Different kinds of experiences lead to
different brain structures.*

—DR. BRUCE D. PERRY,
Baylor College of Medicine

O UR CHILDREN TODAY are being socialized in a way that is vastly different from their parents'. The numbers are overwhelming: over 10,000 hours playing video games, over 200,000 e-mails and instant messages sent and received, over 10,000 hours talking on digital cell phones, over 20,000 hours watching TV (a high percentage fast-speed MTV), over 500,000 commercials seen—all before the kids leave college. And, maybe, *at the very most,* 5,000 hours of book reading. These are today's "Digital Native" students.[1]

In "Digital Natives, Digital Immigrants: Part I," I discussed how the differences between our Digital Native students and their Digital Immigrant teachers lie at the root of a great many of today's educational problems. I suggested that Digital Natives' brains are likely *physically different* as a result of the digital input they received growing up. And I submitted that learning via digital games is one good way to reach Digital Natives in their "native language."

Here I present evidence for why I think this is so. It comes from neurobiology, social psychology, and from studies done on children using games for learning.

>>> neuroplasticity

Although the vast majority of today's educators and teachers grew up with the understanding that the human brain doesn't physically change based on stimulation it receives from the outside—especially after the age of three—it turns out that that view is, in fact, *incorrect*.

Based on the latest research in neurobiology, there is no longer any question that stimulation of various kinds actually changes brain structures and affects the way people think, and that these transformations go on *throughout life*. The brain is, to an extent not at all understood or believed to be when Baby Boomers were growing up, *massively plastic*. It can be, and is, constantly reorganized. (Although the popular term *rewired* is somewhat misleading, the overall idea is right—the brain changes and organizes itself differently based on the inputs it receives.) The old idea that we have a fixed number of brain cells that die off one by one has been replaced by research showing that our supply of brain cells is replenished constantly.[2] The brain *constantly* reorganizes itself all our child and adult lives, a phenomenon technically known as *neuroplasticity*.

One of the earliest pioneers in this field of neurological research found that rats in "enriched" environments showed brain changes compared with those in "impoverished" environments after as little as two weeks. Sensory areas of their brains were thicker, other layers heavier. Changes showed consistent overall growth, leading to the conclusion that *the brain maintains its plasticity for life*.[3]

Other experiments leading to similar conclusions include the following:

- Ferrets' brains were physically rewired, with inputs from the eyes switched to where the hearing nerves went and vice versa. Their brains changed to accommodate the new inputs.[4]

- Imaging experiments have shown that when blind people learn Braille, "visual" areas of their brains light up. Similarly, deaf people use their auditory cortex to read signs.[5]

- Scans of brains of people who tapped their fingers in a complicated sequence that they had practiced for weeks showed a larger area of motor cortex becoming activated than when they performed sequences they hadn't practiced.[6]

- Japanese subjects were able to learn to "reprogram" their circuitry for distinguishing "ra" from "la," a skill they "forget" soon after birth because their language doesn't require it.[7]

- Researchers found that an additional language learned later in life goes into a different place in the brain than the language or languages learned as children.[8]

- Intensive reading instruction experiments with students age ten and up appeared to create lasting chemical changes in key areas of the subjects' brains.[9]

- A comparison of musicians' versus non-players' brains via magnetic resonance imaging showed a 5 percent greater volume in the musicians' cerebellums, ascribed to adaptations in the brain's structure resulting from intensive musical training and practice.[10]

We are only at the very beginning of understanding and applying brain plasticity research. The goal of many who are—such as the company Scientific Learning—is "neuroscience-based education."[11]

>>> malleability

Social psychology also provides strong evidence that one's thinking patterns change depending on one's experiences. Until very recently Western philosophers and psychologists took it for granted that the same basic processes underlie all human thought. While cultural differences might dictate what people think *about*, the *strategies* and *processes* of thought, which include logical reasoning and a desire to understand situations and events in linear terms of cause and effect, were assumed to be the same for everyone. However, this, too, appears to be wrong.

Research by social psychologists[12] shows that people who grow up in different cultures do not just think about different things; they actually *think differently*. The environment and culture in which people are raised affects and even determines many of their thought processes.

"We used to think that everybody uses categories in the same way, that logic plays the same kind of role for everyone in the understanding of everyday life, that memory, perception, rule application and so on are the same," says one. "But we're now arguing that cognitive processes themselves are just far more malleable than mainstream psychology assumed."[13]

We now know that brains that undergo different developmental experiences develop differently, and that people who undergo different inputs from the culture that surrounds them think differently. And while we haven't yet directly observed Digital Natives' brains to see whether they are physically different (such as musicians' appear to be), the indirect evidence for this is extremely strong.

However, brains and thinking patterns do not just change overnight. A key finding of brain plasticity research is that brains do *not* reorganize casually, easily, or arbitrarily. "Brain reorganization takes place only when the animal pays attention to the sensory input and to the task."[14] "It requires very hard work."[15] Biofeedback requires upwards of fifty sessions to produce results.[16] Scientific Learning's Fast ForWard program requires students to spend 100 minutes a day, five days a week, for five to ten weeks to create desired changes, because "it takes sharply focused attention to rewire a brain."[17]

Several hours a day, five days a week, sharply focused attention—does that remind you of anything? Oh, yes—video games! That is exactly what kids have been doing ever since *Pong* arrived in 1974. They have been adjusting or programming their brains to the speed, interactivity, and other factors in the games, much as Boomers' brains were programmed to accommodate television, and literate man's brains were reprogrammed to deal with the invention of written language and reading (where the brain had to be retrained to deal with things in a highly linear way).[18] "Reading does not just happen; it is a terrible struggle."[19] "Reading [has] a different neurology to it than the things that are built into our brain, like spoken language."[20] One of the main focuses of schools for the hundreds of years since reading became a mass phenomenon has been retraining our speech-oriented brains to be able to read. Again, the training involves several hours a day, five days a week, and sharply focused attention.

Of course, just when we'd figured out (more or less) how to retrain brains for reading, they were retrained again by television. And now things have changed *yet again*, and our children are furiously retraining their brains in even newer ways, many of which are antithetical to our older ways of thinking.

Children raised with the computer "think differently from the rest of us. They develop hypertext minds. They leap around. It's as though their cognitive structures were parallel, not sequential."[21]

"Linear thought processes that dominate educational systems now can actually retard learning for brains developed through game and Web-surfing processes on the computer."[22]

Some have surmised that teenagers use different parts of their brain and think in different ways than adults when at the computer.[23] We now know that it goes even further—their brains are almost certainly *physiologically different*. But these differences, most observers agree, are less a matter of kind than a difference of degree. For example, as a result of repeated experiences, particular brain areas are larger and more highly developed, and others are less so.

For example, thinking skills enhanced by repeated exposure to computer games and other digital media include reading visual images as representations of three-dimensional space (representational competence), multidimensional visual-spatial skills, mental maps, "mental paper folding" (i.e., picturing the results of various origami-like folds in your mind without actually doing them), "inductive discovery" (i.e., making observations, formulating hypotheses and figuring out the rules governing the behavior of a dynamic representation), "attentional deployment" (such as monitoring multiple locations simultaneously), and responding faster to expected and unexpected stimuli.[24]

While these individual cognitive skills may not be new, the particular combination and intensity are. We now have a new generation with a very different blend of cognitive skills than its predecessors—the Digital Natives.

>>> what about attention spans?

We hear teachers complain so often about the Digital Natives' attention spans that the phrase "the attention span of a gnat" has become a cliché. But is it really true?

"Sure they have short attention spans—for the old ways of learning," says a professor.[25] Their attention spans are *not* short for games, for example, or for anything else that actually interests them. As a result of their experiences Digital Natives crave *interactivity*—an immediate response to their each and every action. Traditional schooling provides very little of this compared to the rest of their world (one study showed that students in class get to ask a question every *ten hours*).[26] So it generally isn't that Digital Natives *can't* pay attention, it's that they *choose not to*.

Research done for *Sesame Street* reveals that children do not actually watch television continuously, but "in bursts." They tune in just enough to get the gist and be sure it makes sense. In one key experiment, half the children were shown the program in a room filled with toys. As expected, the group with toys was distracted and watched the show only about 47 percent of the time as opposed to 87 percent in the group without toys. But when the children were tested for how much of the show they remembered and understood, the scores were exactly the same. "We were led to the conclusion that the five-year-olds in the toys group were attending quite strategically, distributing their attention between toy play and viewing so that they looked at what was for them the most informative part of the program. The strategy was so effective that the children could gain no more from increased attention."[27]

>>> what have we lost?

Still, we often hear from teachers about increasing problems their students have with reading and thinking. What about this? Has anything been *lost* in the Digital Natives' "reprogramming" process?

One key area that appears to have been affected is *reflection*. Reflection is what enables us, according to many theorists, to generalize, as we create "mental models" from our experience. It is, in many ways, the *process* of "learning from experience." In our twitch-speed world, there is less and less time and opportunity for reflection, and this development concerns many people. One of the most interesting challenges and opportunities in teaching Digital Natives is to figure out and invent ways to *include* reflection and critical thinking in the learning (either built into the instruction or through a process of instructor-led debriefing) *but still do it in the Digital Native language*. We can and must do more in this area.

Digital Natives accustomed to the twitch-speed, multitasking, random-access, graphics-first, active, connected, fun, fantasy, quick-payoff world of their video games, MTV, and the Internet are *bored* by most of today's education, well meaning as it may be. But worse, the many skills that new technologies *have* actually enhanced (e.g., parallel processing, graphics awareness, and random access)—which have profound implications for their learning—are almost totally ignored by educators.

The cognitive differences of the Digital Natives *cry out* for new approaches to education with a better "fit." And, interestingly enough, it turns out that one of the few structures capable of meeting the Digital Natives' changing learning needs and requirements is the very video and computer games they so enjoy. This is why "Digital Game–Based Learning" is beginning to emerge and thrive.

>>> but does it work?

Of course, many criticize today's learning games, and there is much to criticize. But if some of these games don't produce learning it is *not* because they are games, or because the concept of "game-based learning" is faulty. It's because *those particular games are badly designed*. There is a great deal of evidence that children's learning games that *are* well designed *do* produce learning, and lots of it—by and while engaging kids.

While some educators refer to games as "sugarcoating," giving that a strongly negative connotation—and often a sneer—it is a big help to the Digital Natives. After all, this is a medium they are very familiar with and really enjoy.

Elementary school, when you strip out the recesses and the lunch and the in-between times, actually consists of about three hours of instruction time in a typical nine-to-three day.[28] So assuming, for example, that learning games were only 50 percent educational, if you could get kids to play them for six hours over a weekend, you'd effectively add a day a week to their schooling! Six hours is far less than a Digital Native would typically spend over a weekend watching TV and playing video games. The trick, though, is to make the learning games compelling enough to actually be used in their place. They must be *real* games, not just drills with eye candy, combined creatively with *real* content.

The numbers back this up. The Lightspan Partnership, which created PlayStation games for curricular reinforcement, conducted studies in over 400 individual school districts and a "meta-analysis" as well. Their findings were increases in vocabulary and language arts of 24 and 25 percent respectively over the control groups, while the math problem solving and math procedures and algorithms scores were 51 and 30 percent higher.[29]

Click Health, which makes games to help kids self-manage their health issues, did clinical trials funded by the National Institutes of Health. They found, in the case of diabetes, that kids playing their games (as compared to a control group playing a pinball game) showed measurable gains in self-efficacy, communication with parents and diabetes self-care. And more important, urgent doctor visits for diabetes-related problems declined 77 percent in the treatment group.[30]

Scientific Learning's Fast ForWard game-based program for retraining kids with reading problems conducted National Field

Trials using 60 independent professionals at 35 sites across the U.S. and Canada. Using standardized tests, each of the 35 sites reported conclusive validation of the program's effectiveness, with 90 percent of the children achieving significant gains in one or more tested areas.[31]

Again and again it's the same simple story. Practice—time spent on learning—*works*. Kids don't like to practice. Games capture their attention and make it happen. And of course they must be practicing the right things, so *design* is important.

The U.S. military, which has a quarter of a million eighteen-year-olds to educate every year, is a big believer in learning games as a way to reach their Digital Natives. They know their volunteers expect this: "If we don't do things that way, they're not going to want to be in our environment."[32]

What's more, they've observed it working operationally in the field. "We've seen it time and time again in flying airplanes, in our mission simulators." Practical-minded Department of Defense trainers are perplexed by educators who say, "We don't know that educational technology works—we need to do some more studies." "We KNOW the technology works," they retort. "We just want to get on with using it."[33]

So, TODAY'S NEUROBIOLOGISTS and social psychologists agree that brains can and do change with new input. And today's educators with the most crucial learning missions—teaching the handicapped and the military—are already using custom-designed computer and video games as an effective way of reaching Digital Natives. But the bulk of today's tradition-bound educational establishment seems in no hurry to follow their lead.

Yet these educators know *something* is wrong, because they are not reaching their Digital Native students as well as they reached students in the past. So they face an important choice.

On the one hand, they can choose to ignore their eyes, ears, and intuition, pretend the Digital Native/Digital Immigrant issue does not exist, and continue to use their suddenly much less effective traditional methods until they retire and the Digital Natives take over.

Or they can choose instead to *accept* the fact that they have become Immigrants into a new Digital world, and to look to their own creativity, their Digital Native students, their sympathetic administrators and other sources to help them communicate their still-valuable knowledge and wisdom in that world's new language.

The route they ultimately choose—and the education of their Digital Native students—depends very much on us.

notes

1. These numbers are intended purely as "order of magnitude" approximations; they obviously vary widely for individuals. They were arrived at in the following ways (note: I am very interested in any additional data anyone has on this):

   Video Games: Average play time: 1.5 hours/day (Source: "Interactive Videogames," *Mediascope*, June 1996). It is likely to be higher five years later, so $1.8 \times 365 \times 15$ years = 9,855 hours.

   E-mails and Instant Messages: Average 40 per day $\times$ 365 $\times$ 15 years = 219, 000. This is not unrealistic even for pre-teens—in just one instant-messaging connection there may be over 100 exchanges per day—and most people do multiple connections.

TV: "Television in the Home, 1998: Third Annual Survey of Parents and Children, Annenberg Policy Center" (June 22, 1998) gives the number of TV hours watched per day as 2.55. M. Chen, in the *Smart Parents' Guide to Kids' TV*, (1994), gives the number as 4 hours/day. Taking the average, 3.3 hrs/day × 365 days × 18 years = 21,681.

Commercials: There are roughly 18 30-second commercials during a TV hour. 18 commercials/hour × 3.3 hours/day × 365 days × 20 years (infants *love* commercials) = 433,620.

Reading: Eric Leuliette, a voracious (and meticulous) reader who has listed online every book he has ever read (www.csr.utexas.edu/personal/leuliette/fw_table_home.html), read about 1,300 books through college. If we take 1,300 books × 200 pages per book × 400 words per page, we get 104,000,000 words. Read at 400 words/minute, that gives 260,000 minutes, or 4,333 hours. This represents a little over 3 hours/book. Although others may read more slowly, most have read far fewer books than Leuliette.

2. Paul Perry in *American Way*, May 15, 2000.
3. Renate Numella Caine and Geoffrey Caine, *Making Connections: Teaching and the Human Brain* (Addison-Wesley, 1991), p. 31.
4. Dr. Mriganka Sur, *Nature*, April 20, 2000.
5. Sandra Blakeslee, *New York Times*, April 24, 2000.
6. Leslie Ungerlieder, National Institutes of Health.
7. James McLelland, University of Pittsburgh.
8. Cited in *Inferential Focus Briefing*, September 30, 1997.
9. Virginia Berninger, University of Washington, *American Journal of Neuroradiology*, May 2000.
10. Dr. Mark Jude Tramano of Harvard. Reported in *USA Today*, December 10, 1998.

11. *Newsweek*, January 1, 2000.
12. They include Alexandr Romanovich Luria (1902–1977), Soviet pioneer in neuropsychology, author of *The Human Brain and Psychological Processes* (1963), and, more recently, Dr. Richard Nisbett of the University of Michigan.
13. Quoted in Erica Goode, "How Culture Molds Habits of Thought," *New York Times*, August 8, 2000.
14. John T. Bruer, *The Myth of the First Three Years* (The Free Press, 1999), p. 155.
15. G. Reid Lyon, a neuropsychologist who directs reading research funded by the National Institutes of Health, quoted in Frank D. Roylance, "Intensive Teaching Changes Brain," *SunSpot*, Maryland's Online Community, May 27, 2000.
16. Alan T. Pope, research psychologist, Human Engineering Methods, NASA. Private communication.
17. *Time*, July 5, 1999.
18. *The Economist*, December 6, 1997.
19. Kathleen Baynes, neurology researcher, University of California, Davis, quoted in Robert Lee Hotz, "In Art of Language, the Brain Matters," *Los Angeles Times*, October 18, 1998.
20. Dr. Michael S. Gazzaniga, neuroscientist at Dartmouth College, quoted in Robert Lee Hotz, "In Art of Language, the Brain Matters," *Los Angeles Times*, October 18, 1998.
21. William D. Winn, Director of the Learning Center, Human Interface Technology Laboratory, University of Washington, quoted in Moore, *Inferential Focus Briefing* (see note 22).
22. Peter Moore, *Inferential Focus Briefing*, September 30, 1997.
23. Ibid.
24. Patricia Marks Greenfield, *Mind and Media: The Effects of Television, Video Games and Computers* (Harvard University Press, 1984).
25. Dr. Edward Westhead, professor of biochemistry (retired), University of Massachusetts.

26. A. C. Graesser and N. K. Person, "Question Asking During Tutoring," *American Educational Research Journal* 31 (1994), pp. 104–107.

27. Elizabeth Lorch, psychologist, Amherst College, quoted in Malcolm Gladwell, *The Tipping Point: How Little Things Can Make a Big Difference* (Little Brown & Co., 2000), p. 101.

28. John Kernan, President, The Lightspan Partnership. Personal communication.

29. Evaluation of Lightspan, "Research Results from 403 Schools and Over 14,580 Students," February 2000, CD-ROM.

30. Debra A. Lieberman, "Health Education Video Games for Children and Adolescents: Theory, Design and Research Findings," paper presented at the annual meeting of the International Communications Association, Jerusalem, 1998.

31. Scientific Learning Corporation, National Field Trial Results (pamphlet). See also Merzenich et al., "Temporal Processing Deficits of Language-Learning Impaired Children Ameliorated by Training," and Tallal et al., "Language Comprehension in Language-Learning Impaired Children Improved with Acoustically Modified Speech," in *Science* (January 5, 1996), pp. 27–28 and 77–84.

32. Michael Parmentier, Director, Office of Readiness and Training, Department of Defense, The Pentagon. Private briefing.

33. Don Johnson, Office of Readiness and Training, Department of Defense, The Pentagon. Private briefing.

<Steven Johnson>

the internet

**Excerpted from *Everything Bad Is Good for You*
(pp. 116–24).**

STEVEN JOHNSON has authored books on science, technology and personal experience, including *The Ghost Map* (2006), *Everything Bad Is Good for You: How Today's Popular Culture Is Actually Making Us Smarter* (2005), and *Mind Wide Open: Your Brain and the Neuroscience of Everyday Life* (2005). Johnson is contributing editor for *Wired* magazine and columnist for *Discover* magazine, as well as cofounder and editor in chief of FEED. He is a Distinguished Writer-in-Residence at the New York University Department of Journalism. He has published in *The New York Times*, *The Wall Street Journal*, *The Nation*, and many other periodicals, and has appeared on *The Charlie Rose Show*, *The Daily Show* with Jon Stewart, and *The NewsHour* with Jim Lehrer. His website is stevenberlinjohnson.com.

VIEWERS WHO GET LOST in *24*'s social network have a resource available to them that *Dallas* viewers lacked: the numerous online sites and communities that share information about popular television shows. Just as *Apprentice* viewers mulled Troy's shady business ethics in excruciating detail, *24* fans exhaustively document and debate every passing glance and brief allusion in the series, building detailed episode guides and lists of Frequently Asked Questions. One Yahoo! site featured at the time of this writing more than forty thousand individual posts from ordinary viewers, contributing their own analysis of last night's episode, posting questions about plot twists, or speculating on the upcoming season. As the shows have complexified, the resources for making sense of that complexity have multiplied as well. If you're lost in *24*'s social network, you can always get your bearings online.

All of which brings us to another crucial piece in the puzzle of the Sleeper Curve: the Internet. Not just because the online world offers resources that help sustain more complex programming in other media, but because the process of acclimating to the new reality of networked communications has had a salutary effect on our minds. We do well to remind ourselves how quickly the industrialized world has embraced the many forms of participatory electronic media—from e-mail to hypertext to instant messages and blogging. Popular audiences embraced television and the cinema in comparable time frames, but neither required the learning curve of e-mail or the Web. It's one thing to adapt your lifestyle to include time for sitting around watching a moving image on a screen; it's quite another to learn a whole new language of communication and a small army of software tools along with it. It seems almost absurd to think of this now, but when the idea of hypertext documents first entered the popular domain in the early nineties, it was a distinctly avant-garde idea, promoted by an experimentalist literary fringe looking to explode the restrictions of the linear sentence and the page-bound book. Fast-forward less than a decade, and something extraordinary occurs: exploring nonlinear document structures becomes as second nature as dialing a phone for hundreds of millions—if not billions—of people. The mass embrace of hypertext is like the *Seinfeld* "Betrayal" episode: a cultural form that was once exclusively limited to avant-garde sensibilities, now happily enjoyed by grandmothers and third graders worldwide.

I won't dwell on this point, because the premise that increased interactivity is good for the brain is not a new one. (A number of insightful critics—Kevin Kelly, Douglas Rushkoff, Janet Murray, Howard Rheingold, Henry Jenkins—have made variations on this argument over the past decade or so.) But let me say this much: The rise of the Internet has challenged our minds in three fundamental and related ways: by virtue of being participatory, by forcing users to learn new interfaces, and by creating new channels for social interaction.

Almost all forms of sustained online activity are participatory in nature: writing e-mails, sending IMs, creating photo logs, posting two-page analyses of last night's *Apprentice* episode. Steve Jobs likes to describe the difference between television and the Web as the difference between lean-back and sit-forward media. The networked computer makes you lean in, focus, engage, while television encourages you to zone out. (Though not as much as it used to, of course.) This is the familiar interactivity-is-good-for-you argument, and it's proof that the conventional wisdom is, every now and then, actually wise.

There was a point several years ago, during the first wave of Internet cheerleading, when it was still possible to be a skeptic about how participatory the new medium would turn out to be. Everyone recognized that the practices of composing e-mail and clicking on hyperlinks were going to be mainstream activities, but how many people out there were ultimately going to be interested in publishing more extensive material online? And if that turned out to be a small number—if the Web turned out to be a medium where most of the content was created by professional writers and editors—was it ultimately all that different from the previous order of things?

The tremendous expansion of the blogging world over the past two years has convincingly silenced this objection. According to a 2004 study by the Pew Charitable Trust, more than 8 million Americans report that they have a personal weblog or online diary. The wonderful blog-tracking service Technorati reports that roughly 275,000 blog entries are published in the average day—a tiny fraction of them authored by professional writers. After only two years of media hype, the number of active bloggers in the United States alone has reached the audience size of prime-time network television.

So why were the skeptics so wrong about the demand for self-publishing? Their primary mistake was to assume that the content produced in this new era would look like old-school journalism: op-ed pieces, film reviews, cultural commentary. There's plenty of armchair journalism out there, of course, but the great bulk of personal publishing is just that, personal: the online diary is the dominant discursive mode in the blogosphere. People are using these new tools not to opine about social security privatization; they're using the tools to talk about their lives. A decade ago Douglas Rushkoff coined the phrase "screenagers" to describe the first generation that grew up with the assumption that the images on a television screen were supposed to be manipulated; that they weren't just there for passive consumption. The next generation is carrying that logic to a new extreme: the screen is not just something you manipulate, but something you project your identity onto, a place to work through the story of your life as it unfolds.

To be sure, that projection can create some awkward or unhealthy situations, given the public intimacy of the online diary and the potential for identity fraud. But every new technology can be exploited or misused to nefarious ends. For the vast majority of those 8 million bloggers, these new venues for self-expression have been a wonderful addition to their lives. There's no denying that the content of your average online diary can be juvenile. These diaries are, after all, frequently created by juveniles. But thirty years ago those juveniles weren't writing novels or composing sonnets in their spare time; they were watching *Laverne & Shirley*. Better to have minds actively composing the soap opera of their own lives than zoning out in front of someone else's.

The Net has actually had a positive lateral effect on the tube as well, in that it has liberated television from attempting tasks that the medium wasn't innately well suited to perform. As a vehicle for narrative and first-person intimacy, television can be a delightful medium, capable of conveying remarkably complex experiences. But as a source of information, it has its limitations. The rise of the Web has enabled television to off-load some of its information-sharing responsibilities to a platform that was designed specifically for the purposes of sharing information. This passage from Neil Postman's *Amusing Ourselves to Death* showcases exactly how much has changed over the past twenty years:

> Television . . . encompasses all forms of discourse. No one goes to a movie to find out about government policy or the latest scientific advance. No one buys a record to find out the baseball scores or the weather or the latest murder. . . . But everyone goes to television for all these things and more, which is why television resonates so powerfully throughout the culture. Television is our culture's principal mode of knowing about itself.

No doubt in total hours television remains the dominant medium in American life, but there is also no doubt that the Net has been gaining on it with extraordinary speed. If the early adopters are any indication, that dominance won't last for long. And for the types of knowledge-based queries that Postman describes—looking up government policy or sports scores—the Net has become the first place that people consult. Google is *our* culture's principal way of knowing about itself.

The second way in which the rise of the Net has challenged the mind runs parallel to the evolving rule systems of video games: the accelerating pace of new platforms and software applications forces users to probe and master new environments. Your mind is engaged by the interactive content of networked media—posting a response to an article online, maintaining three separate IM conversations at the same time—but you're also exercising cognitive muscles interacting with the form of the media as well: learning the tricks of a new e-mail client, configuring the video chat software properly, getting your bearings after installing a new operating system. This type of problem solving can be challenging in an unpleasant way, of course, but the same can be said for calculus. Just because you don't like troubleshooting your system when your browser crashes doesn't mean you aren't exercising your logic skills in finding a solution. This extra layer of cognitive involvement derives largely from the increased prominence of the interface in digital technology. When new tools arrive, you have to learn what they're good for, but you also have to learn the rules that govern their use. To be an accomplished telephone user, you needed to grasp the essential utility of being able to have real-time conversations with people physically removed from you, and you had to master the interface of the telephone device itself. That same principle holds true for digital technologies; only the interfaces have expanded dramatically in depth and complexity. There's only so much cognitive challenge at stake in learning the rules of a rotary dial phone. But you could lose a week exploring all the nooks and crannies of Microsoft Outlook.

Just as we saw in the world of games, learning the intricacies of a new interface can be a genuine pleasure. This is a story that is not often enough told in describing our evolving relationship with software. There is a kind of exploratory wonder in downloading a new application, and meandering through its commands and dialog boxes, learning its tricks by feel. I've often found certain applications are more fun to explore the first time than they actually are to use—because in the initial exploration, you can delight in features that are clever without being terribly helpful. This sounds like something only a hardened tech geek would say, but I suspect the feeling has become much more mainstream over the past few years. Think of the millions of ordinary music fans who downloaded Apple's iTunes software: I'm sure many of them enjoyed their first walk through the application, seeing all the tools that would revolutionize the way they listened to music. Many of them, I suspect, eschewed the manual altogether, choosing to probe the application the way gamers investigate their virtual worlds: from the inside. That probing is a powerful form of intellectual activity—you're learning the rules of a complex system without a guide, after all. And it's all the more powerful for being fun.

Then there is the matter of social connection. The other concern that Net skeptics voiced a decade ago revolved around a withdrawal from public space: yes, the Internet might connect us to a new world of information, but it would come at a terrible social cost, by confining us in front of barren computer monitors, away from the vitality of genuine communities. In fact, nearly all of the most hyped developments on the Web in the past few years have been tools for augmenting social connection: online personals, social and business network sites such as Friendster, the Meetup.com service so central to the political organization of the 2004 campaign, the many tools designed to enhance conversation between bloggers—not to mention all the handheld devices that we now use to coordinate new kinds of real-world encounters. Some of these tools create new modes of communication that are entirely digital in nature (the cross-linked conversations of bloggers). Others use the networked computer to facilitate a face-to-face encounter (as in Meetup). Others involve a hybrid dance of real and virtual encounters, as in the personals world, where flesh-and-blood dates usually follow weeks of online flirting. Tools like Google have fulfilled the original dream of digital machines becoming extensions of our memory, but the new social networking applications have done something that the visionaries never imagined: they are augmenting our people skills as well, widening our social networks, and creating new possibilities for strangers to share ideas and experiences.

Television and automobile society locked people up in their living rooms, away from the clash and vitality of public space, but the Net has reversed that long-term trend. After a half-century of technological isolation, we're finally learning new ways to connect.

<Maryanne Wolf>

learning to think in a digital world

Originally published in the *Boston Globe*
(September 5, 2007).

MARYANNE WOLF is a professor in the Eliot-Pearson
Department of Child Development at Tufts University. She
is the author of *Proust and the Squid: The Story and Science
of the Reading Brain* (2007) and the RAVE-O Intervention
Program, a fluency comprehension program for struggling
readers. She was awarded the Distinguished Professor of
the Year Award from the Massachusetts Psychological Association, and also the Teaching Excellence Award from the
American Psychological Association.

AS PARENTS INVEST in the latest academic software and
teachers consider how to weave the Internet into lesson
plans for the new school year, it is a good moment to reflect
upon the changing world in which youths are being educated. In a
word, it is digital, with computer notebooks displacing spiraled
notebooks, and Web-based blogs, articles, and e-mails shaping how
we read and communicate. Parents, teachers, and scholars are
beginning to question how our immersion in this increasingly dig-

ital world will shape the next generation's relationship to reading, learning, and to knowledge itself.

As a cognitive neuroscientist and scholar of reading, I am particularly concerned with the plight of the reading brain as it encounters this technologically rich society. Literacy is so much entwined in our lives that we often fail to realize that the act of reading is a miracle that is evolving under our fingertips. Over the last five thousand years, the acquisition of reading transformed the neural circuitry of the brain and the intellectual development of the species. Yet, the reading brain is slowly becoming endangered—the unforeseen consequences of the transition to a digital epoch that is affecting every aspect of our lives, including the intellectual development of each new reader. Three unexpected sources can help us negotiate the historical transition we face as we move from one prevailing mode of communication to another: Socrates, modern cognitive neuroscience, and Proust.

Similarly poised between two modes of communication, one oral and one written, Socrates argued against the acquisition of literacy. His arguments are as prescient today as they were futile then. At the core of Socrates' arguments lay his concerns for the young. He believed that the seeming permanence of the printed word would delude them into thinking they had accessed the heart of knowledge, rather than simply decoded it. To Socrates, only the arduous process of probing, analyzing, and ultimately internalizing knowledge would enable the young to develop a lifelong approach to thinking that would lead them ultimately to wisdom, virtue, and "friendship with [their] god." To Socrates, only the examined word and the "examined life" were worth pursuing, and literacy short-circuited both.

How many children today are becoming Socrates' nightmare, decoders of information who have neither the time nor the motivation to think beneath or beyond their Googled universes? Will they become so accustomed to immediate access to escalating on-screen information that they will fail to probe beyond the information given to the deeper layers of insight, imagination, and knowledge that have led us to this stage of human thought? Or, will the new demands of information technologies to multitask, integrate, and prioritize vast amounts of information help to develop equally, if not more, valuable skills that will increase human intellectual capacities, quality of life, and collective wisdom as a species?

There is surprisingly little research that directly confronts these questions, but knowledge from the neurosciences about how the brain learns to read and how it learns to think about what it reads can aid our efforts. We know, for example, that no human being was born to read. We can do so only because of our brain's protean capacity to rearrange itself to learn something new. Using neuroimaging to scan the brains of novice readers allows us to observe how a new neural circuitry is fashioned from some of its original structures. In the process, that brain is transformed in ways we are only now beginning to fully appreciate. More specifically, in the expert reading brain, the first milliseconds of decoding have become virtually automatic within that circuit. It is this automaticity that allows us the precious milliseconds we need to go beyond the decoded text to think new thoughts of our own—the heart of the reading process.

Perhaps no one was more eloquent about the true purpose of reading than French novelist Marcel Proust, who wrote: "that which is the end of their [the authors'] wisdom is but the beginning of ours." The act of going beyond the text to think new thoughts is a developmental, learnable approach toward knowledge.

Within this context, there should be a developmental perspective on our transition to a digital culture. Our already biliterate children, who nimbly traverse between various modes of print, need to develop an expert reading brain before they become totally immersed in the digital world. Neuroscience shows us the profound miracle of an expert reading brain that uses untold areas across all four lobes and both hemispheres to comprehend sophisticated text and to think new thoughts that go beyond the text.

Children need to have both time to think and the motivation to think for themselves, to develop an expert reading brain, before the digital mode dominates their reading. The immediacy and volume of information should not be confused with true knowledge. As technological visionary Edward Tenner cautioned, "It would be a shame if the very intellect that produced the digital revolution could be destroyed by it." Socrates, Proust, and the images of the expert reading brain help us to think more deliberately about the choices we possess as our next generation moves toward the next great epoch in our intellectual development.

<James Gee>

learning theory, video games, and popular culture

Originally published in Kirsten Drotner and Sonia Livingston, eds., *The International Handbook of Children, Media, and Culture* (2008), pp. 200–203.

JAMES PAUL GEE is the Mary Lou Fulton Presidential Professor of Literacy Studies in the Department of English at Arizona State University. His books include *Social Linguistics and Literacies* (Fourth Edition, 2011) and *What Video Games Have to Teach Us About Learning and Literacy* (Second Edition, 2007). More information can be found at www.jamespaulgee.com.

>>> action-and-goal-directed preparations for, and simulations of, embodied experience

VIDEO GAMES don't just carry the potential to replicate a sophisticated scientific way of thinking. They actually externalize the way in which the human mind works and thinks in a better fashion than any other technology we have.

In history, scholars have tended to view the human mind through the lens of a technology they thought worked like the mind. Locke and Hume, for example, argued that the mind was like a blank slate on which experience wrote ideas, taking the technology of literacy as their guide. Much later, modern cognitive scientists argued that the mind worked like a digital computer, calculating generalizations and deductions via a logic-like rule system (Newell and Simon, 1972). More recently, some cognitive scientists, inspired by distributed parallel-processing computers and complex adaptive networks, have argued that the mind works by storing records of actual experiences and constructing intricate patterns of connections among them (Clark, 1989; Gee, 1992). So we get different pictures of the mind: mind as a slate waiting to be written on, mind as software, mind as a network of connections.

Human societies get better through history at building technologies that more closely capture some of what the human mind can do and getting these technologies to do mental work publicly. Writing, digital computers, and networks each allow us to externalize some functions of the mind. Though they are not commonly thought of in these terms, video games are a new technology in this same line. They are a new tool with which to think about the mind and through which we can externalize some of its functions. Video games of the sort I am concerned with are what I would call "action-and-goal-directed preparations for, and simulations of, embodied experience." A mouthful, indeed, but an important one, and one connected intimately to the nature of human thinking; so, let us see what it means.

Let me first briefly summarize some recent research in cognitive science, the science that studies how the mind works (Bransford et al., 2000). Consider, for instance, the remarks on the following page (in the quotes, the word "comprehension" means "understanding words, actions, events, or things"):

... comprehension is grounded in perceptual simulations
that prepare agents for situated action. (Barsalou, 1999a:
77)

... to a particular person, the meaning of an object, event,
or sentence is what that person can do with the object,
event, or sentence. (Glenberg, 1997: 3)

What these remarks mean is this: human understanding is not
primarily a matter of storing general concepts in the head or applying abstract rules to experience. Rather, humans think and understand best when they can imagine (simulate) an experience in such
a way that the simulation prepares them for actions they need and
want to take in order to accomplish their goals (Clark, 1997; Barsalou, 1999b; Glenberg and Robertson, 1999).

Let us take weddings as an example, though we could just as
well have taken war, love, inertia, democracy, or anything. You
don't understand the word or the idea of weddings by meditating on
some general definition of weddings. Rather, you have had experiences of weddings, in real life and through texts and media. On the
basis of these experiences, you can simulate different wedding scenarios in your mind. You construct these simulations differently for
different occasions, based on what actions you need to take to
accomplish specific goals in specific situations. You can move around
as a character in the mental simulation as yourself, imaging your
role in the wedding, or you can "play" other characters at the wedding (e.g., the minister), imaging what it is like to be that person.

You build your simulations to understand and make sense of
things, but also to help you prepare for action in the world. You can
act in the simulation and test out what consequences follow, before
you act in the real world. You can role-play another person in the
simulation and try to see what motivates their actions or might
follow from them before you respond in the real world. So I am argu-

ing that the mind is a simulator, but one that builds simulations to prepare purposely for specific actions and to achieve specific goals (i.e., they are built around win states).

Video games turn out to be the perfect metaphor for what this view of the mind amounts to, just as slates and computers were good metaphors for earlier views of the mind. Video games usually involve a visual and auditory world in which the player manipulates a virtual character (or characters). They often come with editors or other sorts of software with which the player can make changes to the game world or even build a new game world (much as the mind can edit its previous experiences to form simulations of things not directly experienced). The player can make a new landscape, a new set of buildings, or new characters. The player can set up the world so that certain sorts of action are allowed or disallowed. The player is building a new world, but is doing so by using and modifying the original visual images (really the code for them) that came with the game. One simple example of this is the way in which players can build new skateboard parks in a game like Tony Hawk Pro Skater. The player must place ramps, trees, grass, poles, and other things in space in such a way that players can manipulate their virtual characters to skate the park in a fun and challenging way.

Even when players are not modifying games, they play them with goals in mind, the achievement of which counts as their "win state." Players must carefully consider the design of the world and consider how it will or will not facilitate specific actions they want to take to accomplish their goals. One technical way that psychologists have talked about this sort of situation is through the notion of "affordances" (Gibson, 1979). An affordance is a feature of the world (real or virtual) that will allow for a certain action to be taken, but only if it is matched by an ability in an actor who has the wherewithal to carry out such an action. For example, in the massive multiplayer game World of WarCraft stags can be killed and skinned (for making leather), but only by characters who have learned the skinning skill. So a stag is an affordance for skinning for such a player, but not for one who has no such skill. The large spiders in the game are not an affordance for skinning for any players, since they cannot be skinned at all. Affordances are relationships between the world and actors.

Playing *World of WarCraft*, or any other video game, is all about such affordances. The player must learn to see the game world—designed by the developers, but set in motion by the players, and, thus, co-designed by them—in terms of such affordances (Gee, 2005). Broadly speaking, players must think in terms of: "What are the features of this world that can enable the actions I am capable of carrying out and that I want to carry out in order to achieve my goals?"

The view of the mind I have sketched argues, as far as I am concerned, that the mind works rather like a video game. For humans, effective thinking is more like running a simulation in our heads within which we have a surrogate actor than it is about forming abstract generalizations cut off from experiential realities. Effective thinking is about perceiving the world such that the human actor sees how the world, at a specific time and place (as it is given, but also modifiable), can afford the opportunity for actions that will lead to a successful accomplishment of the actor's goals. Generalizations are formed, when they are, bottom up from experience and imagination of experience. Video games externalize the search for affordances, for a match between character (actor) and world, but this is just the heart and soul of effective human thinking and learning in any situation. They are, thus, a natural tool for teaching and learning.

As a game player you learn to see the world of each different game you play in a quite different way. But in each case you see the world in terms of how it will afford the sorts of embodied actions you (and your virtual character, your surrogate body in the game) need to take to accomplish your goals (to win in the short and long run). For example, you see the world in *Full Spectrum Warrior* as routes (for your squad) between cover (e.g., corner to corner, house to house), because this prepares you for the actions you need to take, namely attacking without being vulnerable to attack yourself. You see the world of *Thief: Deadly Shadows* in terms of light and dark, illumination and shadows, because this prepares you for the different actions you need to take in this world, namely hiding, disappearing into the shadows, sneaking, and otherwise moving unseen to your goal.

While commercial video games often stress a match between worlds and characters like soldiers or thieves, there is no reason why other types of game could not let players experience such a match between the world and the way a particular type of scientist, for instance, sees and acts on the world (Gee, 2004). Such games would involve facing the sorts of problems and challenges that type of scientist does, and living and playing by the rules that type of scientist uses. Winning would mean just what it does to a scientist: feeling a sense of accomplishment through the production of knowledge to solve deep problems.

I have argued for the importance of video games as "action-and-goal-directed preparations for, and simulations of, embodied experience." They are the new technological arena—just as were literacy and computers earlier—around which we can study the mind and externalize some of its most important features to improve human thinking and learning. . . .

<Jakob Nielsen>

usability of websites
for teenagers

**Originally published in *Jakob Nielsen's Alertbox*
(January 31, 2005).**

JAKOB NIELSEN, PH.D., is a principal of Nielsen Norman Group (www.nngroup.com). Noted as "the world's leading expert on Web usability" by *U.S. News & World Report* and "the next best thing to a true time machine" by *USA Today*, he is the author of *Designing Web Usability: The Practice of Simplicity* (1999) and *Eyetracking Web Usability* (2009). From 1994 to 1998, Nielsen was a Sun Microsystems Distinguished Engineer. He holds 79 U.S. patents, mainly on ways of making the Internet easier to use. His website is www.useit.com.

IT'S ALMOST CLICHÉ to say that teenagers live a wired lifestyle, but they do. Teens in our study reported using the Internet for:

- School assignments
- Hobbies or other special interests
- Entertainment (including music and games)

- News
- Learning about health issues that they're too embarrassed to talk about
- E-commerce

And, even when they don't make actual purchases online, teens use websites to do product research and to build gift wish lists for the credit-card-carrying adults in their lives.

>>> user research

We conducted a series of usability studies to determine how website designs can better cater to teenagers. We systematically tested twenty-three websites, asking teenagers to visit the sites, perform given tasks, and think out loud. We also asked test participants to perform Web-wide tasks using any website they wanted. This gave us data about a wider range of sites, along with insight into how teens decide which sites to use. Finally, we interviewed the participants about how and when they use the Web and asked them to show us their favorite sites.

In all, thirty-eight users between the ages of thirteen and seventeen participated in the tests. Most sessions were conducted in the U.S.; we also ran a few tests in Australia to assess the international applicability of the findings. We found no major differences here: factors that make websites easy or difficult for teens to use were the same in both countries, as were the design characteristics that appealed to teens.

The only big difference between the two nations confirmed a stereotype about Australians: they are nuts about sports. When asked to show us their favorite sites, almost every Australian teen nominated a team site from the Australian Football League. An Australian teen also praised Google for offering a feature to search only Australian sites. Localizing websites and offering country-specific content and services is good advice that applies across age groups.

Within the U.S., we conducted studies in a rural Colorado and in three California locations ranging from affluent suburbs to disadvantaged urban areas. We tested a roughly equivalent number of boys and girls.

>>> focus on web usability

Teenagers are heavy users of a broad range of technology products, including music download services and MP3 players, chat and instant messaging, e-mail, mobile phones and SMS texting, on-line diary services, and much more. Nonetheless, we focused our research on teens' use of websites for two reasons:

- There are many existing reports about how teens use computer-mediated communication, mobile devices, and other non-Web technologies. Such studies are not always conducted using proper usability methodology, and they tend to rely too much on surveys of self-reported behavior rather than direct observation of actual behavior. Still, this area has been well covered by other researchers.

- Non-website design is a highly restricted market: there are about three significant vendors of chat and IM software, ten big vendors of mobile phones, and a handful of important music download services. It doesn't make sense to publish a general report for so few readers. In contrast, there are 60 million websites in the world, and a big percentage of them might be interested in how to serve teenagers better.

Web design for teens is a broad enough topic to warrant its own specialized study.

We tested sites in the following genres:

- **School resources** (BBC Schools, California State University, and SparkNotes)

- **Health** (Australian Drug Foundation, KidsHealth, National Institute on Drug Abuse)

- **News and entertainment** (BBC Teens, ChannelOne .com, MTV, and The Orange County Register)

- **E-commerce** (American Eagle Outfitters, Apple, Volcom)

- **Corporate sites** (McDonald's, Pepsi-Cola, The Principal Financial Group, and Procter & Gamble)

- **Government** (Australian government main portal, California's Department of Motor Vehicles, and the U.S. White House)

- **Non-profits** (Alzheimer's Association, The Insite, Museum of Tolerance, National Wildlife Federation)

As this list shows, we tested both specialized sites that explicitly target teenagers and mainstream sites for which teens are part of a larger target audience.

>>> misconceptions about teenagers

Many people think teens are technowizards who surf the Web with abandon. It's also commonly assumed that the best way to appeal to teens is to load up on heavy, glitzy, blinking graphics.

Our study refuted these stereotypes. Teenagers are not in fact superior Web geniuses who can use anything a site throws at them. We measured a **success rate of only 55 percent** for the teenage users in this study, which is substantially lower than the 66 percent success rate we found for adult users in our latest broad test of a wide range of websites. (The success rate indicates the proportion of times users were able to complete a representative and perfectly feasible task on the target site. Thus, anything less than 100 percent represents a design failure and lost business for the site.)

Teens' poor performance is caused by three factors: insufficient **reading skills**, less sophisticated **research strategies**, and a dramatically lower **patience level**.

We did confirm that **teens like cool-looking graphics** and that they pay more attention to a website's visual appearance than adult users do. Still, the sites that our teen users rated the highest for subjective satisfaction were sites with a **relatively modest, clean design**. They typically marked down overly glitzy sites as too difficult to use. Teenagers like to *do* stuff on the Web, and dislike sites that are slow or that look fancy but behave clumsily.

Why are there so many misconceptions about teens? Two reasons. First, most people in charge of websites are at the extreme high end of the brainpower/techno-enthusiasm curve. These people are highly educated and very smart early adopters, and they spend a lot of time online. Most of the teens they know share these characteristics. Rarely do people in the top 5 percent spend any significant time with the 80 percent of the population who constitute the mainstream audience.

Second, when you know several teenagers, the one super-user in the bunch is most likely to stand out in memory and serve as the "typical teen" persona, even though he or she is actually the outlier. Teens who *don't* volunteer to fix your VCR when it's blinking "12:00" are not the ones you remember.

>>> no boring sites

Teens frequently complained about sites that they found boring. Being boring is the kiss of death in terms of keeping teens on your site. That's one stereotype our study confirmed: teens have a short attention span and want to be stimulated. That's also why they leave sites that are difficult to figure out.

Teenagers don't like to read a lot on the Web. They get enough of that at school. Also, the reading skills of many teenagers are not what one might hope for, especially among younger teens. Sites that were easy to scan or that illustrated concepts visually were strongly preferred to sites with dense text.

One surprising finding in this study: **teenagers don't like tiny font sizes** any more than adults do. We've often warned websites about using small text because of the negative implications for senior citizens—and even people in their late forties whose eyesight has begun to decline. We have always assumed that tiny text is predominant on the Web because most Web designers are young and still have perfect vision, so we didn't expect to find issues with font sizes when testing even younger users. However, small type often caused problems or provoked negative comments from the teen users in our study. Even though most teens are sufficiently sharp-eyed, they move too quickly and are too easily distracted to attend to small text.

What's good? The following **interactive features** all worked well because they let teens *do* things rather than simply sit and read:

- Online quizzes
- Forms for providing feedback or asking questions
- Online voting
- Games

- Features for sharing pictures or stories
- Message boards
- Forums for offering and receiving advice
- Features for creating a website or otherwise adding content

These interactive features allow teenagers to make their mark on the Internet and express themselves in various ways—some small, some big.

>>> differences between age groups

The following table summarizes the main differences in Web design approaches for young children, teenagers, and adults. (The findings about children are from our separate tests with six- to twelve-year-old users.)

	Animation and sound effects	Mine sweeping for links	Advertising	Scrolling	Reading
Kids	☺	☺	☺	☹	☹
Teens	😐	☹	😐	😐	☹
Adults	☹	☹	☹	☺	😐

Key:
☺ Enjoyable, interesting, and appealing, or users can easily adjust to it.
😐 Users might appreciate it to some extent, but overuse can be problematic.
☹ Users dislike it, don't do it, or find it difficult to operate.

Clearly, there are many differences between age groups, and the highest usability level for teenagers comes from having designs targeted specifically at their needs and behaviors. Teens have different needs than both adults and young children. This goes for interaction design (as the table indicates) as well as for more obvious factors such as the choice of topics and content style.

Some websites in our study tried to serve both children and teens in a single area, usually titled something like *Kids*. This is a grave mistake; **the word "kid" is a teen repellent**. Teenagers are fiercely proud of their newly won status and they don't want overly childish content (one more reason to ease up on the heavy animations and gory color schemes that actually work for younger audiences). We recommend having separate sections for young children and teens, labeling them *Kids* and *Teens*, respectively.

>>> teenage opportunities

The average participant in our study spent **five to ten hours per week on the Web**. This in addition to the many hours they spent with other technologies.

According to the Pew Internet and American Life Project, **83 percent of U.S. teenagers are online**. Other advanced countries show similar percentages. Websites should improve their design to better meet this huge user group's actual needs and desires, rather than target mistaken stereotypes. The opportunities are there.

<Jakob Nielsen>

user skills improving, but only slightly

Originally published in *Jakob Nielsen's Alertbox*
(February 4, 2008).

ENEMIES OF USABILITY have two **counterarguments** against design guidelines that are based on user research:

- "You're **testing idiots**—most users are smarter and don't mind complexity."
- "You were **right in the past**, but users have now learned how to use advanced websites, so simplicity isn't a requirement anymore."

I decided to put these claims to the test in a new study we're currently conducting. We'll use the new insights generated by the study to update our course on Fundamental Guidelines for Web Usability.

Because we're testing *this year's sites* with *this year's users*, the study automatically assesses the second claim.

We can't directly assess whether our study participants are idiots, since we don't subject them to an IQ test. But participants' comments during all of our studies these past fourteen years indicate that we've mainly had plenty smart test users. Unless a specific study calls for participants with a different profile, we mostly recruit people with respectable jobs—an engineering consultant, an equity trader, a lawyer, an office manager, a real estate agent, a speech therapist, and a teacher, to take some of the job titles from the first week of our current study.

One part of the current study tests B2B sites since many of our seminar audience work on such sites. This time, we chose sites targeting **dentists** in clinical practice, **IT managers** from big corporations, and **CEOs** of small businesses. Thus, we have disproportionally many users with these job descriptions. They aren't stupid.

One way of quantifying the level of users we're currently testing is to look at their annual income. In our screening, we look at the user's personal income, rather than his or her household income. We also recruit an equal number of people making: below $50,000, $50,000–99,999, and $100,000 or more. The following table compares our users with the entire U.S. population (according to the Census Bureau) within the study's target age range (twenty to sixty years; we've covered kids, teens, and seniors in other research):

User's Annual Income	Our Participants	U.S. Population (age 20–60)
<$50,000	33%	70%
$50,000–99,999	33%	22%
>$100,000	33%	8%

We're definitely testing people who are much more successful than the average. We decided to **bias the study in favor of high-salary users** for three reasons:

- We need to test many business professionals and doctors because so many of our seminar participants target these groups, whether for websites or intranets.

- Wealthy users have more money to spend and are thus more important to seminar attendees who work on e-commerce sites.

- Even conference attendees who target a broad consumer audience benefit from presentations that are based mainly on studies of wealthy users, because that fact helps them overcome the "dumb users" objection when they take the guidelines back to their teams.

We're not neglecting poor people—we have enough of them in the study to learn about their needs. But our participant profile is clearly such that no one could claim that the findings don't apply to high-end users.

>>> improved user skills

So, with the qualifications about our research out of the way, what have we found in recent studies? We've seen several indications that users are indeed **getting a bit better** at using the Web. Almost all users:

- are better at **physical operations**, such as mouse movements and scrolling;

- are more **confident** at clicking, and less afraid that they'll break something; and

- know the basics of using **search** and use it more often than we saw in the past.

In addition,

- some users are exhibiting **expert behaviors**, such as opening a second browser window to compare two websites or changing a PDF file's zoom level.

When performing **common tasks on sites they often use**, most users are incredibly **fast and competent**. This fact leads us to two interesting conclusions:

- Many sites are now good enough that users reward them with **loyalty** and frequent use.
- When people revisit such sites, they tend to do the same things repeatedly and develop a high degree of **skilled performance**—something we rarely saw on websites in the past.

As an example, one user failed almost every task on unfamiliar websites, yet was highly confident and extremely fast in using her bank's site to transfer money between two of her accounts.

>>> browsing and research skills still poor

Even though users are remarkably good at repeated tasks on their favorite sites, they're **stumped** by the smallest usability problems when they **visit new sites for the first time**.

People are very bad at coping with information architectures that deviate from their view of the problem space. They also fail to readjust their content interpretation to compensate for **changing contexts**. For example, when users jump from one information architecture area to another, they often continue to think that the information addresses the previous topic.

Users are also **overwhelmed** by the sheer amount of information that many sites dump on them. For example, a beginning investor tested E-Trade, which could be a great site to support his initial investments and might gradually grow his site involvement over time. Instead, E-Trade's first few pages were littered with scary jargon like "ADR" and "ETF." To escape, he clicked the *Active Trading* link, assuming this would help him understand how to trade. In fact, it took him to an area for highly experienced investors and it had even more mumbo jumbo. So, this hot prospect concluded that he didn't dare open an E-Trade account.

First-time visitors to a site don't have the **conceptual model** needed to correctly interpret menu options and navigate to the appropriate place. Lacking this contextual understanding, they waste time in the wrong site areas and misinterpret the area content.

People's **reading skills** are the same as they have always been, emphasizing the importance of writing for the Web. In earlier research, we have studied lower-literacy users, but even the higher-literacy users in our current study had problems with the dense content on many sites. For example, when testing NASA.gov, we asked users to find out when the rings around Saturn were formed. One user did find a page about Saturn, but ended up picking a wrong answer, 1980, which is when additional ringlets were *discovered*.

To help new users find their way, sites must provide much more **handholding** and much more simplified content.

Making comparisons is one of the most important tasks on the Web, and yet users have great difficulty doing so on most sites. The test participants were particularly happy with those websites that **do the comparing and consolidating for them**, like kayak.com.

Why worry about new users' ability to understand your site when your experienced users are clearly having a jolly old time performing frequent tasks? Because people develop into loyal, experienced users only after **passing through the new-user stage**. To grow your business, you have to accommodate first-time visitors for whom small difficulties loom large and often spell defeat.

Also, it's important to **expand your loyal users' interaction vocabulary** to further increase their loyalty. Because they move so fast, experienced users don't waste much time learning new features. Users have **tunnel vision** on their favorite sites: unless a new feature immediately proves its worth, users will stick to safe, familiar territory where they can quickly accomplish their tasks and leave.

By now, our test participants have extensive experience using the Web (mostly three-plus years), and they're still running into substantial problems online. Waiting for people to get *even more* experience is not likely to resolve the issues. Websites are just too darn difficult.

>>> google gullibility

Users live by search, but they also die by search.

People turn to search as their first step—or as their second step, if their first attempt at navigating fails. Users typically **formulate good initial queries**, and vaguely understand how to tickle the search engine into coughing up desired sites when they **appropriately modify their main keywords**. For example, in our new study, a user looking for a modest gift for a football fan searched for "football trinket." Five years ago, such a user would most likely have searched "football" and been buried by the results.

Still, today's users **rarely change their search strategy** when the initial query fails. They might modify their first attempt, but they typically stick with the same general approach rather than try something genuinely new.

For example, one user tested the Mayo Clinic's site to find out how to ensure that a child with a milk allergy would receive sufficient calcium. The user attempted multiple queries with the keyword "calcium," but never tried the words "milk" or "allergy."

Also, users are incredibly **bad at interpreting SERP listings** (SERP = Search Engine Results Page). Admittedly, SERPs from Google and the other main search engines typically offer unreadable gibberish rather than decent website descriptions. Still, an expert searcher (like me) can look at the listings and predict a destination site's quality much better than average users.

When it comes to search, users face three problems:

- Inability to **retarget queries** to a different search strategy

- Inability to understand the search results and **properly evaluate** each destination site's likely usefulness

- Inability to sort through the SERP's polluted mass of **poor results**, whether from blogs or from heavily SEO-optimized sites that are insufficiently specific to really address the user's problem

Given these difficulties, many users are at the search engine's mercy and **mainly click the top links**—a behavior we might call *Google Gullibility*. Sadly, while these top links are often not what they really need, users don't know how to do better.

I use "Google" in labeling the behavior only because it's the search engine used by the vast majority of our test users. People using other search engines have the same problems. Still, it's vital to **reestablish competition** in the search engine field: it would be a tragedy for democracy to let three guys at one company determine what billions of people read, learn, and ultimately think.

>>> guidelines reconfirmed

Our work is generating many interesting **new findings** on questions such as: What makes a website credible? What inspires user loyalty? We're running more studies to dig into these issues, which are among the most important for improving website profitability over the next decade. Once we've analyzed the mountains of data we're collecting, we'll announce the new findings at our upcoming usability conference.

For now, one thing is clear: we're confirming more and more of the old usability guidelines. Even though we have new issues to consider, the old issues aren't going away. A few examples:

- E-mail newsletters remain the best way to drive users back to websites. It's incredible how often our study participants say that a newsletter is their main reason for revisiting a site. Most business professionals are not very interested in podcasts or newsfeeds (RSS).

- **Opening new browser windows** is highly confusing for most users. Although many users can cope with extra windows that they've opened *themselves*, few understand why the Back button suddenly stops working in a new window that *the computer* initiated. Opening new windows was #2 on my list of top ten Web design mistakes of 1999; that this design approach continues to hurt users exemplifies both the longevity of usability guidelines and the limited improvement in user skills.

- Links that don't change color when clicked still create confusion, making users unsure about what they've already seen on a site.

- **Splash screens and intros** are still incredibly
  annoying: users look for the "skip intro" button—if
  not found, they often leave. One user wanted to buy
  custom-tailored shirts and first visited Turnbull &
  Asser because of its reputation. Clicking the
  appropriate link led to a page where a video started
  to play without warning and without a way to skip it
  and proceed directly to actual info about the service.
  The user watched a few seconds, got more and more
  agitated about the lack of options to bypass the intro,
  and finally closed down the site and went to a
  competitor. Customer lost.

- A fairly large minority of users still don't know that
  they can get to a site's home page by clicking its logo,
  so I still have to recommend having an **explicit
  "home" link** on all interior pages (not on the home
  page, of course, because no-op links that point to the
  current page are confusing—yet another guideline
  we saw confirmed again several times last week).
  It particularly irks me to have to retain the "explicit
  home link" guideline, because I had hoped to get rid
  of this stupid extra link. But many users really do
  change very slowly, so we'll probably have to keep this
  guideline in force until 2020—maybe longer. At least
  bread crumbs are a simple way to satisfy this need.

- People are still very wary, sometimes more so than in
  the past, about **giving out personal information**.
  In particular, the B2B sites in this new study failed
  in exactly the same way as most B2B sites in our major
  B2B research: by hitting users with a registration
  screen before they were sufficiently committed to
  the site.

- Nonstandard scrollbars are often overlooked and make people miss most of the site's offerings. Consider two examples from last week's testing.

On the Carl's Jr. hamburger chain website, we asked users to look up nutritional information for various meals. Many participants thought the quick item view menu covered only breakfast items, because those were the only choices visible without scrolling. Users overlooked the nonstandard scrollbar, and instead often suffered through the PDF files available through the *nutrition guide* link. (These PDF files caused many other problems, confirming more age-old usability guidelines. That said, some users are now skillful enough to adjust PDF views so that they're slightly more readable. Still, it's a painful process.)

On the Sundance Resort's site, one user was thrilled to see photos of celebrations hosted at the resort. She eagerly clicked through all five visible thumbnails, but never noticed the small triangles at the top and bottom that let users scroll to see more photos.

Web usability guidelines are not the only guidelines our new studies confirm. On VW's site, we asked participants to use the configurators to customize a car according to their preferences. Unfortunately, this mini-application violated some of the basic application usability guidelines, causing people many problems.

Users can select their car's wheel style from two options. This simple operation was difficult and error prone, however, because the option for the wheel that's currently mounted on the car was grayed out—a GUI convention that's supposed to mean that something is *unavailable*, not that it's the current selection. It would have been much better to show both available wheels at all times, placing a selection rectangle—or some other graphical highlighting convention—around the current selection. (Poor feedback is #4 on my list of top ten mistakes of application design.)

Interface conventions exist for a reason: they allow users to focus on your content (in this case, the car and its options). When all interface elements work as expected, users know how to operate the UI to get the desired effect. Conversely, when you deviate from user expectations, you erect a great barrier between users and their ability to get things done. Some designers think this makes the site more *exciting*. In reality, nonstandard design makes the site more *frustrating* and drastically reduces the user's chance of success. Users are thus more likely to quickly leave the site.

In VW's case, the designers probably suffered from a case of **metaphor overload**: the design mimics the experience of actually assembling a physical car in a real workshop. If you had two wheels on the workshop floor and mounted one on the car, then the chosen wheel would no longer be on the floor.

In reality, though, users are not grease monkeys. They're clicking on interface elements, and they expect the picture of a wheel to behave like a GUI element.

We're confirming hundreds more of the existing usability guidelines every week as our testing continues. Even though we have upscale users and it's a new study testing new sites, most of the findings are the same as we've seen year after year after year. Usability guidelines remain remarkably constant over time, because basic human characteristics stay the same.

<Nicholas Carr>

is google making us stupid?

Originally published in *The Atlantic* (July/August 2008).

NICHOLAS CARR is the author of *The Shallows: What the Internet Is Doing to Our Brains* (2010) and *The Big Switch: Rewiring the World, from Edison to Google* (2008). He has been a columnist for *The Guardian* and executive editor of *Harvard Business Review*, and has written for *The Atlantic, The New York Times, The Wall Street Journal, Wired, The Times* (London), and *The New Republic*. His blog is roughtype.com.

D AVE, STOP. Stop, will you? Stop, Dave. Will you stop, Dave?" So the supercomputer HAL pleads with the implacable astronaut Dave Bowman in a famous and weirdly poignant scene toward the end of Stanley Kubrick's *2001: A Space Odyssey*. Bowman, having nearly been sent to a deep-space death by the malfunctioning machine, is calmly, coldly disconnecting the memory circuits that control its artificial brain. "Dave, my mind is going," HAL says, forlornly. "I can feel it. I can feel it."

I can feel it, too. Over the past few years I've had an uncomfortable sense that someone, or something, has been tinkering with my brain, remapping the neural circuitry, reprogramming the mem-

ory. My mind isn't going—so far as I can tell—but it's changing. I'm
not thinking the way I used to think. I can feel it most strongly
when I'm reading. Immersing myself in a book or a lengthy article
used to be easy. My mind would get caught up in the narrative or
the turns of the argument, and I'd spend hours strolling through
long stretches of prose. That's rarely the case anymore. Now my
concentration often starts to drift after two or three pages. I get
fidgety, lose the thread, begin looking for something else to do. I feel
as if I'm always dragging my wayward brain back to the text. The
deep reading that used to come naturally has become a struggle.

I think I know what's going on. For more than a decade now, I've
been spending a lot of time online, searching and surfing and sometimes adding to the great databases of the Internet. The Web has
been a godsend to me as a writer. Research that once required days
in the stacks or periodical rooms of libraries can now be done in
minutes. A few Google searches, some quick clicks on hyperlinks,
and I've got the telltale fact or pithy quote I was after. Even when
I'm not working, I'm as likely as not to be foraging in the Web's info-
thickets reading and writing e-mails, scanning headlines and blog
posts, watching videos and listening to podcasts, or just tripping
from link to link to link. (Unlike footnotes, to which they're sometimes likened, hyperlinks don't merely point to related works; they
propel you toward them.)

For me, as for others, the Net is becoming a universal medium,
the conduit for most of the information that flows through my eyes
and ears and into my mind. The advantages of having immediate
access to such an incredibly rich store of information are many, and
they've been widely described and duly applauded. "The perfect
recall of silicon memory," *Wired*'s Clive Thompson has written, "can
be an enormous boon to thinking." But that boon comes at a price.
As the media theorist Marshall McLuhan pointed out in the 1960s,
media are not just passive channels of information. They supply the
stuff of thought, but they also shape the process of thought. And

what the Net seems to be doing is chipping away my capacity for concentration and contemplation. My mind now expects to take in information the way the Net distributes it: in a swiftly moving stream of particles. Once I was a scuba diver in the sea of words. Now I zip along the surface like a guy on a Jet Ski.

I'm not the only one. When I mention my troubles with reading to friends and acquaintances—literary types, most of them—many say they're having similar experiences. The more they use the Web, the more they have to fight to stay focused on long pieces of writing. Some of the bloggers I follow have also begun mentioning the phenomenon. Scott Karp, who writes a blog about online media, recently confessed that he has stopped reading books altogether. "I was a lit major in college, and used to be [a] voracious book reader," he wrote. "What happened?" He speculates on the answer: "What if I do all my reading on the Web not so much because the way I read has changed, i.e., I'm just seeking convenience, but because the way I THINK has changed?"

Bruce Friedman, who blogs regularly about the use of computers in medicine, also has described how the Internet has altered his mental habits. "I now have almost totally lost the ability to read and absorb a longish article on the Web or in print," he wrote earlier this year. A pathologist who has long been on the faculty of the University of Michigan Medical School, Friedman elaborated on his comment in a telephone conversation with me. His thinking, he said, has taken on a "staccato" quality, reflecting the way he quickly scans short passages of text from many sources online. "I can't read *War and Peace* anymore," he admitted. "I've lost the ability to do that. Even a blog post of more than three or four paragraphs is too much to absorb. I skim it."

Anecdotes alone don't prove much. And we still await the long-term neurological and psychological experiments that will provide a definitive picture of how Internet use affects cognition. But a recently published study of online research habits, conducted by scholars from University College London, suggests that we may well be in the midst of a sea change in the way we read and think. As part of the five-year research program, the scholars examined computer logs documenting the behavior of visitors to two popular research sites, one operated by the British Library and one by a U.K. educational consortium, that provide access to journal articles, e-books, and other sources of written information. They found that people using the sites exhibited "a form of skimming activity," hopping from one source to another and rarely returning to any source they'd already visited. They typically read no more than one or two pages of an article or book before they would "bounce" out to another site. Sometimes they'd save a long article, but there's no evidence that they ever went back and actually read it. The authors of the study report:

> It is clear that users are not reading online in the traditional sense; indeed there are signs that new forms of "reading" are emerging as users "power browse" horizontally through titles, contents pages and abstracts going for quick wins. It almost seems that they go online to avoid reading in the traditional sense.

Thanks to the ubiquity of text on the Internet, not to mention the popularity of text-messaging on cell phones, we may well be reading more today than we did in the 1970s or 1980s, when television was our medium of choice. But it's a different kind of reading, and behind it lies a different kind of thinking—perhaps even a new sense of the self. "We are not only *what* we read," says Maryanne Wolf, a developmental psychologist at Tufts University and the author of *Proust and the Squid: The Story and Science of the Reading Brain*. "We are *how* we read." Wolf worries that the style of reading promoted by the Net, a style that puts "efficiency" and "immediacy" above all else, may be weakening our capacity for the kind of deep reading that emerged when an earlier technology, the printing press, made long and complex works of prose common-place. When we read online, she says, we tend to become "mere decoders of information." Our ability to interpret text, to make the rich mental connections that form when we read deeply and without distraction, remains largely disengaged.

Reading, explains Wolf, is not an instinctive skill for human beings. It's not etched into our genes the way speech is. We have to teach our minds how to translate the symbolic characters we see into the language we understand. And the media or other tech-nologies we use in learning and practicing the craft of reading play an important part in shaping the neural circuits inside our brains. Experiments demonstrate that readers of ideograms, such as the Chinese, develop a mental circuitry for reading that is very differ-ent from the circuitry found in those of us whose written language employs an alphabet. The variations extend across many regions of the brain, including those that govern such essential cognitive functions as memory and the interpretation of visual and auditory stimuli. We can expect as well that the circuits woven by our use of the Net will be different from those woven by our reading of books and other printed works.

Sometime in 1882, Friedrich Nietzsche bought a typewriter—a Malling-Hansen Writing Ball, to be precise. His vision was failing, and keeping his eyes focused on a page had become exhausting and painful, often bringing on crushing headaches. He had been forced to curtail his writing, and he feared that he would soon have to give it up. The typewriter rescued him, at least for a time. Once he had mastered touch-typing, he was able to write with his eyes closed, using only the tips of his fingers. Words could once again flow from his mind to the page.

But the machine had a subtler effect on his work. One of Nietzsche's friends, a composer, noticed a change in the style of his writing. His already terse prose had become even tighter, more telegraphic. "Perhaps you will through this instrument even take to a new idiom," the friend wrote in a letter, noting that, in his own work, his "'thoughts' in music and language often depend on the quality of pen and paper."

"You are right," Nietzsche replied, "our writing equipment takes part in the forming of our thoughts." Under the sway of the machine, writes the German media scholar Friedrich A. Kittler, Nietzsche's prose "changed from arguments to aphorisms, from thoughts to puns, from rhetoric to telegram style."

The human brain is almost infinitely malleable. People used to think that our mental meshwork, the dense connections formed among the 100 billion or so neurons inside our skulls, was largely fixed by the time we reached adulthood. But brain researchers have discovered that that's not the case. James Olds, a professor of neuroscience who directs the Krasnow Institute for Advanced Study at George Mason University, says that even the adult mind "is very plastic." Nerve cells routinely break old connections and form new ones. "The brain," according to Olds, "has the ability to reprogram itself on the fly, altering the way it functions."

As we use what the sociologist Daniel Bell has called our "intellectual technologies"—the tools that extend our mental rather than our physical capacities—we inevitably begin to take on the qualities of those technologies. The mechanical clock, which came into common use in the fourteenth century, provides a compelling example. In *Technics and Civilization*, the historian and cultural critic Lewis Mumford described how the clock "disassociated time from human events and helped create the belief in an independent world of mathematically measurable sequences." The "abstract framework of divided time" became "the point of reference for both action and thought."

The clock's methodical ticking helped bring into being the scientific mind and the scientific man. But it also took something away. As the late MIT computer scientist Joseph Weizenbaum observed in his 1976 book, *Computer Power and Human Reason: From Judgment to Calculation*, the conception of the world that emerged from the widespread use of timekeeping instruments "remains an impoverished version of the older one, for it rests on a rejection of those direct experiences that formed the basis for, and indeed constituted, the old reality." In deciding when to eat, to work, to sleep, to rise, we stopped listening to our senses and started obeying the clock.

The process of adapting to new intellectual technologies is reflected in the changing metaphors we use to explain ourselves to ourselves. When the mechanical clock arrived, people began thinking of their brains as operating "like clockwork." Today, in the age of software, we have come to think of them as operating "like computers." But the changes, neuroscience tells us, go much deeper than metaphor. Thanks to our brain's plasticity, the adaptation occurs also at a biological level.

The Internet promises to have particularly far-reaching effects on cognition. In a paper published in 1936, the British mathematician Alan Turing proved that a digital computer, which at the time existed only as a theoretical machine, could be programmed to perform the function of any other information-processing device. And that's what we're seeing today. The Internet, an immeasurably powerful computing system, is subsuming most of our other intellectual technologies. It's becoming our map and our clock, our printing press and our typewriter, our calculator and our telephone, and our radio and TV.

When the Net absorbs a medium, that medium is re-created in the Net's image. It injects the medium's content with hyperlinks, blinking ads, and other digital gewgaws, and it surrounds the content with the content of all the other media it has absorbed. A new e-mail message, for instance, may announce its arrival as we're glancing over the latest headlines at a newspaper's site. The result is to scatter our attention and diffuse our concentration.

The Net's influence doesn't end at the edges of a computer screen, either. As people's minds become attuned to the crazy quilt of Internet media, traditional media have to adapt to the audience's new expectations. Television programs add text crawls and pop-up ads, and magazines and newspapers shorten their articles, introduce capsule summaries, and crowd their pages with easy-to-browse info-snippets. When, in March of this year, *The New York Times* decided to devote the second and third pages of every edition to article abstracts, its design director, Tom Bodkin, explained that the "shortcuts" would give harried readers a quick "taste" of the day's news, sparing them the "less efficient" method of actually turning the pages and reading the articles. Old media have little choice but to play by the new-media rules.

Never has a communications system played so many roles in our lives—or exerted such broad influence over our thoughts—as the Internet does today. Yet, for all that's been written about the Net, there's been little consideration of how, exactly, it's reprogramming us. The Net's intellectual ethic remains obscure.

About the same time that Nietzsche started using his type-writer, an earnest young man named Frederick Winslow Taylor carried a stopwatch into the Midvale Steel plant in Philadelphia and began a historic series of experiments aimed at improving the efficiency of the plant's machinists. With the approval of Midvale's owners, he recruited a group of factory hands, set them to work on various metalworking machines, and recorded and timed their every movement as well as the operations of the machines. By breaking down every job into a sequence of small, discrete steps and then testing different ways of performing each one, Taylor created a set of precise instructions—an "algorithm," we might say today—for how each worker should work. Midvale's employees grumbled about the strict new regime, claiming that it turned them into little more than automatons, but the factory's productivity soared.

More than a hundred years after the invention of the steam

engine, the Industrial Revolution had at last found its philosophy and its philosopher. Taylor's tight industrial choreography—his "system," as he liked to call it—was embraced by manufacturers throughout the country and, in time, around the world. Seeking maximum speed, maximum efficiency, and maximum output, factory owners used time-and-motion studies to organize their work and configure the jobs of their workers. The goal, as Taylor defined it in his celebrated 1911 treatise, *The Principles of Scientific Management*, was to identify and adopt, for every job, the "one best method" of work and thereby to effect "the gradual substitution of science for rule of thumb throughout the mechanic arts." Once his system was applied to all acts of manual labor, Taylor assured his followers, it would bring about a restructuring not only of industry but of society, creating a utopia of perfect efficiency. "In the past the man has been first," he declared; "in the future the system must be first."

Taylor's system is still very much with us; it remains the ethic of industrial manufacturing. And now, thanks to the growing power that computer engineers and software coders wield over our intellectual lives, Taylor's ethic is beginning to govern the realm of the mind as well. The Internet is a machine designed for the efficient and automated collection, transmission, and manipulation of information, and its legions of programmers are intent on finding the "one best method"—the perfect algorithm—to carry out every mental movement of what we've come to describe as "knowledge work."

Google's headquarters, in Mountain View, California—the Googleplex—is the Internet's high church, and the religion practiced inside its walls is Taylorism. Google, says its chief executive, Eric Schmidt, is "a company that's founded around the science of measurement," and it is striving to "systematize everything" it does. Drawing on the terabytes of behavioral data it collects through its search engine and other sites, it carries out thousands of experiments a day, according to the *Harvard Business Review*, and it uses the results to refine the algorithms that increasingly control how people find information and extract meaning from it. What Taylor did for the work of the hand, Google is doing for the work of the mind.

The company has declared that its mission is "to organize the world's information and make it universally accessible and useful." It seeks to develop "the perfect search engine," which it defines as something that "understands exactly what you mean and gives you back exactly what you want." In Google's view, information is a kind of commodity, a utilitarian resource that can be mined and processed with industrial efficiency. The more pieces of information we can "access" and the faster we can extract their gist, the more productive we become as thinkers.

Where does it end? Sergey Brin and Larry Page, the gifted young men who founded Google while pursuing doctoral degrees in computer science at Stanford, speak frequently of their desire to turn their search engine into an artificial intelligence, a HAL-like machine that might be connected directly to our brains. "The ultimate search engine is something as smart as people—or smarter," Page said in a speech a few years back. "For us, working on search is a way to work on artificial intelligence." In a 2004 interview with *Newsweek*, Brin said, "Certainly if you had all the world's information directly attached to your brain, or an artificial brain that was smarter than your brain, you'd be better off." Last year, Page told a convention of scientists that Google is "really trying to build artificial intelligence and to do it on a large scale."

Such an ambition is a natural one, even an admirable one, for a pair of math whizzes with vast quantities of cash at their disposal and a small army of computer scientists in their employ. A fundamentally scientific enterprise, Google is motivated by a desire to use technology, in Eric Schmidt's words, "to solve problems that have never been solved before," and artificial intelligence is the hardest problem out there. Why wouldn't Brin and Page want to be the ones to crack it?

Still, their easy assumption that we'd all "be better off" if our brains were supplemented, or even replaced, by an artificial intelligence is unsettling. It suggests a belief that intelligence is the output of a mechanical process, a series of discrete steps that can be isolated, measured, and optimized. In Google's world, the world we enter when we go online, there's little place for the fuzziness of contemplation. Ambiguity is not an opening for insight but a bug to be fixed. The human brain is just an outdated computer that needs a faster processor and a bigger hard drive.

The idea that our minds should operate as high-speed data-processing machines is not only built into the workings of the Internet, it is the network's reigning business model as well. The faster we surf across the Web—the more links we click and pages we view—the more opportunities Google and other companies gain to collect information about us and to feed us advertisements. Most of the proprietors of the commercial Internet have a financial stake in collecting the crumbs of data we leave behind as we flit from link to link—the more crumbs, the better. The last thing these companies want is to encourage leisurely reading or slow, concentrated thought. It's in their economic interest to drive us to distraction.

Maybe I'm just a worrywart. Just as there's a tendency to glorify technological progress, there's a countertendency to expect the worst of every new tool or machine. In Plato's *Phaedrus*, Socrates bemoaned the development of writing. He feared that, as people came to rely on the written word as a substitute for the knowledge they used to carry inside their heads, they would, in the words of one of the dialogue's characters, "cease to exercise their memory and become forgetful." And because they would be able to "receive a quantity of information without proper instruction," they would "be thought very knowledgeable when they are for the most part quite ignorant." They would be "filled with the conceit of wisdom instead of real wisdom." Socrates wasn't wrong—the new technology did often have the effects he feared—but he was shortsighted. He couldn't foresee the many ways that writing and reading would serve to spread information, spur fresh ideas, and expand human knowledge (if not wisdom).

The arrival of Gutenberg's printing press, in the fifteenth century, set off another round of teeth gnashing. The Italian humanist Hieronimo Squarciafico worried that the easy availability of books would lead to intellectual laziness, making men "less studious" and weakening their minds. Others argued that cheaply printed books and broadsheets would undermine religious authority, demean the work of scholars and scribes, and spread sedition and debauchery. As New York University professor Clay Shirky notes, "Most of the arguments made against the printing press were correct, even prescient." But, again, the doomsayers were unable to imagine the myriad blessings that the printed word would deliver.

So, yes, you should be skeptical of my skepticism. Perhaps those who dismiss critics of the Internet as Luddites or nostalgists will be proved correct, and from our hyperactive, data-stoked minds will spring a golden age of intellectual discovery and universal wisdom. Then again, the Net isn't the alphabet, and although it may replace the printing press, it produces something altogether different. The kind of deep reading that a sequence of printed pages promotes is valuable not just for the knowledge we acquire from the author's words but for the intellectual vibrations those words set off within our own minds. In the quiet spaces opened up by the sustained, undistracted reading of a book, or by any other act of contemplation, for that matter, we make our own associations, draw our own inferences and analogies, foster our own ideas. Deep reading, as Maryanne Wolf argues, is indistinguishable from deep thinking.

If we lose those quiet spaces, or fill them up with "content," we will sacrifice something important not only in our selves but in our culture. In a recent essay, the playwright Richard Foreman eloquently described what's at stake:

> I come from a tradition of Western culture, in which the
> ideal (my ideal) was the complex, dense and "cathedral-
> like" structure of the highly educated and articulate per-
> sonality—a man or woman who carried inside themselves
> a personally constructed and unique version of the entire
> heritage of the West. [But now] I see within us all (myself
> included) the replacement of complex inner density with a
> new kind of self—evolving under the pressure of informa-
> tion overload and the technology of the "instantly avail-
> able."

As we are drained of our "inner repertory of dense cultural inheri-
tance," Foreman concluded, we risk turning into "'pancake people'—spread wide and thin as we connect with that vast network of
information accessed by the mere touch of a button."

I'm haunted by that scene in *2001*. What makes it so poignant,
and so weird, is the computer's emotional response to the disas-
sembly of its mind: its despair as one circuit after another goes
dark, its childlike pleading with the astronaut—"I can feel it. I can
feel it. I'm afraid"—and its final reversion to what can only be called
a state of innocence. HAL's outpouring of feeling contrasts with the
emotionlessness that characterizes the human figures in the film
who go about their business with an almost robotic efficiency. Their
thoughts and actions feel scripted, as if they're following the steps
of an algorithm. In the world of *2001*, people have become so
machinelike that the most human character turns out to be a
machine. That's the essence of Kubrick's dark prophecy: as we come
to rely on computers to mediate our understanding of the world, it
is our own intelligence that flattens into artificial intelligence.

<Gary Small>
<Gigi Vorgan>

your brain is evolving right now

Excerpted from *iBrain* (pp. 1–22).

GARY SMALL is the Parlow-Solomon Professor on Aging at the David Geffen School of Medicine at UCLA and Director of the UCLA Center on Aging. He has written more than 500 scientific works. *Scientific American* magazine named him one of the world's top innovators in science and technology. He is also the author or coauthor of five popular books, including *The Memory Bible* (2003) and *iBrain: Surviving the Technological Alteration of the Modern Mind* (2008). More information at www.DrGarySmall.com.

GIGI VORGAN wrote, produced, and appeared in numerous feature films and television projects before joining her husband, Dr. Gary Small, to cowrite *The Memory Bible*. She also coauthored with him *The Memory Prescription* (2005), *The Longevity Bible* (2007), *The Naked Lady Who Stood on Her Head: A Psychiatrist's Stories of His Most Bizarre Cases* (2010), and *iBrain: Surviving the Technological Alteration of the Modern Mind*. Contact: gigi@vorgan.com.

T HE CURRENT EXPLOSION of digital technology not only is changing the way we live and communicate but is rapidly and profoundly altering our brains. Daily exposure to high technology—computers, smartphones, video games, search engines like Google and Yahoo—stimulates brain cell alteration and neurotransmitter release, gradually strengthening new neural pathways in our brains while weakening old ones. Because of the current technological revolution, our brains are *evolving* right now—at a speed like never before.

Besides influencing how we think, digital technology is altering how we feel, how we behave, and the way in which our brains function. Although we are unaware of these changes in our neural circuitry or brain wiring, these alterations can become permanent with repetition. This evolutionary brain process has rapidly emerged over a *single* generation and may represent one of the most unexpected yet pivotal advances in human history. Perhaps not since Early Man first discovered how to use a tool has the human brain been affected so quickly and so dramatically.

Television had a fundamental impact on our lives in the past century, and today the average person's brain continues to have extensive daily exposure to TV. Scientists at the University of California, Berkeley, recently found that on average Americans spend nearly three hours each day watching television or movies, or much more time spent than on *all* leisure physical activities combined. But in the current digital environment, the Internet is replacing television as the prime source of brain stimulation. Seven out of ten American homes are wired for high-speed Internet. We rely on the Internet and digital technology for entertainment, political discussion, and even social reform as well as communication with friends and coworkers.

As the brain evolves and shifts its focus toward new technological skills, it drifts away from fundamental social skills, such as reading facial expressions during conversation or grasping the emotional context of a subtle gesture. A Stanford University study found that for every hour we spend on our computers, traditional face-to-face interaction time with other people drops by nearly thirty minutes. With the weakening of the brain's neural circuitry controlling human contact, our social interactions may become awkward, and we tend to misinterpret, and even miss, subtle, non-verbal messages. Imagine how the continued slipping of social skills might affect an international summit meeting ten years from now when a misread facial cue or a misunderstood gesture could make the difference between escalating military conflict or peace.

The high-tech revolution is redefining not only how we communicate but how we reach and influence people, exert political and social change, and even glimpse into the private lives of coworkers, neighbors, celebrities, and politicians. An unknown innovator can become an overnight media magnet as news of his discovery speeds across the Internet. A cell phone video camera can capture a momentary misstep of a public figure and in minutes it becomes the most downloaded video on YouTube. Internet social networks like MySpace and Facebook have exceeded a hundred million users, emerging as the new marketing giants of the digital age and dwarfing traditional outlets such as newspapers and magazines.

Young minds tend to be the most exposed, as well as the most sensitive, to the impact of digital technology. Today's young people in their teens and twenties, who have been dubbed Digital Natives, have never known a world without computers, twenty-four-hour TV news, Internet, and cell phones—with their video, music, cameras, and text messaging. Many of these Natives rarely enter a library, let alone look something up in a traditional encyclopedia; they use Google, Yahoo, and other online search engines. The neural networks in the brains of these Digital Natives differ dramatically from those of Digital Immigrants: people—including all baby boomers—who came to the digital/computer age as adults but whose basic brain wiring was laid down during a time when direct social interaction was the norm. The extent of their early technological communication and entertainment involved the radio, telephone, and TV.

As a consequence of this overwhelming and early high-tech stimulation of the Digital Native's brain, we are witnessing the beginning of a deeply divided *brain gap* between younger and older minds—in just one generation. What used to be simply a *generation gap* that separated young people's values, music, and habits from those of their parents has now become a huge divide resulting in two separate cultures. The brains of the younger generation are digitally hardwired from toddlerhood, often at the expense of neural circuitry that controls one-on-one people skills. Individuals of the older generation face a world in which their brains *must* adapt to high technology or they'll be left behind—politically, socially, and economically.

Young people have created their own digital social networks, including a shorthand type of language for text messaging, and studies show that fewer young adults read books for pleasure now than in any generation before them. Since 1982, literary reading has declined by 28 percent in eighteen- to thirty-four-year-olds. Professor Thomas Patterson and colleagues at Harvard University reported that only 16 percent of adults age eighteen to thirty read a daily newspaper, compared with 35 percent of those thirty-six and older. Patterson predicts that the future of news will be in the electronic digital media rather than the traditional print or television forms.

These young people are not abandoning the daily newspaper for a stroll in the woods to explore nature. Conservation biologist Oliver Pergams at the University of Illinois recently found a highly significant correlation between how much time people spend with new technology, such as video gaming, Internet surfing, and video watching, and the decline in per capita visits to national parks.

Digital Natives are snapping up the newest electronic gadgets and toys with glee and often putting them to use in the workplace. Their parents' generation of Digital Immigrants tends to step more reluctantly into the computer age, not because they don't want to make their lives more efficient through the Internet and portable devices but because these devices may feel unfamiliar and might upset their routine at first.

During this pivotal point in brain evolution, Natives and Immigrants alike can learn the tools they need to take charge of their lives and their brains, while both preserving their humanity and keeping up with the latest technology. We don't all have to become techno-zombies, nor do we need to trash our computers and go back to writing longhand. Instead, we all should help our brains adapt and succeed in this ever-accelerating technological environment.

>>> it's all in your head

Every time our brains are exposed to new sensory stimulation or information, they function like camera film when it is exposed to an image. The light from the image passes through the camera lens and causes a chemical reaction that alters the film and creates a photograph.

As you glance at your computer screen or read this book, light impulses from the screen or page will pass through the lens of your eye and trigger chemical and electrical reactions in your retina, the membrane in the back of the eye that receives images from the lens and sends them to the brain through the optic nerve. From the optic nerve, neurotransmitters send their messages through a complex network of neurons, axons, and dendrites until you become consciously aware of the screen or page. All this takes a minuscule fraction of a second.

Perception of the image may stir intense emotional reactions, jog repressed memories, or simply trigger an automatic physical response—like turning the page or scrolling down the computer screen. Our moment-to-moment responses to our environment lead to very particular chemical and electrical sequences that shape who we are and what we feel, think, dream, and do. Although initially transient and instantaneous, enough repetition of any stimulus—whether it's operating a new technological device or simply making a change in one's jogging route—will lay down a corresponding set of neural network pathways in the brain, which can become permanent.

Your brain—weighing about three pounds—sits cozily within your skull and is a complex mass of tissue, jam-packed with an estimated hundred billion cells. These billions of cells have central bodies that control them, which constitute the brain's *gray matter*, also known as the cortex, an extensive outer layer of cells or neurons. Each cell has extensions, or wires (axons), that make up the brain's *white matter* and connect to dendrites, allowing the cells to communicate and receive messages from one another across synapses, or connection sites.

The brain's gray matter and white matter are responsible for memory, thinking, reasoning, sensation, and muscle movement. Scientists have mapped the various regions of the brain that correspond to different functions and specialized neural circuitry. These regions and circuits manage everything we do and experience, including falling in love, flossing our teeth, reading a novel, recalling fond memories, and snacking on a bag of nuts.

The amount and organizational complexity of these neurons, their wires, and their connections are vast and elaborate. In the average brain, the number of synaptic connection sites has been estimated at 1,000,000,000,000,000, or a million times a billion. After all, it's taken millions of years for the brain to evolve to this point. The fact that it has taken so long for the human brain to evolve such complexity makes the current single-generation, high-tech brain evolution so phenomenal. We're talking about significant brain changes happening over mere decades rather than over millennia.

>>> young plastic brains

The process of laying down neural networks in our brains begins in infancy and continues throughout our lives. These networks or pathways provide our brains an organizational framework for incoming data. A young mind is like a new computer with some basic programs built in and plenty of room left on its hard drive for additional information. As more and more data enter the computer's memory, it develops shortcuts to access that information. E-mail, word processing, and search engine programs learn the user's preferences and repeated keywords, for which they develop shortcuts, or macros, to complete words and phrases after only one or two keys have been typed. As young malleable brains develop shortcuts to access information, these shortcuts represent new neural pathways being laid down. Young children who have learned their times tables by heart no longer use the more cumbersome neural pathway of figuring out the math problem by counting their fingers or multiplying on paper. Eventually they learn even more effective shortcuts, such as ten times any number simply requires adding a zero, and so on.

In order for us to think, feel, and move, our neurons or brain cells need to communicate with one another. As they mature, neurons sprout abundant branches, or dendrites, that receive signals from the long wires or axons of neighboring brain cells. The amount of cell connections, or synapses, in the human brain reaches its peak early in life. At age two, synapse concentration maxes out in the frontal cortex, when the weight of the toddler's brain is nearly that of an adult's. By adolescence, these synapses trim themselves down by about 60 percent and then level off for adulthood. Because there are so many potential neural connections, our brains have evolved to protect themselves from "overwiring" by developing a selectivity and letting in only a small subset of information. Our brains cannot function efficiently with too much information.

The vast number of potentially viable connections accounts for the young brain's *plasticity,* its ability to be malleable and ever-changing in response to stimulation and the environment. This plasticity allows an immature brain to learn new skills readily and much more efficiently than the trimmed-down adult brain. One of the best examples is the young brain's ability to learn language. The fine-tuned and well-pruned adult brain can still take on a new language, but it requires hard work and commitment. Young children are more receptive to the sounds of a new language and much quicker to learn the words and phrases. Linguistic scientists have found that the keen ability of normal infants to distinguish foreign-language sounds begins declining by twelve months of age.

Studies show that our environment molds the shape and function of our brains as well, and it can do so to the point of no return. We know that normal human brain development requires a balance of environmental stimulation and human contact. Deprived of these, neuronal firing and brain cellular connections do not form correctly. A well-known example is visual sensory deprivation. A baby born with cataracts will not be able to see well-defined spatial stimuli in the first six months of life. If left untreated during those six months, the infant may never develop proper spatial vision. Because of ongoing development of visual brain regions early in life, children remain susceptible to the adverse effects of visual deprivation until they are about seven or eight years old. Although exposure to new technology may appear to have a much more subtle impact, its structural and functional effects are profound, particularly on a young, extremely plastic brain.

Of course, genetics plays a part in our brain development as well, and we often inherit cognitive talents and traits from our parents. There are families in which musical, mathematical, or artistic talents appear in several family members from multiple generations. Even subtle personality traits appear to have genetic determinants. Identical twins who were separated at birth and then reunited as adults have discovered that they hold similar jobs, have given their children the same names, and share many of the same tastes and hobbies, such as collecting rare coins or painting their houses green.

But the human genome—the full collection of genes that produces a human being—cannot run the whole show. The relatively modest number of human genes—estimated at twenty thousand—is tiny compared with the billions of synapses that eventually develop in our brains. Thus, the amount of information in an individual's genetic code would be insufficient to map out the billions of complex neural connections in the brain without additional environmental input. As a result, the stimulation we expose our minds to every day is critical in determining how our brains work.

>>> natural selection

Evolution essentially means change from a primitive to a more specialized or advanced state. When your teenage daughter learns to upload her new iPod while IM'ing on her laptop, talking on her cell phone, and reviewing her science notes, her brain adapts to a more advanced state by cranking out neurotransmitters, sprouting dendrites, and shaping new synapses. This kind of moment-to-moment, day-in and day-out brain morphing in response to her environment will eventually have an impact on future generations through evolutionary change.

One of the most influential thinkers of the nineteenth century, Charles Darwin, helped explain how our brains and bodies evolve through *natural selection*, an intricate interaction between our genes and our environment, which Darwin simply defined as a "preservation of favorable variations and the rejection of injurious variations." Genes, made up of DNA—the blueprint of all living things—define who we are: whether we'll have blue eyes, brown hair, flexible joints, or perfect pitch. Genes are passed from one generation to the next, but occasionally the DNA of an offspring contains errors or mutations. These errors can lead to differing physical and mental attributes that could give certain offspring an advantage in some environments. For example, the genetic mutation leading to slightly improved visual acuity gave the "fittest" ancestral hunters a necessary advantage to avoid oncoming predators and go on to kill their prey. Darwin's principle of *survival of the fittest* helps explain how those with a genetic edge are more likely to survive, thrive, and pass their DNA on to the next generation. These DNA mutations also help explain the tremendous diversity within our species that has developed over time.

Not all brain evolution is about survival. Most of us in developed nations have the survival basics down—a place to live, a grocery store nearby, and the ability to dial 911 in an emergency. Thus, our brains are free to advance in creative and academic ways, achieve higher goals, and, it is hoped, increase our enjoyment of life.

Sometimes an accident of nature can have a profound effect on the trajectory of our species, putting us on a fast-track evolutionary course. According to anthropologist Stanley Ambrose of the University of Illinois, approximately three hundred thousand years ago, a Neanderthal man realized he could pick up a bone with his hand and use it as a primitive hammer. Our primitive ancestors soon learned that this tool was more effective when the other object was steadied with the opposite hand. This led our ancestors to develop right-handedness or left-handedness. As one side of the brain evolved to become stronger at controlling manual dexterity, the opposite side became more specialized in the evolution of language.

The area of the modern brain that controls the oral and facial muscle movement necessary for language—Broca's area—is in the frontal lobe just next to the fine muscle area that controls hand movement.

Nine out of ten people are right-handed, and their Broca's area, located in the left hemisphere of their brain, controls the right side of their body. Left-handers generally have their Broca's area in the right hemisphere of their brain. Some of us are ambidextrous, but our handedness preference for the right or the left tends to emerge when we write or use any handheld tool that requires a precision grip.

In addition to handedness, the coevolution of language and tool-making led to other brain alterations. To create more advanced tools, prehuman Neanderthals had to have a goal in mind and the planning skills to reach that goal. For example, ensuring that a primitive spear or knife could be gripped well and kill prey involved planning a sequence of actions, such as cutting and shaping the tool and collecting its binding material. Similar complex planning was also necessary for the development of grammatical language, including stringing together words and phrases and coordinating the fine motor lingual and facial muscles, which are thought to have further accelerated frontal lobe development.

In fact, when neuroscientists perform functional magnetic resonance imaging (MRI) studies while volunteers imagine a goal and carry out secondary tasks to achieve that goal, the scientists can pinpoint areas of activation in the most anterior, or forward, part of the frontal lobe. This frontal lobe region probably developed at the same time that language and tools evolved, advancing our human ancestors' ability to hold in mind a main goal while exploring secondary ones—the fundamental components of our human ability to plan and reason.

Brain evolution and advancement of language continue today in the digital age. In addition to the shorthand that has emerged through e-mail and instant messaging, a whole new lexicon has developed through text messaging, based on limiting the number of words and letters used when communicating on handheld devices. Punctuation marks and letters are combined in creative ways to indicate emotions, such as LOL = laugh out loud, and :-) = happy or good feelings. Whether our communications involve talking, written words, or even just emoticons, different brain regions control and react to the various types of communications. Language—either spoken or written—is processed in Broca's area in our frontal lobes. However, neuroscientists at Tokyo Denki University in Japan found that when volunteers viewed emoticons during functional MRI scanning, the emoticons activated the right inferior frontal gyrus, a region that controls nonverbal communication skills.

>>> honey, does my brain look fat?

Natural selection has literally enlarged our brains. The human brain has grown in intricacy and size over the past few hundred thousand years to accommodate the complexity of our behaviors. Whether we're painting, talking, hammering a nail or answering e-mail, these activities require elaborate planning skills, which are controlled in the front part of the brain.

As Early Man's language and toolmaking skills gradually advanced, brain size and specialization accelerated. Our ancestors who learned to use language began to work together in hunting groups, which helped them survive drought and famine. Sex-specific social roles evolved further as well. Males specialized in hunting, and those males with better visual and spatial abilities (favoring the right brain) had the hunting advantage. Our female ancestors took on the role of caring for offspring, and those with more developed language skills (left brain) were probably more nurturing to their offspring, so those offspring were more likely to survive. Even now, women tend to be more social and talk more about their feelings, while men, no longer hunters, retain their highly evolved right-brain visual-spatial skills, thus often refusing to use the GPS navigation systems in their cars to get directions.

The printing press, electricity, telephone, automobile, and air travel were all major technological innovations that greatly affected our lifestyles and our brains in the twentieth century. Medical discoveries have brought us advances that would have been considered science fiction just decades ago. However, today's technological and digital progress is likely causing our brains to evolve at an unprecedented pace. . . .

>>> your brain, on google

We know that the brain's neural circuitry responds every moment to whatever sensory input it gets, and that the many hours people spend in front of the computer—doing various activities, including trolling the Internet, exchanging e-mail, videoconferencing, IM'ing, and e-shopping—expose their brains to constant digital stimulation. Our UCLA research team wanted to look at how much impact this extended computer time was having on the brain's neural circuitry, how quickly it could build up new pathways, and whether or not we could observe and measure these changes as they occurred.

I enlisted the help of Drs. Susan Bookheimer and Teena Moody, UCLA experts in neuropsychology and neuroimaging. We hypothesized that computer searches and other online activities cause measurable and rapid alterations to brain neural circuitry, particularly in people without previous computer experience.

To test our hypotheses, we planned to use functional MRI scanning to measure the brain's neural pathways during a common

Internet computer task: searching Google for accurate information. We first needed to find people who were relatively inexperienced and naive to the computer. Because the Pew Internet project surveys had reported that about 90 percent of young adults are frequent Internet users compared with less than 50 percent of older people, we knew that people naive to the computer did exist and that they tended to be older.

After initial difficulty finding people who had not yet used computers, we were able to recruit three volunteers in their midfifties and sixties who were new to computer technology yet willing to give it a try. To compare the brain activity of these three computer-naive volunteers, we also recruited three computer-savvy volunteers of comparable age, gender, and socioeconomic background. For our experimental activity, we chose searching on Google for specific and accurate information on a variety of topics, ranging from the health benefits of eating chocolate to planning a trip to the Galápagos.

Next, we had to figure out a way to do MRI scanning on the volunteers while they used the Internet. Because the study subjects had to be inside a long narrow tube of an MRI scanner during the experiment, there would be no space for a computer, keyboard, or mouse. To re-create the Google-search experience inside the scanner, the volunteers wore a pair of special goggles that presented images of website pages designed to simulate the conditions of a typical Internet search session. The system allowed the volunteers to navigate the simulated computer screen and make choices to advance their search by simply pressing one finger on a small keypad, conveniently placed.

To make sure that the functional MRI scanner was measuring the neural circuitry that controls Internet searches, we needed to factor out other sources of brain stimulation. To do this, we added a control task that involved the study subjects reading pages of a book projected through the specialized goggles during the MRI.

This task allowed us to subtract from the MRI measurements any nonspecific brain activations, from simply reading text, focusing on a visual image, or concentrating. We wanted to observe and measure only the brain's activity from those mental tasks required for Internet searching, such as scanning for targeted key words, rapidly choosing from among several alternatives, going back to a previous page if a particular search choice was not helpful, and so forth. We alternated this control task—simply reading a simulated page of text—with the Internet searching task. We also controlled for nonspecific brain stimulations caused by the photos and drawings that are typically displayed on an Internet page.

Finally, to determine whether we could train the brains of Internet-naive volunteers, after the first scanning session we asked each volunteer to search the Internet for an hour each day for five days. We gave the computer-savvy volunteers the same assignment and repeated the functional MRI scans on both groups after the five days of search-engine training.

As we had predicted, the brains of computer-savvy and computer-naive subjects did not show any difference when they were reading the simulated book text; both groups had years of experience in this mental task, and their brains were quite familiar with reading books. By contrast, the two groups showed distinctly different patterns of neural activation when searching on Google. During the baseline scanning session, the computer-savvy subjects used a specific network in the left front part of the brain, known as the dorsolateral prefrontal cortex. The Internet-naive subjects showed minimal, if any, activation in this region.

One of our concerns in designing the study was that five days would not be enough time to observe any changes, but previous research suggested that even Digital Immigrants can train their brains relatively quickly. Our initial hypothesis turned out to be correct. After just five days of practice, the exact same neural circuitry in the front part of the brain became active in the Internet-naive subjects. Five hours on the Internet, and the naive subjects had already rewired their brains.

This particular area of the brain controls our ability to make decisions and integrate complex information. It also controls our mental process of integrating sensations and thoughts, as well as working memory, which is our ability to keep information in mind for a very short time—just long enough to manage an Internet search task or dial a phone number after getting it from directory assistance.

The computer-savvy volunteers activated the same frontal brain region at baseline and had a similar level of activation during their second session, suggesting that for a typical computer-savvy individual, the neural circuit training occurs relatively early and then remains stable. But these initial findings raise several unanswered questions. If our brains are so sensitive to just an hour a day of computer exposure, what happens when we spend more time? What about the brains of young people, whose neural circuitry is even more malleable and plastic? What happens to their brains when they spend their average eight hours daily with their high-tech toys and devices?

>>> techno-brain burnout

In today's digital age, we keep our smartphones at our hip and their earpieces attached to our ears. A laptop is always within reach, and there's no need to fret if we can't find a landline—there's always Wi-Fi (short for *wireless fidelity*, which signifies any place that supplies a wireless connection to the Internet) to keep us connected. As technology enables us to cram more and more work into our days, it seems as if we create more and more work to do.

Our high-tech revolution has plunged us into a state of *continu-*

ous partial attention, which software executive Linda Stone describes as continually staying busy—keeping tabs on everything while never truly focusing on anything. Continuous partial attention differs from multitasking, wherein we have a purpose for each task and we are trying to improve efficiency and productivity. Instead, when our minds partially attend, and do so continuously, we scan for an opportunity for any type of contact at every given moment. We virtually chat as our text messages flow, and we keep tabs on active buddy lists (friends and other screen names in an instant message program); everything, everywhere is connected through our peripheral attention. Although having all our pals online from moment to moment seems intimate, we risk losing personal touch with our real-life relationships and may experience an artificial sense of intimacy compared with when we shut down our devices and devote our attention to one individual at a time. But still, many people report that if they're suddenly cut off from someone's buddy list, they take it personally—deeply personally.

When paying partial continuous attention, people may place their brains in a heightened state of stress. They no longer have time to reflect, contemplate, or make thoughtful decisions. Instead, they exist in a sense of constant crisis—on alert for a new contact or bit of exciting news or information at any moment. Once people get used to this state, they tend to thrive on the perpetual connectivity. It feeds their egos and sense of self-worth, and it becomes irresistible.

Neuroimaging studies suggest that this sense of self-worth may protect the size of the hippocampus—that horseshoe-shaped brain region in the medial (inward-facing) temporal lobe, which allows us to learn and remember new information. Dr. Sonia Lupien and associates at McGill University studied hippocampal size in healthy younger and older adult volunteers. Measures of self-esteem correlated significantly with hippocampal size, regardless of age. They also found that the more people felt in control of their lives, the larger the hippocampus.

But at some point, the sense of control and self-worth we feel when we maintain partial continuous attention tends to break down—our brains were not built to maintain such monitoring for extended time periods. Eventually, the endless hours of unrelenting digital connectivity can create a unique type of brain strain. Many people who have been working on the Internet for several hours without a break report making frequent errors in their work. Upon signing off, they notice feeling spaced out, fatigued, irritable, and distracted, as if they are in a "digital fog." This new form of mental stress, what I term techno-brain burnout, is threatening to become an epidemic.

Under this kind of stress, our brains instinctively signal the adrenal gland to secrete cortisol and adrenaline. In the short run, these stress hormones boost energy levels and augment memory, but over time they actually impair cognition, lead to depression, and alter the neural circuitry in the hippocampus, amygdala, and prefrontal cortex—the brain regions that control mood and thought. Chronic and prolonged techno-brain burnout can even reshape the underlying brain structure.

Dr. Sara Mednick and colleagues at Harvard University were able to experimentally induce a mild form of techno-brain burnout in research volunteers; they then were able to reduce its impact through power naps and by varying mental assignments. Their study subjects performed a visual task: reporting the direction of three lines in the lower left corner of a computer screen. The volunteers' scores worsened over time, but their performance improved if the scientists alternated the visual task between the lower left and lower right corners of the computer screen. This result suggests that brain burnout may be relieved by varying the location of the mental task.

The investigators also found that the performance of study subjects improved if they took a quick twenty- to thirty-minute nap. The neural networks involved in the task were apparently refreshed during rest; however, optimum refreshment and reinvigoration

for the task occurred when naps lasted up to sixty minutes—
the amount of time it takes for rapid eye movement (REM) sleep to
kick in.

>>> the new, improved brain

Young adults have created computer-based social networks through
sites like MySpace and Facebook, chat rooms, instant messaging,
videoconferencing, and e-mail. Children and teenagers are cyber-
savvy too. A fourteen-year-old girl can chat with ten of her friends
at one time with the stroke of a computer key and find out all the
news about who broke up with whom in seconds—no need for ten
phone calls or, heaven forbid, actually waiting to talk in person the
next day at school.

These Digital Natives have defined a new culture of communication—no longer dictated by time, place, or even how one looks at the
moment unless they're video chatting or posting photographs of
themselves on MySpace. Even baby boomers who still prefer communicating the traditional way—in person—have become adept at
e-mail and instant messaging. Both generations—one eager, one
often reluctant—are rapidly developing these technological skills
and the corresponding neural networks that control them, even if
it's only to survive in the ever-changing professional world.

Almost all Digital Immigrants will eventually become more
technologically savvy, which will bridge the brain gap to some
extent. And, as the next few decades pass, the workforce will be
made up of mostly Digital Natives; thus, the brain gap as we now
know it will cease to exist. Of course, people will always live in a
world in which they will meet friends, date, have families, go on job
interviews, and interact in the traditional face-to-face way. However, those who are most fit in these social skills will have an adaptive advantage. For now, scientific evidence suggests that the

consequences of early and prolonged technological exposure of a young brain may in some cases never be reversed, but early brain alterations can be managed, social skills learned and honed, and the brain gap bridged.

Whether we're Digital Natives or Immigrants, altering our neural networks and synaptic connections through activities such as e-mail, video games, Googling (verb: to use the Google search engine to obtain information on the Internet [from Wikipedia, the free encyclopedia]), or other technological experiences does sharpen some cognitive abilities. We can learn to react more quickly to visual stimuli and improve many forms of attention, particularly the ability to notice images in our peripheral vision. We develop a better ability to sift through large amounts of information rapidly and decide what's important and what isn't—our mental filters basically learn how to shift into overdrive. In this way, we are able to cope with the massive amounts of information appearing and disappearing on our mental screens from moment to moment.

Initially, the daily blitz of data that bombards us can create a form of attention deficit, but our brains are able to adapt in a way that promotes rapid information processing. According to Professor Pam Briggs of North Umbria University in the United Kingdom, Web surfers looking for information on health spend two seconds or less on any particular website before moving on to the next one. She found that when study subjects did stop and focus on a particular site, that site contained data relevant to the search, whereas those they skipped over contained almost nothing relevant to the search. This study indicates that our brains learn to swiftly focus attention, analyze information, and almost instantaneously decide on a go or no-go action. Rather than simply catching "digital ADD," many of us are developing neural circuitry that is customized for rapid and incisive spurts of directed concentration.

While the brains of today's Digital Natives are wiring up for rapid-fire cybersearches, the neural circuits that control the more traditional learning methods are neglected and gradually diminished. The pathways for human interaction and communication weaken as customary one-on-one people skills atrophy. Our UCLA research team and other scientists have shown that we can intentionally alter brain wiring and reinvigorate some of these dwindling neural pathways, even while the newly evolved technology circuits bring our brains to extraordinary levels of potential.

Although the digital evolution of our brains increases social isolation and diminishes the spontaneity of interpersonal relationships, it may well be increasing our intelligence in the way we currently measure and define IQ. Average IQ scores are steadily rising with the advancing digital culture, and the ability to multitask without errors is improving. Neuroscientist Paul Kearney at Unitec in New Zealand reported that some computer games can actually improve cognitive ability and multitasking skills. He found that volunteers who played the games eight hours each week improved multitasking skills by two and a half times.

Other research at Rochester University has shown that video game playing can improve peripheral vision as well. As the modern brain continues to evolve, some attention skills improve, mental response times sharpen, and the performance of many brain tasks becomes more efficient. These new brain proficiencies will be even greater in future generations and alter our current understanding and definition of intelligence.

section two

social life, personal life, school

>>>

<Sherry Turkle>

identity crisis

Excerpted from *Life on the Screen* (pp. 255–62).

SHERRY TURKLE is Abby Rockefeller Mauzé Professor of
the Social Studies of Science and Technology in the Program
in Science, Technology, and Society at MIT. Her books
include *The Second Self: Computers and the Human Spirit*
(1984), *Life on the Screen: Identity in the Age of the Internet*
(1995), and *Alone Together: Why We Expect More from Technology and Less from Each Other* (2011).

EVERY ERA CONSTRUCTS its own metaphors for psychological well-being. Not so long ago, stability was socially valued
and culturally reinforced. Rigid gender roles, repetitive
labor, the expectation of being in one kind of job or remaining in
one town over a lifetime, all of these made consistency central to
definitions of health. But these stable social worlds have broken
down. In our time, health is described in terms of fluidity rather
than stability. What matters most now is the ability to adapt and
change—to new jobs, new career directions, new gender roles, new
technologies.

In *Flexible Bodies*, the anthropologist Emily Martin argues that
the language of the immune system provides us with metaphors for

the self and its boundaries.[1] In the past, the immune system was described as a private fortress, a firm, stable wall that protected within from without. Now we talk about the immune system as flexible and permeable. It can only be healthy if adaptable.

The new metaphors of health as flexibility apply not only to human mental and physical spheres, but also to the bodies of corporations, governments, and businesses. These institutions function in rapidly changing circumstances; they too are coming to view their fitness in terms of their flexibility. Martin describes the cultural spaces where we learn the new virtues of change over solidity. In addition to advertising, entertainment, and education, her examples include corporate workshops where people learn wilderness, camping, high-wire walking, and zip-line jumping. She refers to all of these as flexibility practicums.

In her study of the culture of flexibility, Martin does not discuss virtual communities, but these provide excellent examples of what she is talking about. In these environments, people either explicitly play roles (as in MUDs—multiuser domains) or more subtly shape their online selves. Adults learn about being multiple and fluid— and so do children. "I don't play so many different people online— only three," says June, an eleven-year-old who uses her mother's Internet account to play in MUDs. During our conversation, I learn that in the course of a year in RL, she moves among three households—that of her biological mother and stepfather, her biological father and stepmother, and a much-loved "first stepfather," her mother's second husband. She refers to her mother's third and current husband as "second stepfather." June recounts that in each of these three households the rules are somewhat different and so is she. Online switches among personae seem quite natural. Indeed, for her, they are a kind of practice. Martin would call them practicums.

>>> "logins r us"

On a WELL (Whole Earth 'Lectronic Link) discussion group about online personae (subtitled "boon or bête-noire"), participants shared a sense that their virtual identities were evocative objects for thinking about the self. For several, experiences in virtual space compelled them to pay greater attention to what they take for granted in the real. "The persona thing intrigues me," said one. "It's a chance for all of us who aren't actors to play [with] masks. And think about the masks we wear every day."[2]

In this way, online personae have something in common with the self that emerges in a psychoanalytic encounter. It, too, is significantly virtual, constructed within the space of the analysis, where its slightest shifts can come under the most intense scrutiny.[3]

What most characterized the WELL discussion about online personae was the way many of the participants expressed the belief that life on the WELL introduced them to the many within themselves. One person wrote that through participating in an electronic bulletin board and letting the many sides of ourselves show, "We start to resemble little corporations, 'LoginRUs,' and like any company, we each have within us the bean-counter, the visionary, the heart-throb, the fundamentalist, and the wild child. Long may they wave."[4] Other participants responded to this comment with enthusiasm. One, echoing the social psychologist Kenneth Gergen,[5] described identity as a "pastiche of personalities" in which "the test of competence is not so much the integrity of the whole but the apparent correct representation appearing at the right time, in the right context, not to the detriment of the rest of the internal 'collective.'"[6] Another said that he thought of his ego "as a hollow tube, through which, one at a time, the 'many' speak through at the appropriate moment. . . . I'd like to hear more . . . about the possibilities surrounding the notion that what we perceive as 'one' in any context is, perhaps, a conglomerate of 'ones.'" This writer went on:

Hindu culture is rooted in the "many" as the root of spiritual experience. A person's momentary behavior reflects
some influence from one of hundreds of gods and/or god-
desses. I am interested in . . . how this natural assumption
of the "many" creates an alternative psychology.[7]

Another writer concurred:

Did you ever see that cartoon by R. Crumb about "Which
is the real R. Crumb?" He goes through four pages of incar-
nations, from successful businessman to street beggar,
from media celebrity to gut-gnawing recluse, etc., etc.
Then at the end he says: "Which is the real one?" . . . "It all
depends on what mood I'm in!"
    We're all like that online.[8]

Howard Rheingold, the member of the WELL who began the discussion topic, also referred to Gergen's notion of a "saturated self,"
the idea that communication technologies have caused us to "colo-
nize each other's brains." Gergen describes us as saturated with the
many "voices of humankind—both harmonious and alien." He
believes that as "we absorb their varied rhymes and reasons, they
become part of us and we of them. Social saturation furnishes us
with a multiplicity of incoherent and unrelated languages of the
self." With our relationships spread across the globe and our knowledge of other cultures relativizing our attitudes and depriving us of
any norm, we "exist in a state of continuous construction and recon-
struction; it is a world where anything goes that can be negotiated.
Each reality of self gives way to reflexive questioning, irony, and
ultimately the playful probing of yet another reality. The center
fails to hold."[9]
    Although people may at first feel anguish at what they sense as
a breakdown of identity, Gergen believes they may come to embrace

the new possibilities. Individual notions of self vanish "into a stage of relatedness. One ceases to believe in a self independent of the relations in which he or she is embedded."[10] "We live in each other's brains, as voices, images, words on screens," said Rheingold in the online discussion. "We are multiple personalities and we include each other."[11]

Rheingold's evocation of what Gergen calls the "raptures of multiplicitous being" met with support on the WELL. One participant insisted that all pejorative associations be removed from the notion of a saturated self. "Howard, I *like* being a saturated self, in a community of similarly saturated selves. I grew up on TV and pop music, but it just ain't enough. Virtual communities are, among other things, the co-saturation of selves who have been, all their lives, saturated in isolation."[12] To which Rheingold could only reply, "I like being a saturated self too."[13] The cybersociety of the WELL is an object-to-think-with for reflecting on the positive aspects of identity as multiplicity.

>>> identity and multiplicity

Without any principle of coherence, the self spins off in all directions. Multiplicity is not viable if it means shifting among personalities that cannot communicate. Multiplicity is not acceptable if it means being confused to a point of immobility.[14] How can we be multiple and coherent at the same time? In *The Protean Self*, Robert Jay Lifton tries to resolve this seeming contradiction. He begins by assuming that a unitary view of self corresponded to a traditional culture with stable symbols, institutions, and relationships. He finds the old unitary notion no longer viable because traditional culture has broken down and identifies a range of responses. One is a dogmatic insistence on unity. Another is to return to systems of belief, such as religious fundamentalism, that enforce conformity. A third is to embrace the idea of a fragmented self.[15] Lifton says this is a dangerous option that may result in a "fluidity lacking in moral content and sustainable inner form." But Lifton sees another possibility, a healthy protean self. It is capable, like Proteus, of fluid transformations but is grounded in coherence and a moral outlook. It is multiple but integrated.[16] You can have a sense of self without being one self.

Lifton's language is theoretical. Experiences in MUDS, on the WELL, on local bulletin boards, on commercial network services, and on the World Wide Web are bringing his theory down to earth. On the Web, the idiom for constructing a "home" identity is to assemble a "home page" of virtual objects that correspond to one's interests. One constructs a home page by composing or "pasting" on it words, images, and sounds, and by making connections between it and other sites on the Internet or the Web. Like the agents in emergent AI, one's identity emerges from whom one knows, one's associations and connections. People link their home page to pages about such things as music, paintings, television shows, cities, books, photographs, comic strips, and fashion models. As I write this book I am in the process of constructing my own home page. It now contains links to the text of my curriculum vitae, to drafts of recent papers (one about MUDS, one about French psychoanalysis), and to the reading lists for the two courses I shall teach next fall. A "visitor" to my home page can also click a highlighted word and watch images of Michel Foucault and Power Rangers "morph," one into the other, a visual play on my contention that children's toys bring postmodernism down to earth. This display, affectionately referred to as "The Mighty Morphin' Michel Foucault," was a present from my assistant at MIT, Cynthia Col. A virtual home, like a real one, is furnished with objects you buy, build, or receive as gifts.

My future plans for my home page include linking to Paris (the city has a home page), the bot Julia, resources on women's studies,

Imari china, and recent research on migraines. I am not limited in
the number of links I can create. If we take the home page as a real
estate metaphor for the self, its decor is postmodern. Its different
rooms with different styles are located on computers all over the
world. But through one's efforts, they are brought together to be of
a piece.

Home pages on the Web are one recent and dramatic illustration
of new notions of identity as multiple yet coherent; in this book we
have met others. Recall Case, the industrial designer who plays the
female lawyer Mairead in MedievalMUSH. He does not experience
himself as a unitary self, yet says that he feels in control of "him-
selves" and "herselves." He says that he feels fulfilled by his real
and virtual work, marriage, and friendships. While conventional
thinking tends to characterize multiple personae in pathological
terms, this does not seem to capture what is most meaningful about
Case playing Mairead or Garrett (introduced in Chapter 8) playing
Ribbit.

Within the psychoanalytic tradition, there have been schools
that departed from the standard unitary view of identity. As we
have seen, the object-relations theorists invented a language for
talking about the many voices that we bring inside ourselves in the
course of development. Jungian psychology encouraged the individual to become acquainted with a whole range of personae and to
understand them as manifestations of universal archetypes, such
as innocent virgins, mothers and crones, eternal youths and old
men.[17] Jung believed that for each of us, it is potentially most liberating to become acquainted with our dark side, as well as the other-
gendered self, called anima in men and animus in women. Jung
was banished from the ranks of orthodox Freudians for such suggestions. The object-relations school, too, was relegated to the mar-
gins. As America became the center of psychoanalytic politics in the
mid–twentieth century, ideas about a robust executive ego became
the psychoanalytic mainstream.

Through the fragmented selves presented by patients and through theories that stress the decentered subject, contemporary psychology confronts what is left out of theories of the unitary self. Now it must ask, What is the self when it functions as a society?[18] What is the self when it divides its labors among its constituent "alters"?[19] Those burdened by post-traumatic dissociative disorders suffer these questions; here I have suggested that inhabitants of virtual communities play with them.

Ideas about mind can become a vital cultural presence when they are carried by evocative objects-to-think-with.[20] I said earlier that these objects need not be material. For example, dreams and slips of the tongue were objects-to-think-with that brought psychoanalytic ideas into everyday life. People could play with their own and others' dreams and slips. Today, people are being helped to develop ideas about identity as multiplicity by a new practice of identity as multiplicity in online life. Virtual personae are objects-to-think-with.

When people adopt an online persona they cross a boundary into highly charged territory. Some feel an uncomfortable sense of fragmentation, some a sense of relief. Some sense the possibilities for self-discovery, even self-transformation. Serena, a twenty-six-year-old graduate student in history, says, "When I log on to a new MUD and I create a character and know I have to start typing my description, I always feel a sense of panic. Like I could find out something I don't want to know." Arlie, a twenty-year-old undergraduate, says, "I am always very self-conscious when I create a new character. Usually, I end up creating someone I wouldn't want my parents to know about. It takes me, like, three hours. But that someone is part of me." In these ways, and others, many more of us are experimenting with multiplicity than ever before.

With this last comment, I am not implying that MUDs or computer bulletin boards are causally implicated in the dramatic increase of people who exhibit symptoms of multiple personality disorder (MPD), or that people on MUDs have MPD, or that MUD-ding is like having MPD. What I am saying is that the many manifestations of multiplicity in our culture, including the adoption of online personae, are contributing to a general reconsideration of traditional, unitary notions of identity.

The history of a psychiatric symptom is inextricably tied up with the history of the culture that surrounds it. When I was in graduate school in psychology in the 1970s, clinical psychology texts regarded multiple personality as so rare (perhaps one in a million) as to be barely worthy of mention. In these rare cases, there was typically one alter personality in addition to the host personality.[21] Today, cases of multiple personality are much more frequent and typically involve up to sixteen alters of different ages, races, genders, and sexual orientations.[22] In multiple personality disorder, it is widely believed that traumatic events have caused various aspects of the self to congeal into virtual personalities, the "ones" often hiding from the "others" and hiding too from that special alter, the host personality. Sometimes, the alters are known to each other and to the host; some alters may see their roles as actively helping others. Such differences led the philosopher Ian Hacking to write about a "continuum of dissociation."[23] These differences also suggest a way of thinking about the self in terms of a continuum of how accessible its parts are to each other.

At one extreme, the unitary self maintains its oneness by repressing all that does not fit. Thus censored, the illegitimate parts of the self are not accessible. This model would of course function best within a fairly rigid social structure with clearly defined rules and roles. At the other extreme is the MPD sufferer whose multiplicity exists in the context of an equally repressive rigidity. The parts of the self are not in easy communication. Communication is highly stylized; one personality must speak to another personality. In fact, the term "multiple personality" is misleading, because the different parts of the self are not full personalities.

They are split-off, disconnected fragments. But if the disorder in multiple personality disorder is the need for the rigid walls between the selves (blocking the secrets those selves protect), then the study of MPD may begin to furnish ways of thinking about healthy selves as nonunitary but with fluid access among their many aspects. Thus, in addition to the extremes of unitary self and MPD, we can imagine a flexible self.

The essence of this self is not unitary, nor are its parts stable entities. It is easy to cycle through its aspects, and these are themselves changing through constant communication with each other. The philosopher Daniel Dennett speaks to the flexible self in his multiple drafts theory of consciousness.[24] Dennett's notion of multiple drafts is analogous to the experience of having several versions of a document open on a computer screen where the user is able to move between them at will. The presence of the drafts encourages a respect for the many different versions while it imposes a certain distance from them. No one aspect can be claimed as the absolute, true self. When I got to know French Sherry, I no longer saw the less confident English-speaking Sherry as my one authentic self. What most characterizes the model of a flexible self is that the lines of communication between its various aspects are open. The open communication encourages an attitude of respect for the many within us and the many within others.

As we sense our inner diversity we come to know our limitations. We understand that we do not and cannot know things completely, not the outside world and not ourselves. Today's heightened consciousness of incompleteness may predispose us to join with others. The historian of science Donna Haraway equates a "split and contradictory self" with a "knowing self." She is optimistic about its possibilities: "The knowing self is partial in all its guises, never finished, whole, simply there and original; it is always constructed and stitched together imperfectly; and therefore able to join with another, to see together without claiming to be another."[25]

When identity was defined as unitary and solid, it was relatively easy to recognize and censure deviation from a norm. A more fluid sense of self allows a greater capacity for acknowledging diversity. It makes it easier to accept the array of our (and others') inconsistent personae—perhaps with humor, perhaps with irony. We do not feel compelled to rank or judge the elements of our multiplicity. We do not feel compelled to exclude what does not fit.

notes

1. Emily Martin, *Flexible Bodies* (Beacon Press, 1994), pp. 161–225.
2. mcdee, The WELL, conference on virtual communities (vc.20.17), April 18, 1992.
3. The sentiment that life online could provide a different experience of self was seconded by a participant who described himself as a man whose conversational abilities as an adult were impaired by having been a stutterer as a child. Online he was able to discover the experience of participating in the flow of a conversation.

> I echo [the previous contributor] in feeling that my online persona differs greatly from my persona offline. And, in many ways, my online persona is more "me." I feel a lot more freedom to speak here. Growing up, I had a severe stuttering problem. I couldn't speak a word without stuttering, so I spoke only when absolutely necessary. I worked through it in my early twenties and you wouldn't even notice it now (except when I'm stressed out), but at thirty-seven I'm still shy to speak. I'm a lot more comfortable with listening than with talking. And when I do

speak I usually feel out of sync: I'll inadvertently step on
other people's words, or lose people's attention, or talk
through instead of to. I didn't learn the dynamic of conversation that most people take for granted, I think.
Here, though, it's completely different: I have a feel for
the flow of the "conversations," have the time to measure
my response, don't have to worry about the balance of
conversational space—we all make as much space as we
want just by pressing "r" to respond. It's been a wonder-
fully liberating experience for me. (Anonymous)

4. spoonman, The WELL, conference on virtual communities
   (vc.20.65), June 11, 1992.
5. Kenneth Gergen, *The Saturated Self: Dilemmas of Identity in
   Contemporary Life* (Basic Books, 1991).
6. bluefire (Bob Jacobson), The WELL, conference on virtual reality
   (vr.85.146), August 15, 1993.
7. The WELL, conference on virtual reality (vr.85.148), August 17,
   1993.
8. Art Kleiner, The WELL, conference on virtual reality (vr.47.41),
   October 2, 1990.
9. Gergen, *The Saturated Self*, p. 6.
10. Ibid., p. 17.
11. hlr (Howard Rheingold), The WELL, conference on virtual reality
    (vr.47.351), February 2, 1993.
12. McKenzie Wark, The WELL, conference on virtual reality
    (vr.47.361), February 3, 1993.
13. hlr (Howard Rheingold), The WELL, conference on virtual reality
    (vr.47.362), February 3, 1993.
14. James M. Glass, *Shattered Selves: Multiple Personality in a Post-
    modern World* (Cornell University Press, 1993).
15. Robert Jay Lifton, *The Protean Self: Human Resilience in an Age
    of Fragmentation* (Basic Books, 1993), p. 192.

16. Ibid., pp. 229–32.

17. See, for example, "Aion: Phenomenology of the Self," in *The Portable Jung*, ed. Joseph Campbell, trans. R. F. C. Hull (Penguin, 1971).

18. See, for example, Marvin Minsky, *The Society of Mind* (Simon & Schuster, 1985).

19. See, for example, Colin Ross, *Multiple Personality Disorder: Diagnosis, Clinical Features, and Treatment* (John Wiley & Sons, 1989).

20. Claude Levi-Strauss, *The Savage Mind* (University of Chicago Press, 1960).

21. Ian Hacking, *Rewriting the Soul: Multiple Personality and the Sciences of Memory* (Princeton University Press, 1995), p. 21.

22. Ibid., p. 29.

23. Ibid., pp. 96ff.

24. Daniel C. Dennett, *Consciousness Explained* (Little, Brown & Co., 1991).

25. Donna Haraway, "The Actors Are Cyborg, Nature Is Coyote, and the Geography Is Elsewhere: Postscript to 'Cyborgs at Large,'" in *Technoculture,* eds. Constance Penley and Andrew Ross (University of Minnesota Press, 1991), p. 22.

<Douglas Rushkoff>

they call me cyberboy

Originally published in *Time Digital* (1996).

DOUGLAS RUSHKOFF is the author of best-selling books on media and society, including *Media Virus!: Hidden Agendas in Popular Culture* (1994) and *Coercion: Why We Listen to What They Say* (1999), winner of the Marshall McLuhan Award for Best Media Book. He made the PBS Frontline documentaries *Merchants of Cool*, *The Persuaders*, and *Digital Nation*. He teaches at New York University's Interactive Telecommunications Program and in Graduate Media Studies at The New School. His website is http://rushkoff.com.

N OT SO LONG AGO, I could freak people out by talking about cyberculture. It was fun. They'd laugh nervously when I'd say they'd be using e-mail someday. They'd call me "cyberboy" and mean it as an insult. I felt like a renegade.

However frustrating it was to be an Internet evangelist in the late 1980s, it beat what I'm feeling now having won the battle. A journey into cyberspace is about as paradigm-threatening as an afternoon at the mall. The Internet is better, bigger, faster, and brighter, but the buzz is gone.

I remember when following Internet culture or, better, actually participating in it, meant witnessing the birth of a movement as radically novel as psychedelia, punk, or, I liked to imagine, the Renaissance itself.

Here was a ragtag collection of idealistic Californians, bent on wiring up the global brain, one node at a time. Every new account on the WELL—the Bay Area's pre-eminent online bulletin board, Whole Earth 'Lectronic Link—meant another convert to the great digital hot tub. The struggle of obtaining the computer, the modem, the software, the phone number and the appropriate protocol was a journey of Arthurian proportion. The community you'd find when you'd got there was as political, high-minded, and tightly knit as the Round Table. No wonder "universal access" became our Holy Grail.

Conceived on the bong-water-stained rugs of Reed College dorm rooms, the Apple personal computer bent over backwards to bring even the most stoned of us into the mix. The Macintosh soon became the central metaphor for our collective challenge to God himself. We held more than a forbidden fruit: we had the whole world in our hands. Access was power.

Our arrogance was matched only by our naïveté. Like hippies scheming to dose the city's reservoir with LSD, Internet enthusiasts took a by-any-means-necessary attitude towards digital enlightenment. Getting a friend to participate in a USENET group was as rewarding to us as scoring a convert is to a Mormon.

And the beauty of it was that we were the freaks! Not just nerds, but deeply and beautifully twisted people from the very fringes of culture had finally found a home. We all had the sense that we were the first settlers of a remote frontier. We had migrated online together in order to create a new society from the ground up.

Cyberculture was hard to describe—and a good number of us got book contracts paying us to try—but it was undeniably real when experienced firsthand. It was characterized by Californian idealism, do-it-yourselfer ingenuity, and an ethic of tolerance above all else. You couldn't go to a hip party in San Francisco without someone switching on a computer and demonstrating the brand-new Mosaic browser for the fledgling World Wide Web. The patience with which experienced hackers walked newbies through their virgin hypertext voyages would make a sexual surrogate ashamed.

Coaxing businesses online was simply an extension of this need to share. It was less an act of profiteering than an effort to acquire some long-awaited credibility. Somehow it seemed like the revolution was taking too long; so our best-spoken advocates loaded up their laptops and made presentations to the Fortune 500. Then something happened on NASDAQ, and cyberculture was turned upside down.

It should have come as no surprise that big corporations, whose bottom line depends on public relations, direct selling, and "staying ahead of the curve," would eventually become the driving force behind cyberculture's evolution. Once the conversation itself was no longer the highest priority, marketing took its place. Though the diehards protested with the fervor of Christ ejecting moneychangers from the temple, the Internet became the domain of businessmen.

To be sure, commercial interests have taken this technology a long way. Thanks to Internet Explorer 4.0, America Online, and banner advertisements, the holy grail of universal access is within our reach. But universal access to what? Direct marketing, movies-on-demand, and up-to-the-second stock quotes?

Even if the Internet has not yet been rendered ubiquitous, it has certainly absorbed the same mainstream culture that denied its existence and resisted its ethos for an awfully long time. True, cyberculture has inalterably changed its co-opter, but in the process it has become indistinguishable from it as well.

Every day, more people conduct their daily business online. The Internet makes their lives more convenient.

I can't bring myself to see mere convenience as a victory. Sadly, cyberspace has become just another place to do business. The question is no longer how browsing the Internet changes the way we look at the world; it's which browser we'll be using to buy products from the same old world.

The only way I can soothe myself is to imagine that the essentially individualistic and countercultural vibe of the Internet I once knew has simply gone into remission. Corporate money is needed to build the infrastructure that will allow the real world to get access to networking technology. By the time Microsoft and the others learn that the Web is not the direct marketing paradise they're envisioning, it will be too late. They'll have put the tools in our hands that allow us to create the interactive world we were dreaming of.

In the meantime, I now get paid for saying the same sorts of things that got me teased before. But I preferred tweaking people for free. That's why they called me cyberboy.

<Douglas Rushkoff>

the people's net

Originally published in *Yahoo Internet Life* (2001).

T O THOSE OF US who really love it, the Internet is looking and feeling more social, more alive, more participatory, and more, well, more Internet-y than ever before. This might sound surprising, given the headlines proclaiming the official bursting of the technology bubble. Likewise, analysts on the financial cable channels and the venture capitalists of Silicon Alley now shun any company whose name ends in .com and have moved on to more promising new buzzwords, such as wireless.

But the statistics fly in the face of conventional wisdom. In terms of real hours spent online and the number of people getting new accounts every day, Internet use is up. We spent an average of 20.2 hours looking at Internet sites in March 2001, up from 15.9 hours last year and 12.8 hours the year before, according to the latest data from Jupiter Media Metrix. More surprisingly, while countless dot-coms have gone under for failure to meet investor demands, e-commerce is actually up—it rose more than 30 percent compared with last year. More than 100 million Americans now buy goods and services online.

The Internet is more capable now than it ever was of supporting the vast range of individual, community, and commercial interests that hope to exploit the massive power of networking. Still, countless investors, analysts, and pundits have fallen off the Internet bandwagon.

Good riddance, I say. The experts jumping ship today can't see the Internet as anything other than an investment opportunity that has dried up. Sure, the Internet made a lot of people money, but its real promise has always been much greater than a few upward stock ticks. If we can look past the size of our 401(k) plans to the underlying strength of our fledgling networked society, all signs are actually quite good. The Internet has never been in better health.

Maybe this kind of optimism requires us to look at the Internet less as an investment opportunity and more as a new life-form. That's the way we used to see it in ancient times, anyway. Back in the 2,400-band, ASCII text era of ten long years ago, the Internet had nothing to do with the Nasdaq Index. Until 1991, you had to sign an agreement promising not to conduct any business online just to get access to the Internet! Imagine that. It was a business-free zone.

How could such rules ever have been put in place? Because the Internet began as a public project. It was created to allow scientists at universities and government facilities to share research and computing resources. Everyone from the Pentagon to Al Gore saw the value of a universally accessible information-sharing network and invested federal funds to build a backbone capable of connecting computers around the world.

What they didn't realize was that they were doing a whole lot more than connecting computers to one another. They were connecting people, too. Before long, all those scientists who were supposed to be exchanging research or comparing data were exchanging stories about their families and comparing notes on movies. People around the world were playing games, socializing, and crossing cultural boundaries never crossed before. Since no one was using the network to discuss military technology anymore, the government turned it over to the public as best it could.

The Internet's unexpected social side effect turned out to be its incontrovertible main feature. Its other functions fall by the wayside. The Internet's ability to network human beings is its very lifeblood. It fosters communication, collaboration, sharing, helpfulness, and community. When word got out, the nerdiest among us found out first. Then came those of us whose friends were nerds. Then their friends, and so on. Someone would insist he had found something you needed to know about—the way a childhood friend lets you in on a secret door leading to the basement under the junior high school.

How many of you can remember that first time you watched that friend log on? How he turned the keyboard over to you and asked what you wanted to know, where you wanted to visit, or whom you wanted to meet? That was the moment when you got it: Internet fever. There was a whole new world out there, unlimited by the constraints of time and space, appearance and prejudice, gender and power.

It's no wonder so many people compared the 1990s Internet to the psychedelic 1960s. It seemed all we needed to do was get a person online, and he or she would be changed forever. And people were. A sixty-year-old Midwestern businessman I know found himself logging on every night to engage in a conversation about Jungian archetypes. It lasted for four weeks before he realized the person with whom he was conversing was a sixteen-year-old boy from Tokyo.

It felt as though we were wiring up a global brain. Techno visionaries of the period, such as Ted Nelson—who coined the word *hyper-*

text—told us how the Internet could be used as a library for everything ever written. A musician named Jaron Lanier invented a bizarre interactive space he called "virtual reality" in which people would be able to, in his words, "really see what the other means."

The Internet was no longer a government research project. It was alive. Out of control and delightfully chaotic. What's more, it promoted an agenda all its own. It was as if using a computer mouse and keyboard to access other human beings on the other side of the monitor changed our relationship to the media and the power the media held. The tube was no longer a place that only a corporate conglomerate could access. It was Rupert Murdoch, Dan Rather, and Heather Locklear's turf no more. The Internet was our space.

The Internet fostered a do-it-yourself mentality. We called it "cyberpunk." Why watch packaged programming on TV when you can make your own online? Who needs corporate content when you can be the content? This was a world we could design ourselves, on our own terms. That's why it fostered such a deep sense of community. New users were gently escorted around the Internet by veterans. An experienced user delighted in setting up a newbie's connection. It was considered an honor to rush out to fix a fellow user's technical problem. To be an Internet user was to be an Internet advocate.

It's also why almost everything to do with the Internet was free. Software was designed by people who wanted to make the Internet a better place. Hackers stayed up late coding new programs and then distributed them free of charge. In fact, most of the programs we use today are based on this shareware and freeware. Internet Explorer and Netscape are fat versions of a program created at the University of Illinois. Streaming media is a dolled-up version of CUSeeMe, a program developed at Cornell. The Internet was built for love, not profit.

And that was the problem—for business, anyway. Studies showed a correlation between time spent on the Internet and time not spent consuming TV programs and commercials. Something had to be done.

Thus began the long march to turn the Internet into a profitable enterprise. It started with content. Dozens, then hundreds, of online magazines sprang up. But no one wanted to pay a subscription charge for content. It just wasn't something one did online. So most of these magazines went out of business.

The others . . . well, they invented the next great Internet catastrophe: the banner ad. Web publishers figured they could sell a little strip atop each page to an advertiser, who'd use it as a billboard for commercials. But everyone hated them. They got in the way. And the better we got at ignoring banner ads, the more distractingly busy they grew, and the more time-consuming they were to download. They only taught us to resent whichever advertiser was inhibiting our movement.

So advertising gave way to e-commerce. The Internet would be turned into a direct-marketing platform. An interactive mail-order catalog! This scheme seemed to hold more promise for Wall Street investors. Not many of these e-commerce businesses actually made money, but they looked as if they could someday. Besides, Wall Street cares less about actual revenue and more about the ability to create the perception that there might be revenue at some point in the future. That's why it's called speculation. Others might call it a pyramid scheme.

Here's how it works: Someone writes a business plan for a new kind of e-commerce company. That person finds "angel investors"— very in-the-know people who give him money to write a bigger business plan and hire a CEO. Then come the first and second rounds, where other, slightly less in-the-know people invest a few million more. Then come the institutional investors, who underwrite the now-infamous IPO. After that, at the bottom of the pyramid, come retail investors. That's you and me. We're supposed to log on to an e-trading site and invest our money, right when the investors at the top are executing their "exit strategy." That's another way of saying *carpetbagging.*

What's all that got to do with the Internet, you ask? Exactly. The Internet was merely the sexy word, the come-hither, the bright idea at the top of the pyramid. Sure, there were and still are lots of entrepreneurs creating vibrant online businesses. But the Internet was not born to support the kind of global economic boom that venture capitalists envisioned. And by turning its principal use from socializing to monetizing, business went against the Internet's very functionality.

People doing what comes naturally online—such as sending messages to one another—don't generate revenue. The object of the game, for Internet business, was to get people's hands off the keyboard and onto the mouse. Less collaboration, more consumption. Sites were designed to be "sticky" so people wouldn't leave. And "information architecture" turned into the science of getting people to click on the Buy button.

Anyone logging on to the Internet for the first time in the year 2000 encountered a place very different from the interactive playground of ten years earlier. Browsers and search engines alike were designed to keep users either buying products or consuming commercial content. Most of those helpful hackers were now vested employees of dot-com companies. And most visions of the electronic future had dollar signs before them.

But the real Internet was hiding underneath this investment charade the whole time. It was a little harder to find, perhaps, and few in the mainstream press were writing about it anymore. Nevertheless, plenty of people were still sharing stories, e-mailing relatives, finding new communities, and educating themselves.

This is why so many of the business schemes were doomed to fail. The behavior control being implemented by more nefarious online merchants, the mercenary tactics of former hackers, and the commercial priorities of the Internet's investors were a blatant contradiction of the Internet's true nature. Sure, the Internet could support some business guests, the way a tree can support some mushrooms at its base and a few squirrels in its branches. But businesses attacked the Internet like men with chain saws. They needed to be rejected.

The inevitable collapse of the dot-com pyramid was not part of some regular business cycle. And it most certainly was not the collapse of anything having to do with the Internet. No, what we witnessed was the Internet fending off an attack. It's no different from when the government abandoned the Internet in the '80s, after scientists online began talking about science fiction instead of defense contracts. The Internet never does what it's supposed to do. It has a mind, and life, of its own. That's because we're alive, too.

Now that the Internet's role in business has faded into the background, the many great applications developed to make our lives better are taking center stage. They are compelling, and surpass some of our wildest dreams of what the Internet might someday achieve. This past spring, for example, as one dot-com after another was folding, M.I.T. announced a new Web curriculum. This leading university promised that, over the next ten years, it will carry online the lecture notes, course outlines, and assignments for almost all of its 2,000 courses in the sciences, humanities, and arts. Instituting a policy that would make an Internet investor shudder, M.I.T. plans to release all of this material, to anyone in the world, for free.

Or have a look at Blogger. It's not just a website; it's also a set of publishing tools that allows even a novice to create a weblog, automatically add content to a website, or organize links, commentary, and open discussions. In the short time Blogger has been available, it has fostered an interconnected community of tens of thousands of users. These people don't simply surf the Web; they are now empowered to create it.

Taking their cue from old-school Internet discussion groups like

Usenet, websites such as MetaFilter let people begin discussions about almost anything they've found online. Each conversation begins with a link, then grows as far as its participants can take it. This is the real beauty of hypertext, and it's finally catching on. Although hackers have used bulletin board interfaces on sites such as Slashdot since the Web's inception, more commercially minded endeavors—e.g., Plastic—are adopting the same model to generate dialogues about culture and media.

On Yahoo! the biggest growth area is conversation. Yahoo! Groups, a set of bulletin board discussions and mailing lists, contains thousands of the best discussions happening online—and almost all of them have been started by real people. Based on an old but still widely used style of e-mail conversation called Listserv, it allows group members to read postings and add to the conversation without ever opening their browsers. Some of these special-interest groups are narrowcast to a degree possible only on a global network where people interested in anything from absinthe drinking to zither tuning can find one another across great distances.

And now that international trade and open markets are no longer the Internet's chief global agenda, more humanitarian efforts are taking shape. Back in 1999, my friend Paul Meyer helped launch Internet Project Kosovo (IPKO) just days after NATO stopped shelling the Serbs. A single satellite dish let Albanian refugees find lost family members, and enabled aid agencies to allocate their resources. Today, Meyer and others are helping people in this and other war-torn and developing regions to network, and even open businesses.

For those whose refugee status ended long ago, Ellis Island has teamed with the Mormon Church to create a database containing arrival records for the 22 million immigrants who came through the New York port between 1892 and 1924. Linked databases, accessible to anyone via the Internet. Is this starting to sound familiar?

Or remember how the Internet was supposed to provide us with alternative sources of news and information? Although it was almost lost under the avalanche of content during the dot-com gold rush, AlterNet has emerged as a vibrant source of news and opinions you won't see in your evening paper anytime soon. It's the ultimate alternative newsweekly, available on the Web or by e-mail, using the Internet to collect and syndicate content from sources that just couldn't get published any other way. And it's free.

It's not that the original Internet community went into some sort of remission. No, not all. While e-commerce customers were waiting for return authorization numbers for misordered merchandise from Pets.com, the participants in AOL's chat rooms were exchanging tips on caring for their Chihuahuas. While DoubleClick was reckoning with plummeting click-through rates on its banner ads, the personal ads in the Nerve singles classifieds were exploding. While the value of many E*Trade portfolios was falling into the red, people who'd never sold anything before were making money peddling items through the auctions on eBay.

Likewise, as headlines panicked investors about the failure of broadband, the massive communities built on IRC chat channels and other early live networking platforms were finding new, more advanced avenues for social and intellectual exchange. For-profit streaming media companies like Icebox may have failed, but the streaming technologies they used have survived and flourished as social tools such as iVisit and NetMeeting. And while the client lists of business-to-business service companies have shrunk, peer-to-peer networks, from Napster to Hotline, still grow in popularity and resist all efforts to quell the massive exchange of data, illegal or not.

In fact, the average American home now has more information and broadcast resources than a major television network newsroom did in the '70s. A single Apple laptop is a video production studio, allowing even for the complex editing of independent films. Add a fast Internet connection, and a home producer can broadcast around the globe. My own Aunt Sophie, armed with a scanner and e-mail account, has inundated the family with photos of all our relatives' new babies.

Independent radio stations run through DSL and cable modems out of studio apartments around the world find loyal audiences through Shoutcast and other amateur media networks. And, as the word "amateur" suggests, these stations are born out of love for a particular genre of music. They allow aficionados from anywhere to enjoy their favorite styles—from raga to reggae—round the clock.

The early Internet was often compared to the Wild West—an anarchic realm where a lone hacker could topple any empire—and that spirit of independence still dominates the culture of the interactive space. Any group or individual, however disenfranchised, can serve as the flash point for an extraordinarily widespread phenomenon.

Online sensations—such as the spoof of the Japanese video game at All Your Base Are Belong to Us! and the parody of Budweiser's "Wassup?" commercial at Budwizer.com: Wassup Page—are launched by teenagers and distributed by e-mail to millions of office cubicles, eventually finding their way to the evening news. Think about it: The mind-melding of some fourteen-year-old kid and his computer—such as Neil Cicierega, who created the brilliant parody of consumer culture called Hyakugojyuuichi!!—becomes a conversation piece around the water cooler in thousands of offices all over the world. Powerful stuff.

It gets better. Thousands of hackers worldwide still represent a threat to major software companies, the DVD industry, and any corporation whose interests rely on closed-source computer code or encrypted files. No sooner is a new closed standard released than it is decoded and published by a lone hacker—or by a team of hackers working in tandem from remote and untraceable locations. Activists of all stripes have also seized upon the Internet to cultivate relationships across vast distances and promote new alliances between formerly unaffiliated groups. The Internet-organized demonstrations against World Trade Organization meetings in Seattle and Quebec are only the most notable examples of such networking.

In spite of the many efforts to direct its chaotic, organismic energy toward the monolithic agenda of Wall Street, the Internet can't help but empower the real people whose spirit it embodies. I've mentioned only a few of the thousands of equally vital new buds blooming on the Internet today. They thrive because they promote the life of the Internet itself. They are not parasites but fruit, capable of spreading their own seeds and carrying the Internet's tendrils even further. They are the Internet.

They share the very qualities that make the Internet so compelling and valuable: transparency, participation, openness, and collaboration. Theirs are the ideals and communities that allowed the Internet to fend off efforts to harness its power for a single, selfish objective. They are also what will keep the Internet resilient enough to withstand the next attack.

So do not mourn. Rejoice. While you may never be able to sell that great dot-com name or make a bundle on that tech stock you bought last year, you're getting to participate in something that no civilization in the history of the planet has ever had the privilege of experiencing until now: the Internet.

<Douglas Rushkoff>

social currency

Originally published in *TheFeature.com* (2003).

N O MATTER HOW COLORFUL you make it, content will never be king in a wireless world. It's not the content that matters—it's the contact.

Wireless providers are busy investing in content. Or, more accurately, in deals with content "partners" who can provide data with file sizes huge enough to justify the industry's massive expenditure on multimedia-ready platforms and networks. Cart before the horse, as always, the cellular industry may have just speculated itself off yet another cliff.

Like the lunatics responsible for the dot-com boom and bust, these entrepreneurs still don't get it: in an interactive space, content is not king. Contact is.

What made the Internet special was not the newfound ability to download data from distant hard drives. No, none of us were so very excited by the idea of accessing News Corp.'s databases of text, for a fee. What made the Internet so sexy was that it let us interact with one another. First asynchronously, through e-mail or bulletin boards, and then live. It was the people.

Content only matters in an interactive space or even the real world, I'd argue, because it gives us an excuse to interact with one another. When I was a kid, we'd buy records not solely because we wanted to hear whoever was on them; we wanted an excuse for someone else to come over! "What are you doing after school? I got the new Stones album. . . ."

In this sense, our content choices are just means to an end—social currency through which we can make connections with others. Jokes are social currency. They help break the ice at a party. "Hey, let's invite Joe. He tells good jokes." We're not even listening for the punch line—we're busy memorizing the joke so that we'll have something to tell at our next party.

Or consider the history of bubblegum and baseball cards. When my dad was a kid, a clever bubble-gum card company decided to give themselves a competitive advantage by offering a free baseball card inside each pack of gum. That's how baseball cards started. The cards did so well that by the time I was a kid, a pack of ten baseball cards would only have one stick of gum. Today, baseball cards are sold with no gum at all. The free prize has replaced the original product! That's because, to use industry terms, baseball cards are a stickier form of content than bubble gum.

Meaning, they are a better form of social currency. They can be traded, played for, compared and contrasted. They create more opportunities for social interactions between the kids who buy them.

As the wireless industry begins on its long, misguided descent into the world of content creation, it must come to terms with the fact that the main reason people want content is to have an excuse—or a way—to interact with someone else.

Ideally, this means giving people the tools to create their own content that they can send to friends. Still, cameras are a great start. Some form of live digital video would be fun, too. ("We're at the Grand Canyon, Mom—look!" or "Here's the new baby!")

But elaborately produced content—like prepackaged video shorts, inscrutable weather maps, and football game TV replays—are not only inappropriate for a two-inch screen, they are inappropriate as social currency. Sorry, but people won't use their cell phones to buy content any more than they used their Internet connections to buy content—unless that content is something that gives them a reason to call someone else.

And that kind of content better be something that can be translated into simple mouth sounds—meaning spoken language, the natural content of telephony. Movie schedules, restaurant addresses, stock quotes, sports scores. No, it's not sexy. But data never are.

It's time for the wireless industry to come to grips with the fact that no matter how sleek the phones or colorful the pictures on their little screens, nobody wants to have sex with either. They want to have sex with each other. Either help them, or get out of the way.

<Don Tapscott>

the eight net gen norms

Excerpted from *Grown Up Digital* (pp. 73–96).

DON TAPSCOTT is chairman of Moxie Insight, a fellow of the World Economic Forum, and Adjunct Professor at the Joseph L. Rotman School of Management, University of Toronto. *Macrowikinomics: Rebooting Business and the World* (2010, coauthored with Anthony Williams) follows 2007's best-selling business book in the U.S., *Wikinomics* (also co-authored with Anthony Williams). Other books include *Grown Up Digital: How the Net Generation Is Changing Your World* (2009), a sequel to *Growing Up Digital: The Rise of the Net Generation* (1997). He holds an M.Ed. specializing in research methodology, and three Doctor of Laws (Hon) granted from the University of Alberta, from Trent University, and from McMaster University.

WHEN *Growing Up Digital* was published in 1997, my daughter Niki had just turned fourteen. She did her homework on the computer in her room and, like most girls her age, she loved to talk with friends on the phone. We had a phone curfew of 10 p.m., and after a while we noticed she wasn't talking on the phone anymore. That seemed like a good thing, until we discovered that Niki was talking to her friends on the Internet via ICQ—one of the early instant messaging systems—from the moment she walked into her bedroom until she turned out the light. As her parents, our first reaction was to feel like she had tricked us, and the issue of ICQ became a sore spot for us all. But my wife and I were torn, because she was getting very good grades, and it was clear that all her friends were connected this way.

Since I was in the business of observing the impact of the Internet, I started pestering Niki with questions at the dinner table about what she was doing online. She was checking her horoscope, downloading music, researching for her homework, playing games, checking the movie schedule, and, of course, talking with friends. Niki tried to put an end to it, with a plea: "Can we have a normal conversation at the dinner table?"

For Niki, her link to the Internet was a sweet taste of freedom. She could talk to whomever she wanted, find out whatever she wanted, and be who she wanted to be, without interference from parents or other adults.

We all want that sense of freedom, but this generation has learned to expect it. They expect it because growing up digital gave kids like Niki the opportunity to explore the world, find out things, talk to strangers, and question the official story from companies and governments. When teenagers in my era did a geography project, they might have cut out some pictures from their parents' *National Geographic* and included some information sent by the PR department of the foreign country's local consulate. Niki, on the other hand, could find significantly more interesting information just by tapping her fingers on her computer in her bedroom.

Niki and her younger brother Alex, who started playing games and drawing pictures on the Internet at age seven, were the inspiration for *Growing Up Digital*. It seemed that every week they would do something amazing with technology or through technology that I had not seen before. Through my experience with them and the 300 other youngsters we studied, I concluded that these kids were very different from their boomer parents. I refer to these differences as "norms"—distinctive attitudinal and behavioral characteristics that differentiate this generation from their baby-boom parents and other generations. These norms were tested in the nGenera survey of 6,000 Net Geners around the world. The list stood up pretty well.

>>> freedom

When my generation graduated from college, we were grateful for that first job. We hung on to it like a life preserver. But times have changed. Kids see no reason to commit, at least not to the first job. High performers are on their fifth job by the time they are twenty-seven and their average tenure at a job is 2.6 years.[1] They revel in the freedom. My son Alex, for instance, is thinking about getting an MBA or a law degree. But when I asked him about his immediate plans for a job, he put it this way: "A commitment of three years or more would make me hesitate. I don't want to get locked in to something I may not enjoy ten years down the road. I want the freedom to try new and different things. If I like what I'm doing, if it challenges me and engages me and is fun, then I would definitely commit to it, I guess. I think about the time I reach age thirty, I would settle on something. I view my twenties as a period of self-discovery and self-realization."

Alex is typical of his generation. The Internet has given them the freedom to choose what to buy, where to work, when to do things like buy a book or talk to friends, and even who they want to be. Politicians like Barack Obama have tapped into it. Obama's iconic line, "Yes we can," has spawned a music video by will.i.am of the Black Eyed Peas, plus the spoofs—proof positive that it went viral. These three words speak volumes about the Net Gen's belief that they can do anything, that no one can tell them not to. "Yes we can" was perfectly tuned to this generation, just as the peace sign was for mine. They're on a quest for freedom, and it's setting up expectations that may surprise and infuriate their elders.

Our research suggests that they expect to choose where and when they work; they use technology to escape traditional office space and hours; and they integrate their home and social lives with work life. More than half of the Net Geners we surveyed online in North America say they want to be able to work in places other than an office. This is particularly true of white- and some gray-collar workers. An almost equal number say they want their job to have flexible hours, again with some differences among the various employee types.[2]

Alex doesn't buy the line that young people expect their first employers to accommodate them with flexible hours and telecommuting. "It makes young people look childish. We're not going to start making demands about hours." Alex says he and his friends want to work hard, be productive, and succeed. "I'm not sure it's a young–old thing."

Yet, in my research and in my work as a consultant to major corporations and governmental institutions, I see signs of a generational trend. They prefer flexible hours and compensation that is based on their performance and market value—not based on face time in the office. And they're not afraid to leave a great job if they find another one that offers more money, more challenging work, the chance to travel, or just a change. As one twenty-six-year-old woman who answered our online survey put it: "We're given the technology that allows us to be mobile, so I don't understand why we need to be restricted to a desk; it feels like you're being micro-managed."

Intel gets it. Many of its employees telework, while other staffers take advantage of flextime, compressed workweeks, part-time hours, and job shares. All the company's major work sites offer employees great amenities, such as fitness centers, locker rooms, basketball and volleyball courts, dry cleaning, sundries, and food court–style cafes with menus that change daily.[3] Studies repeatedly show that perks such as those offered by Intel boost employee satisfaction and performance.[4]

So does Google. Its engineers are asked to spend 20 percent of their workplace time on projects that are of personal interest to them. Google says it has a strong business case for making such an offer. If Google's employees are the best and brightest available— and Google believes they are—then whatever piques their personal interest could open new avenues of business for the company.

While flexible work hours and workplace amenities are routine practice at many high-tech firms, the flexible workplace philosophy is making inroads in other sectors. Best Buy, America's leading electronics retailer, is trying to revamp its corporate culture to make its workplace more appealing to young employees. The endeavor, called ROWE, for results-only work environment, lets corporate employees do their work anytime, anywhere, as long as they get their work done. "This is like TiVo for your work," says the program's cofounder, Jody Thompson.[5] By June of 2008, 3,200 of Best Buy's 4,000 corporate staffers are participating in the ROWE program. The company plans to introduce the program into its stores, something no retailer has tried before.[6]

There are even signs that more Net Geners will seek to own their own business, especially after they worked for a traditional bureaucratic company for a while. The appeal is having more creative control, more freedom, and no boss to answer to. In recent years, YouTube, Facebook, and Digg have emerged as outstandingly successful examples of organizations started by individuals under the age of twenty-five. Such stories inspire other youthful entrepreneurs to pursue their dreams.

Young people insist on freedom of choice. It's a basic feature of their media diet. Instead of listening to the top ten hits on the radio, Net Geners compose iPod playlists of thousands of songs chosen from the millions of tunes available. So when they go shopping, they assume they'll have a world of choice. Curious whether the African Pygmy hedgehog makes a good pet for a pre-teen? Google offers more than 25,000 links to "African Pygmy Hedgehog" to help the Net Gener decide. Interested in buying a book? Amazon offers millions of choices. Search for a digital camera on Froogle, Google's shopping search engine, and more than 900,000 pages appear. The number is even greater in Asia, which has far more choice in consumer electronics than North America.

Baby boomers often find variety burdensome, but the Net Geners love it. When faced with thousands of choices, they show no signs of anxiety, from what we could see in our online survey of 1,750 North American kids. Only 13 percent strongly agree with the statement "There is so much to choose from that when I buy something, I tend to wonder if I have made the right decision."

Typical Net Gen shoppers know what they are going to buy before they leave the house. They've already checked out all the choices online, and they are well informed and confident in their decisions—83 percent say they usually know what they want before they go to buy a product.[7] With the proliferation of media, sales channels, product types, and brands, Net Geners use digital technologies to cut through the clutter and find the product that fits their needs. And if it turns out to be the wrong choice, Net Geners want to be able to change their mind. They are attracted to companies that make it easy to exchange the product for something different or get their money back.

The search for freedom is transforming education as well. At their fingertips they have access to much of the world's knowledge. Learning for them should take place where and when they want it. So attending a lecture at a specific time and place, given by a mediocre professor in a room where they are passive recipients, seems oddly old-fashioned, if not completely inappropriate. The same is true for politics. They have grown up with choice. Will a model of democracy that gives them only two choices and relegates them, between elections, to four years of listening to politicians endlessly repeating the same speeches actually meet their needs?

>>> customization

Last year, someone sent me an iTouch PDA. It was sitting in a box on my desk at home when Niki and her boyfriend spied it. They were astonished I hadn't opened it up, so Moritz opened the box, and then hacked into the iTouch so he could give it some special features—lots of widgets, some of my favorite movies, like *The Departed*, plus some music from my computer, including a couple of great tunes pounded out by my band, Men In Suits, with Niki singing lead vocals and me on the keyboard. They kindly left the horrid PDA on my desk with a little note. It sat there for months, until someone took it away. It's not that I wasn't grateful. I just wanted the PDA to work. I didn't need it to work for me. That's the difference between me and the Net Gen.

As a typical boomer, I took what I got and hoped it would work. Net Geners get something and customize it to make it theirs. This is the generation that has grown up with personalized mobile phones, TiVo, Slingbox, and podcasts. They've grown up getting what they want, when they want it, and where, and they make it fit their personal needs and desires.

Half of them tell us they modify products to reflect who they are.[8] Niki, for example, has a phone with white-and-orange swirly "wallpaper" on the screen, plus a ringtone that sings out a techno version of "Taking Care of Business."

My son Alex has a special mouse for his laptop. Now, most of us have a mouse with two or three buttons. Alex has five. "My mouse is called the Mighty Mouse," he tells me. "Each of those buttons does a separate thing, according to my interests and what I need to use it for. My left button clicks on something. The right button opens up a window, just like a regular one. The middle button is a track wheel, so if I'm on a Web page or a window in my operating system I can scroll 360 degrees. On the side, if I click on one button every single window that's open on my computer will shrink down so I can choose individually. On the other side is a button that opens up my dashboard, basically, which shows me different widgets—a news widget, a wild widget, a sports widget, a weather widget, a time zone widget, and a widget that monitors the health and productivity of my computer." See what I mean? "It's funny," Alex notes. "I'm actually in the middle to the low end of technological advancement in my peer group."

Today, the "timer" car-customization industry, largely fueled by Net Geners, is worth more than $3 billion in North America. The trend snuck in under the radar of the big auto companies. At least one auto company, Toyota, is trying to pounce on it by introducing the Scion niche brand back in 2003. Company research shows owners spend $1,000–$3,000 on customization and accessories, from paint jobs to XM satellite radios with Bazooka subwoofers. These are kids in their twenties, and they "have changed every category they have touched so far," says Jim Farley, VP of Scion. "It's the most diverse generation ever seen."[9]

Our research at nGenera also shows that the potential to personalize a product is important to the Net Generation, even if the individual decides not to make any changes. The desire is about personalizing and accessorizing—it is more aesthetic than functional. Personalized online space is now almost obligatory; witness the popularity of sites such as MySpace and Facebook. Net Geners also customize their media. Two-thirds of early technology adopters say they watch their favorite TV shows when they want to rather than at the time of broadcast. With YouTube, television networks run the risk of becoming quaint relics. The industry will still produce programming, but where and when the programming is watched will be up to the viewer.

At work, the Net Geners will want to customize their jobs. In our online survey of 1,750 kids in North America, more than half of Net Geners said they liked working offsite.[10] They enjoyed the change of scenery, they said, and their ability to work outside the office showed their employer they could be trusted to get the job done. They may even want to customize their job descriptions, although they still welcome some structure and want to know what is expected of them. Ideally, companies will replace job descriptions with work goals, and give Net Geners the tools, latitude, and guidance to get the job done. They may not do it on day one, though. "Demanding to customize a job description is a bit brash if you've only just started a job," Alex told me. "But after a while, I think it's fine to make suggestions on how the job could be changed or improved."

>>> scrutiny

On April Fools' Day 2005, I decided to play a bit of a gag on my employees and associates. I asked my executive assistant to send them the following e-mail:

> Through Don's connections at the World Economic Forum, Angelina Jolie (she's an actress who has become involved in social responsibility), who attended the last Forum meetings, is interested in Don's work and wants to come to Toronto for a meeting to discuss transparency in the global economy.
>
> This has been arranged for Thursday, May 26th.
>
> Don will be having a private lunch with her and will come to the office afterwards so she can meet others here and continue the discussions. The day will end with a cocktail party at Verity.
>
> She'll bring some of her friends.
>
> Please confirm your attendance.
>
> Thanks,
> Antoinette

In my dreams. Anyway, not a single young member of my staff fell for the joke. I would get responses like "Nice try" and "You and Angelina. Right."

However, associates my age reacted in a completely different manner. They were falling over themselves to join the afternoon discussions and attend the cocktail party. I believe the expression is they fell for it hook, line, and ink. And they were not happy to find out that Angelina was not going to appear.

Net Geners are the new scrutinizers. Given the large number of information sources on the Web, not to mention unreliable information—spam, phishers, inaccuracies, hoaxes, scams, and misrepresentations—today's youth have the ability to distinguish between fact and fiction. They appear to have high awareness about the world around them and want to know more about what is happening. They use digital technologies to find out what's really going on. Imagine if Orson Welles had directed the radio version of *War of the Worlds* today, instead of in 1938, when it caused widespread panic as many listeners believed that Martians had actually landed. In a couple of clicks, Net Geners would figure out it was a play, not a news broadcast. No one would have had to flee their homes!

The Net Generation knows to be skeptical whenever they're online.[11] When baby boomers were young, a picture was a picture; it documented reality. Not so today. "Trust but verify" would be an apt motto for today's youth. They accept few claims at face value. No wonder the 74-second "Evolution" video was such a big hit when it was posted on YouTube in October 2006. The video showed an ordinary attractive girl—the director's girlfriend, in fact—being transformed into a billboard model—with considerable help from Photoshop, which lengthened her neck, reshaped her head, and widened her eyes. You could see, before your very eyes, how fake the image of beauty is in magazines and billboards. The video was made for Dove soap by a young Australian working for the Ogilvy & Mather ad agency in Toronto. It instantly struck a chord among Net Geners worldwide. Unilever, the British conglomerate that owns Dove, estimates it was seen by at least 18.5 million people worldwide on the Net,[12] not including how many saw it on TV, where it was prominently featured on morning talk shows. Not bad for a video that cost only $135,000 to make.

But the story didn't end so well for Dove's parent Unilever. Very quickly, some young consumers took note that Unilever was also the maker of Axe, a men's cologne with a campaign of ads featuring highly sexual and exploitative photos of women. The theme was that if you bought Axe, women would be dying to strip and submit to you. As fast as you can say "mockumentary," videos began appearing on YouTube pointing out the contradiction. One, "A message from Unilever, the makers of Axe and Dove," ends with the tagline "Tell your daughters before Unilever gets to them."

For anyone wanting to reach this age group, the best strategy is candor. They should provide Net Geners with ample product information that is easy to access. The more they have scrutinized a product, the better they feel about purchases, especially ones requiring a large financial or emotional investment. Boomers marvel at the consumer research available online; Net Geners expect it. When they go shopping, almost two-thirds of Net Geners tell us, they search for information about products that interest them before they buy.[13] They compare and contrast product information, online, and look for the cheapest price without sacrificing value. They read blogs, forums, and reviews. They're skeptical about online reviews. Instead, they consult their friends. They can be very picky. Our survey found that 69 percent of the "Bleeding Edge" (first adopters) said they "wouldn't buy a product unless it has the exact features I want." Only 46 percent of Luddites (technophobes) felt that way.[14] It's easy to be a smart shopper in the digital world, and it's about to get easier. As Niki tells me, "You'll be able to scan the bar code of a product on the store shelf and up will pop information on what the product costs at other stores." Bar codes that can hold that amount of information are already registered with the patent office.[15] It's only a matter of time.

Since companies are increasingly naked, they better be buff.[16] Corporate strategies should be built on good products, good prices, and good values. The Progressive Group of Insurance Companies website is ideally suited to the Net Generation. It provides potential customers with an online insurance quote and calculates how much the company's competitors would charge for the same package. Progressive believes it offers the best value in most cases, and backs its beliefs with facts.

Companies should expect employee scrutiny. Two-thirds of the Bleeding Edge say that they've searched a great deal for online information about the organization they are currently working for or about people working in their organization. Sixty percent of the same subgroup say they would thoroughly research an employer before accepting a job offer. Respondents say they want to prepare for a job interview, learn about corporate culture, and ensure that the company and job fit their needs and desired lifestyle.

Scrutiny, as we have seen, can go the other way, too. Many Net Geners still don't realize that the private information they disclose on social networking sites like Facebook may come back to bite them when they're applying for a big job or public office.

>>> integrity

Recently, Niki received an alarming message from one of her high school friends. The young woman, who was volunteering in Ecuador, reported that she had seen the horrible conditions of people working in the fields of roses—the dreadful chemicals sprayed on the flowers, the long hours, the child labor. Niki instantly sent the message to all her friends on her Facebook network. Now, whenever she buys roses, Niki asks questions about where they come from. She won't buy flowers from a company that sprays poisonous chemicals on plants that children pick. It's a small, but telling, example of the values Niki shares with her generation.

The stereotype that this generation doesn't give a damn is not supported by the facts. Net Geners care about integrity—being honest, considerate, transparent, and abiding by their commitments. This is also a generation with profound tolerance. Alex had an experience that drove this home for me. I asked him to describe it.

My junior year, I decided to study abroad in London, England. I will always remember what one of my fellow students said the very first day. Before we began, he stood up in front of an auditorium of 250 students, faculty, and program coordinators and made this announcement:

"Hi everyone, my name is Steve, I am from St. Louis, Missouri, and, like the rest of you, I am really excited about being in London. But perhaps unlike the rest of you, I have Tourette syndrome. So if you think you hear a donkey or a sheep in the back of the classroom, don't hide your lunches because it is just me. Sometimes I can't help making animal noises. Also, don't be distracted if you hear any swear words or grunting either, because that's me too. Thanks for hearing me out."

With that, most people in the class just shrugged their shoulders and began making small talk with the people around them. Sure enough, the head of the program was barely able to get out a "Welcome to London" before Steve started BAAAAing away. At first, some people did seem distracted. I personally was fascinated with him, both for his peculiar problem, and with his ballsy move at the beginning of class. I was impressed with his confidence and how honest and direct he could be about his illness, and I think everyone else was too. After a couple of minutes, it was like his illness wasn't even there (even though his grunting and cursing still was).

Alex's story made me flash back to when I was a kid. There would have been no student in my class with Tourette's syndrome. More likely, he would have never made it to any university, or worse, would have been locked up in a mental institution. If he had gotten into our class, how would we have reacted to such a seemingly bizarre thing? Would we even have known about psychiatric conditions like this? Would we have just shrugged it off as Alex and his 250 classmates did? Would we have had such tolerance for diversity and such instant compassion for someone with an illness like this? Or would the stigma of mental illness have gotten the better of us? And would we have had Alex's admiration for the courage and determination his fellow students showed?

It's not surprising that Net Geners display such tolerance, and even wisdom, compared with previous generations. They have been exposed to a ton of scientific, medical, and other pertinent information that wasn't available to their parents. The world around them has changed, too. So it's not surprising that they care about honesty. Among other things, they have seen the giants of corporate corruption, the CEOs of Enron and other major companies, being led away in handcuffs, convicted, and sent to jail. It's far easier for Net Geners than it was for boomers to tell whether a company president is doing one thing and saying another. They can use the Internet to find out, and then use social communities like Facebook to tell all their friends.

They expect other people to have integrity, too. They do not want to work for, or buy a product from, an organization that is dishonest. They also expect companies to be considerate of their customers, employees, and the communities in which they operate. Net Geners are also more aware of their world than ever before, due to the abundance of information on the Internet.

This astuteness of the Net Generation has big implications for companies that want to sell things to Net Geners or employ them. At a time of uncertainty, young people look for companies they can trust. They have a low tolerance for companies that lie when they're trying to sell something, and they can find out pretty quickly if that's the case.

In a crowded marketplace, a company's integrity becomes an important point of difference. Net Geners don't like to be misled or hit with costly surprises, whether measured in money, time, quality, or function. Seventy-seven percent agreed with the statement "If a company makes untrue promises in their advertising, I'll tell my friends not to buy their products."[17] They get angry when they feel they were wronged: "Blockbuster says no late fees. It is all a lie!" said one fifteen-year-old boy. "After a week you have to pay $1.25 and then you have to buy the movie after two weeks. They trick you!"

Although Net Geners are quick to condemn, they are also quick to forgive if they see signs that the company is truly sorry for an error. Seventy-one percent said they would continue to do business with a company if it corrected a mistake honestly and quickly.[18]

Integrity, to the Net Gener, primarily means telling the truth and living up to your commitments. Does it also mean doing good? Would Net Geners shun a company that pollutes on a massive scale or mistreats its employees? The survey data are not clear. Our research suggests that only a quarter take into account a company's policies on social responsibility or the environment when making a big purchase. About 40 percent would abandon a product they love if they discovered that the company has suspect social practices.[19]

Yet my interviews with Net Geners suggest that significant numbers of them think about values before they buy. It's not because they're necessarily better human beings. It's because they can easily find out how a product is made, and what's in it. Knowledge leads to action. When you can scrutinize the environmental and labor practices of a company as readily as Net Geners like Niki can, you can make decisions on the basis of what that company is doing—not just what it's saying.

Integrity swings both ways, though. You can find plenty of Net Geners who judge companies by a very strict ethical standard, and yet they are downloading music for free—which the music industry regards as stealing. A third of iPod owners are downloading illegally, according to a study by Jupiter Research.[20] My research suggests that's an underestimation. According to nGenera research, 77 percent of Net Geners have downloaded music, software, games, or movies without paying for them.[21] What's more, 72 percent of file-sharers age eighteen to twenty-nine say they don't care about the copyright status of the files they share, according to a Pew Internet and American Life Project.[22] Most don't view it as stealing, or if they do, they justify it in different ways. They see the music industry as a big business that deserves what it gets, or they think the idea of owning music is over. Some even think they're doing small bands a favor.

There's one clear sign that Net Geners value the act of doing good: a record number of Net Geners are volunteering for civic causes. One of them even launched a magazine, aptly called *Good* magazine. Niki says 70 percent of her crowd is volunteering, and she's an enthusiastic example. This winter, she helped organize a big fundraiser for Toronto's Centre for Addiction and Mental Health. "We want to end the stigma against mental illness," says Niki. Her friends have taken a big step in this direction. "A lot of my friends have anorexia or depression, and like most I've got mental illness in my own extended family. It's time to take a stand. We can talk about it. It's not swept under the carpet."

Integrity is driving their behavior in other institutions as well. They want their universities, schools, governments, and politicians to be honest, considerate of their interests, accountable, and open. As parents, the early evidence suggests, they want to run their families based on such values. This is such a hopeful finding—the biggest generation ever is demanding that companies and other institutions behave with integrity. What a powerful force for a better world.

>>> collaboration

At most companies, employees chat over coffee, in front of the fax machine, or by the water cooler. But at Best Buy, Net Gen store employees—some as young as nineteen—helped to create an entirely new kind of digital chat zone. It's The Watercooler, a mass-communication and dialogue tool for all employees at all levels. It's part of Best Buy's big effort to tap the unique skills of its Net Gen employees, especially in using digital technology to get the front-line staff to contribute ideas. "The Watercooler fills a huge hole we've had," said Best Buy's senior manager of communications, Jennifer Rock. It's "a direct line between employees in stores and all locations to talk about business topics directly with corporate leaders, teams, and with each other. In the first three months, we've gained 85,000 active users."

The Watercooler is the best place for employees to get answers to their questions about things like best practices for home theater installation, or why they do not sell Dell products in their stores. It gives the company a way to mine the knowledge and experience of the entire employee population for input on weighty business decisions. "Being that Best Buy, like most companies, has traditionally communicated at employees instead of with them, we didn't forecast how quickly The Watercooler would become this business communication tool," said Rock. "But our employees were obviously ready."

Net Geners are natural collaborators. This is the relationship generation. As much as I thought that I, as a ten-year-old, had a relationship with the fabulous teenager Annette Funicello on *The Mickey Mouse Club*, it wasn't so. (She did eventually answer my letters, but today I wonder if they were really her answers.)

They collaborate online in chat groups, play multiuser video games, use e-mail, and share files for school, work, or just for fun.

They influence one another through what I call N-Fluence networks, where they discuss brands, companies, products, and services. They bring a culture of collaboration with them to work and the marketplace and are comfortable using new online tools to communicate. They like to be in touch with their friends on their BlackBerrys or cell phones wherever they are—on the street, in the store, or at work. It gives them a sense of virtual community all day long. It makes them feel like they have a friend in their pocket.

Their eagerness to collaborate can be a bonus for companies. Net Geners want to work hand-in-hand with companies to create better goods and services, something their parents never dreamed of. Companies never thought of it either: without the Internet for a free two-way dialogue with customers, they conceived new products in secret.

Today, Net Geners are helping companies develop advertising campaigns. In one early experiment in advertising collaboration, GM invited consumers to a newly built website that offered video clips and simple editing tools they could use to create ads for the Chevy Tahoe SUV. The site gained online fame after environmentalists hijacked the site's tools to build and post ads on the site condemning the Tahoe as an eco-unfriendly gas guzzler. GM didn't take the ads down, which caused even more online buzz. Some pundits said GM was being foolhardy, but the numbers proved otherwise. The website quickly attracted more than 620,000 visitors, two-thirds of whom went on to visit Chevy.com. For three weeks running, the new site funneled more people to the Chevy site than either Google or Yahoo did. Most important, sales of the Tahoe soared.[23] To be sure, concern for the environment did not impede the young car enthusiasts from purchasing the Tahoe. For them, the competing norms resolved in GM's favor.

Many Net Geners are happy to help with product design. They believe they offer useful insights and like to feel part of a knowledgeable and exclusive group. They are willing to test product prototypes and answer survey questions. Half of Net Geners are willing to tell companies the details of their lives if the result is a product that better fits their needs. This number rises to 61 percent of Early Adopters and 74 percent of the Bleeding Edge. However, they hesitate to share the data if they feel a company might misuse the information, sell it to other companies, or inundate them with junk mail and spam.[24]

Now, Net Gen consumers are taking the next step and becoming producers, cocreating products and services with companies. Alvin Toffler coined the term "prosumer" in his 1970s book *Future Shock*.[25] I called it "prosumption" a decade ago.[26] I can see it happening now, as the Internet transforms itself from a platform for presenting information to a place where you can collaborate and where individuals can organize themselves into new communities. In the Web 2.0, new communities are being formed in social networks such as Facebook and MySpace, and these communities are starting to go into production. People are making things together. So prosumption was an idea waiting to happen, waiting for a generation who had a natural instinct to collaborate and co-innovate.

Collaboration extends to other aspects of the Net Geners' lives. At work, they want to feel that their opinion counts. While they acknowledge their lack of experience, they feel they have relevant insights—especially about technology and the Internet—and they want the opportunity to influence decisions and change work processes to make them more efficient. Making this happen requires a receptive corporate culture and the work tools, such as blogs and wikis, that encourage collaboration.

The new collaboration is not traditional teamwork at all. The difference today is that individual efforts can be harnessed on a large scale to achieve collective outcomes, like Wikipedia, the online encyclopedia written by 75,000 active volunteers and continually edited by hundreds of thousands of readers around the world who perform millions of edits per month. That would have been impossible to achieve without a new generation of collaboration tools.

These tools make collaboration on an international scale so easy, as my daughter Niki found last year while working for an international consulting company. She'd cook up an idea for a widget that might be useful for a client, and at the end of the day she'd send a message to a team of four computer developers in the Czech Republic. The next morning, there it was: a new widget ready for her to check out. "There's an old saying that two heads are better than one," she says. "Well, I say that ten thousand heads are better than two. There are lots of smart people out there, and we should be using new technologies to tap into their talents."

Net Geners are collaborators in every part of their lives. As civic activists, they're tapping into the collaborative characteristic with aplomb. The Net Gen wants to help. They'll help companies make better products and services. They're volunteering in record numbers, in part because the Internet offers so many ways, big and small, to help out.

Educators should take note. The current model of pedagogy is teacher focused, one-way, one size fits all. It isolates the student in the learning process. Many Net Geners learn more by collaborating—both with their teacher and with each other. They'll respond to the new model of education that's beginning to surface—student-focused and multiway, which is customized and collaborative.

>>> entertainment

In the high-tech world, where employers put a premium on attracting the brightest Net Geners they can find, some work sites look like playgrounds. You can play foosball at Microsoft's Redmond campus—or baseball on the company diamond or soccer or volleyball. There's even a private lake. You can take your pick of the twenty-five cafeterias on campus, along with the requisite Starbucks stands. Xbox consoles are stashed in alcoves. Nearly three thousand works of art hang on the walls. You can even go on whale-watching excursions. Over at Google, there's a rock-climbing wall on the premises, along with a company pool, a beach volleyball pit, a gym, plus pool tables. You'll feel like you're right back in college. You can even bring your pet.

These employers know that for Net Geners, work should be fun. Net Geners see no clear dividing line between the two. This may be anathema to corporate types who enjoy the grind. The old paradigm was that there was a time of day when one worked and a time of day when one relaxed and had fun. These two models have now become merged in the same activity because Net Geners believe in enjoying what they do for a living. Net Geners expect their work to be intrinsically satisfying. They expect to be emotionally fulfilled by their work. They also see nothing wrong with taking time off from work to check their profile on Facebook or play an online game. Eighty-one percent of teens play online games—and once they get jobs, they're likely to play online games at work to blow off steam.

Employers often growl when they see Net Geners goofing off online at work. But I think that employers should cool it. What's wrong with spending twenty minutes playing an online game at work? Why is that any worse than what my generation did—amble downstairs for a coffee, a smoke, and a shared complaint, usually about management? Immersion in digital technology has taught this generation to switch very quickly between one line of thought and another. Switching off for a few minutes by playing a game can generate fresh ways to solve problems. It's arguably more productive than hunkering down and spinning your wheels for hours on end.

The Internet gives them plenty of opportunity to amuse themselves online. The Web is the fun tool of choice with which to catch up on news headlines, Google, check e-mail, and IM with friends. There's entertainment from around the world from websites, chatting with "Net pals," and online gaming. There's niche entertainment that caters to their interests, such as HollywoodStockExchange .com for movie buffs, or StyleDiary.net for fashionistas. Many Net Geners maximize their interactions by engaging in multiple "netivities" simultaneously, such as chatting with friends on MSN while listening to their media player and surfing the Net. YouTube raises the bar for interactive entertainment. Users upload hundreds of thousands of videos daily, either snippets of television programs they like or content they've created. Users vote and comment on the submissions.

To be sure, employers who allow Net Geners to amuse themselves online or wear headphones need proper work design and policies to maximize productivity. In some situations, listening to music on headphones at work is fine, while in other situations it might not be. Notwithstanding the Net Gen ability to multitask, it's best to minimize distractions, including online ones, for work that requires deep thinking.

Net Geners' love of entertainment also has important implications for companies that want to sell things to them. Nearly three-quarters of Net Geners agreed with the following statement: "Having fun while using a product is just as important as the product doing what it is supposed to do." Net Geners value the experience of using the product beyond its primary function. They find amusement in accessory options and playing with tactile features, particularly younger males. Net Geners become bored easily, so playing with their tech devices keeps them interested.[27]

Still, making a product fun as well as useful presents a challenge to companies targeting the generation. How, for instance, do you make a mortgage fun? Well, take a look at what MtvU, the national network for college students, is doing as part of its campaign to help Darfur. On the site, the network launched an audacious game that asked players to put themselves in the shoes of a teenager in Darfur faced with a terrible decision of whether to go and get water before the bloodthirsty militia roll in. Millions of kids have played the game online—a testament to the power of the "games for change movement."

>>> speed

When I began working with computers, I used a 360-bits-per-second dial-up modem to write my first book from my home office. Fifteen years later, when I wrote *Growing Up Digital*, the typical access rate was 9,600 bits per second. Many young people today access the Web at between 5 million bits per second and 65 million bytes per second!

Having grown up digital, they expect speed—and not just in video games. They're used to instant response, 24/7. Video games give them instant feedback; Google answers their inquiries within nanoseconds. So they assume that everyone else in their world will respond quickly, too. Every instant message should draw an instant response. If a member of their peer group doesn't respond instantly, they become irritated and worried. They fear it may be a negative comment on their status and a personal slight. "IM has made this worse, because if someone sees you online and you don't answer, they *know* you are ignoring them," a twenty-eight-year-old man said in our online survey.

Net Geners also expect to receive an item they have purchased within a matter of days. They are no longer willing to wait four to six weeks to receive their secret decoder ring after sending in their cereal box tops. Corporations that are quick to respond to inquiries are praised and viewed as trustworthy, while long wait times are criticized. Needless to say, Net Geners do not like being put on hold.

When they e-mail a company, 80 percent expect an answer back quickly. But when they talk to their friends, e-mail is too slow for this generation, too cumbersome. They prefer the speed of instant messaging. They're impatient, and they know it. When we asked them what they thought of the following statement—"I have little patience and I can't stand waiting for things"—56 percent agreed.[28]

It makes working in the conventional office hard. "Working in a typical company can really sap one's energy, because things happen so slowly," said Net Gener Moritz Kettler. "A lot of my friends tell me they are frustrated with the glacial pace of decision making. There is a lack of urgency. There's no 'let's get this done.' There is a big culture clash in the workplace with my generation and the bosses, who can often be much older."

The pressure of living in an instantaneous environment can overwhelm some Net Geners. They know others are expecting an immediate response from them, and many experience feelings of saturation, craziness, and never having a moment of peace. Some wish they could disconnect by turning off their cell phones and logging off their computer, but they're reluctant to do this because they fear missing an important message and don't want to feel detached from their social environment.

E-mail is faster than talking, which is why Net Geners often prefer to communicate with people at work via electronic means rather than meeting them—unless it's a first-time meeting or an important negotiation.

Many Net Geners would like their careers to progress at the same fast pace as the rest of their lives. They appreciate continual performance feedback from employers. It helps them gauge their progress and enhances their professional self-esteem and sense of career momentum. Loyalty is strengthened when Net Geners regularly receive feedback that helps them feel "on track" to being successful at the company. Conversely, loyalty may weaken if requests for regular feedback are not acknowledged in a short time frame. This alone may not cause them to switch jobs, but they will feel less emotionally satisfied at work.

>>> innovation

When I was a kid, the pace of innovation was glacial. I remember when the transistor radio came on the scene. I got one and took it to summer camp. We all had one. It was a wonderful innovation. And that radio and its predecessors didn't really change for years. I also remember our first television. That thing lasted for many years as well, until a new innovation—color—appeared on the scene.

This generation, on the other hand, has been raised in a culture of invention. Innovation takes place in real time. Compare my transistor radio that lasted for years with today's mobile devices that improve, sometimes dramatically, every few weeks. Today my kids want the new mobile device every few months, because the current one doesn't have the capability of the new one. And as for televisions, flat-panel technology is an engine of innovation, dropping in price significantly every few months or so.

For marketers, there is no doubt that Net Geners want the latest and greatest product available—in ways that supersede the needs of their parents. The Net Geners live to stay current, whether it's with their cell phone, iPod, or game console. The latest product makes their friends envious and contributes to their social status and their positive self-image.

Motorola came out three years ago with the RAZR, its ultrathin cell phone with built-in camera and music player. Samsung Group answered within a year with the Blade. Motorola responded with its SLVR, a phone even sleeker than its predecessor. "It's like having a popular nightclub. You have to keep opening new ones. To stay cool, you have to speed up," says Michael Greeson, president of market researcher The Diffusion Group.[29]

For Niki, her latest innovation is the Nike+ iPod Sport Kit. The Sport Kit allows a Nike+ shoe to talk to an iPod nano. The sensor uses a sensitive accelerometer to measure a runner's activity; then it wirelessly transfers this data to the receiver on the runner's iPod nano. As Apple's website says: "You don't just take iPod nano on your run. You let it take you. Music is your motivation. But what if you want to go further? Thanks to a unique partnership between Nike and Apple, your iPod nano becomes your coach. Your personal trainer. Your favorite workout companion." As you run, iPod nano tells you your time, distance, pace, and calories burned via voice feedback that adjusts music volume as it plays. In addition to prog- ress reports, voice feedback congratulates you when you've reached a personal best—your fastest pace, longest distance and time, or most calories burned. Voice feedback occurs automatically, accord- ing to predetermined intervals that vary by workout type. Niki loves her Nikes and nano: they help keep her fit.

In the workplace, innovation means rejecting the traditional command-and-control hierarchy and devising work processes that encourage collaboration and creativity. Former chairman and chief mentor N. R. Narayana Murthy at the Bangalore-based Infosys Technologies introduced the company's "voice of youth" program eight years ago. Each year, nine top-performing young employees— all under thirty—participate in eight senior management council meetings, presenting and discussing their ideas with the top lead- ership team. "We believe these young ideas need the senior-most attention for them to be identified and fostered," says Sanjay Puro- hit, associate vice president and head of corporate planning. Info- sys CEO Nandan M. Nilekani concurs: "If an organization becomes too hierarchical, ideas that bubble up from younger people [aren't going to be heard]."[30]

Infosys is on the right track. Net Geners don't want to toil in the same old bureaucracies as their parents. They've grown up in an era of constant innovation and change, and want the workplace to be equally innovative and creative. Net Geners told us an innova- tive work environment is perceived to be leading edge, dynamic, creative, and efficient. Not surprisingly, an innovative workplace is expected to have leading-edge technology.

These are the eight norms of the Net Generation. They value freedom—freedom to be who they are, freedom of choice. They want to customize everything, even their jobs. They learn to be skeptical, to scrutinize what they see and read in the media, including the Internet. They value integrity—being honest, considerate, transparent, and abiding by their commitments. They're great collaborators, with friends online and at work. They thrive on speed. They love to innovate. This is the Net Generation, and in the next few chapters, we will explore how those characteristics are displayed in different spheres of the Net Gen life and how, if you understand these norms, you can change your company, school or university, government, or family for the twenty-first century.

notes

1. "Idea Paper," Syndicated Research Project, nGenera, 2008.
2. "The Net Generation: A Strategic Investigation," Syndicated Research Project, nGenera, 2008 (survey of 1,750 respondents aged thirteen to twenty-nine, September–October 2006).
3. Tamina Vahidy, "Best Commuter Workplaces," *Line 56*, October 20, 2006.
4. Frank Giancola, "Flexible Schedules: A Win-Win Reward," *Workspan*, July 10, 2005, www.worldatwork.org.
5. Michelle Conlin, "Smashing the Clock," *BusinessWeek*, December 11, 2006.
6. Bill Ward, "Power to the People," *Minneapolis Star Tribune*, June 2, 2008.

7. "The Net Generation: A Strategic Investigation," Syndicated Research Project, nGenera, 2008 (survey of 1,750 respondents aged thirteen to twenty-nine, September–October 2006).

8. Ibid.

9. Lillie Guyer, "Scion Connects in Out of Way Places: Toyota Reaches Out to Gen Y Drivers Without Screaming, 'Buy This Car!'" *Advertising Age*, February 21, 2005, adage.com.

10. "The Net Generation: A Strategic Investigation," Syndicated Research Project, nGenera, 2008 (survey of 1,750 respondents aged thirteen to twenty-nine, September–October 2006).

11. Almost two-thirds of Net Genera tell us they search for information about products that interest them before purchase. They compare and contrast product information online; they read blogs, forums, and reviews; and they consult friends. In the digital world, it's easy to be a smart shopper. Those at the top of the technology-adoption curve were the most demanding: our survey found that 69 percent of the Bleeding Edge or first adopters said they "wouldn't buy a product unless it has the exact features I want." This number slowly dropped as one went down the technology scale, reaching a level of 46 percent for Luddites. Almost two-thirds of Net Genera say they take the time to find the lowest price, which isn't surprising, since many work for minimum wage or a limited salary. They want value without jeopardizing quality. Interestingly, most Net Geners are dubious about online reviews, thinking many are the product of disgruntled buyers. "People who write reviews are those who are really bitter about stupid little things," a twenty-two-year-old woman told our researchers. Only 15 percent of Net Genera as a whole agreed with the statement; however, when we study the statement "I frequently write online reviews for products I have bought," the number jumps to 42 percent of those atop the technology-adoption pyramid.

12. "Campaign for Real Beauty," internally computed numbers, Dove, www.youtube.com, April 30, 2008. Number of views tabulated on

April 30, 2008, includes multiple copies of identical videos posted to YouTube; includes only videos with more than 100,000 views.

13. "The Net Generation: A Strategic Investigation," Syndicated Research Project, nGenera, 2008 (survey of 1,750 respondents aged thirteen to twenty-nine, September–October 2006).

14. Ibid.

15. U.S. Patent No. 6820062 (issued November 16, 2004).

16. Don Tapscott and David Ticoll, *The Naked Corporation: How the Age of Transparency Will Revolutionize Business* (Free Press, 2003).

17. "The Net Generation: A Strategic Investigation," Syndicated Research Project, nGenera, 2008 (survey of 1,750 respondents aged thirteen to twenty-nine, September–October, 2006).

18. Ibid.

19. Ibid.

20. David Richards, "Free Illegal Music Beats iTunes," SmartHouse, November 30, 2005, www.smarthouse.com.au.

21. "The Net Generation: A Strategic Investigation," Syndicated Research Project, nGenera, 2008 (survey of 1,750 respondents aged thirteen to twenty-nine, September–October 2006).

22. Mary Madden and Amanda Lennart, "Pew Internet Project Data Memo," Pew Internet and American Life Project, July 31, 2003.

23. Frank Rose, "And Now, a Word from Our Customers," *Wired* 14, no. 12, December 2006.

24. "The Net Generation: A Strategic Investigation," Syndicated Research Project, nGenera, 2008 (survey of 1,750 respondents aged thirteen to twenty-nine, September–October 2006).

25. Alvin Toffler, *Future Shock* (Bantam Books, 1971).

26. Don Tapscott, *The Digital Economy: Promise and Peril in the Age of Networked Intelligence* (McGraw-Hill, 1995).

27. "The Net Generation: A Strategic Investigation," Syndicated Research Project, nGenera, 2008 (survey of 1,750 respondents aged thirteen to twenty-nine, September–October 2006).

28. Ibid.
29. Steve Hamm and Ian Rowley, "Speed Demons," *BusinessWeek*, March 27, 2006.
30. Jena McGregor, "The World's Most Innovative Companies," *BusinessWeek*, April 24, 2006.

<Henry Jenkins>

love online

Excerpted from *Fans, Bloggers, and Gamers*
(pp. 173–77).

HENRY JENKINS is Provost's Professor of Communication,
Journalism and Cinematic Arts at the University of Southern
California. His publications include *Confronting the Challenges
of Participatory Culture* (2009), *Convergence Culture* (2006),
and *Fans, Bloggers, and Gamers: Exploring Participatory Culture*
(2006). He holds a Ph.D. in communication arts from the
University of Wisconsin and a master's degree in communication studies from the University of Iowa. More information at henryjenkins.org.

WHEN MY SON, HENRY, was fifteen, we made a trip from
Cambridge to Omaha so that he could meet his girlfriend face-to-face for the first time. Though they met
online, this is not the story of a virtual relationship; their feelings
were no less real to them than the first love of any other teenager,
past or present. When I was suffering the first pangs of unrequited
adolescent longing, there weren't a lot of girls in my immediate
vicinity who would risk the stigma involved in going out with me.
One summer I met a few girls at a camp for honors students, but
our relationships withered once we returned to our own schools and

neighborhoods. My son, finding slim pickings at school, cast a wider net, seeking kindred spirits wherever they dwelt in a neighborhood as big as cyberspace itself. Online, he had what it took—good communication skills.

He met Sarah in an online discussion group; they talked through private e-mail; after getting to know her a little he finally got the courage to phone her. They dated in chat rooms. They sent each other virtual candy, flowers, and cards downloaded off various websites. They spoke of "going out," even though they sat thousands of miles apart.

Sarah's father often screened her telephone calls and didn't want her to talk with boys. He didn't pay the same degree of attention to what she did online. He quickly ran up against the difference between his expectations of appropriate courtship and the realities of online love. He felt strongly that boys should not talk to his daughter on the telephone or ask her out on dates unless they were personally known to him. Henry had to go through the ritual of meeting him on the telephone and asking his permission to see her before we could make the trip.

Long-distance communication between lovers is hardly new. The exchange of love letters was central to the courtship of my grandparents (who were separated by the First World War) and of my parents (who were separated by my father's service after the Second World War). By the time my wife and I were courting, we handed our love letters back and forth in person and read them aloud to each other. Our courtship was conducted face-to-face or through late-night telephone conversations. The love letter was a residual form—though we still have a box of yellowing letters we periodically reread with misty-eyed nostalgia.

Sarah and Henry's romantic communications might seem, at first, more transient, bytes passing from computer to computer. Yet he backlogged all of their chats and surprised Sarah with a printout. In this fashion, he preserved not only the carefully crafted love letters but the process of an evolving relationship. It was as if my wife and I had tape-recorded our first strolls in the park together.

Henry and Sarah would not have met outside the virtual communities the Internet facilitates. But they were both emphatic that purely digital communication could not have sustained their relationship. The first time Sarah confirmed that she shared my son's affections, she spoke her words of love on a chat room without realizing that he had been accidentally disconnected. By the time he was able to get back online, she had left in frustration. Wooing must be difficult if you can't even be sure the other party is there.

The medium's inadequacies are, no doubt, resulting in significant shifts in the vocabulary of love. In cyberspace, there is no room for the ambiguous gestures that characterized another generation's fumbling first courtships. In a multiuser domain, one doesn't type, "Henry smiles. He moves his hand subtly toward her in a gesture that might be averted at the last moment if she seems not to notice or to be shocked." The language of courtly love emerged under similar circumstances: distant lovers putting into writing what they could not say aloud.

They may have met online, but they communicated through every available channel. Their initial exchange of photographs produced enormous anxiety as they struggled to decide what frozen image or images should anchor their more fluid online identities. In choosing, my son attempted to negotiate between what he thought would be desirable to another fifteen-year-old and what wouldn't alienate her conservative parents.

The photographs were followed by other tangible objects, shipped between Nebraska and Massachusetts. These objects were cherished because they had achieved the physical intimacy still denied the geographically isolated teens. Henry sent her, for example, the imprint of his lips, stained in red wine on stationery. In some cases, they individually staged rituals they could not perform together. Henry preserved a red rose he purchased for himself the day she first agreed to go steady. Even in an age of instant communication, they still sent handwritten notes. These two teens longed for the concrete, for being together in the same space, for things materially passed from person to person.

Barring that, they cherished their weekly telephone calls. Talking on the telephone helped make Sarah real for Henry. When his friends at school challenged his inability to "produce" his girlfriend for inspection and asked how he knew she wasn't a guy, he cited their telephone conversations. Even for these teens, the fluidity of electronic identities posed threats. Once, early in their relationship, Henry jokingly told Sarah that they went to the same school, never imagining that she would believe him. The results were both farcical and tragic as she searched in vain for her mystery date.

After a while, they started to fear that they might break up without ever having seen each other in the flesh, and they didn't want it to end that way. After some pleading, I agreed to accompany Henry on the trip. Henry and Sarah first "met" in an airport. He almost didn't recognize her since she was so different from the single photograph she had sent. From the start, their interaction was intensely physical. Henry said that what had given him the most pleasure was being able to play with her hair, and Sarah punched him in the arm so many times he was black and blue. Sarah's mother and I watched two slouching teens shuffle through the terminal, learning to walk in rhythm.

As would-be dramatists, they wondered what they should say at that first meeting. Sarah solved the problem by shouting "Sony PlayStation" across the crowded airport. The two of them had a running debate about the relative merits of different game systems. Their first date was to an arcade where Sarah made good her longstanding boasts and beat him at *Street Fighter II* before Henry got his revenge on *NFL GameDay*. Sarah made the state finals in a video-game competition, so it was no surprise this proved central to the time they spent together. Sarah's mother purchased some new games and—ever the chaperone—brought the game system down to the parlor from Sarah's room so they could play together.

If we are going to talk, from Cambridge to Omaha, with people we've never met before, we need something to talk about. For Henry and Sarah, that common culture consisted not only of different games and game systems, but also a shared enthusiasm for professional wrestling. They met on rec.sport.pro-wrestling, brought together by a shared interest in the Undertaker, a star of the World Wrestling Federation. They both were participants in an electronic pro wrestling role-playing game. Henry brought a cardboard sign with him to a televised wrestling event, pushed his way through the crowd, and got on camera so he could send Sarah a broadcast message.

Popular culture also helped to bridge the awkward silences in my exchanges with Sarah's parents. I had wondered what a media scholar from "the People's Republic of Cambridge" would say to two retired Air Force officers from Nebraska. As Sarah's mother and I sat in the arcade, trying to dodge religion and politics, we found common ground discussing *Star Trek*, the original *Saturday Night Live* cast, and of course, *Mutual of Omaha's Wild Kingdom*.

Henry and Sarah broke up sometime after that trip—not because they had met online or because the real-life experience hadn't lived up to their expectations but because they were fifteen, their interests shifted, and they never really overcame her father's opposition. Henry's next relationship was also online—with a girl from Melbourne, Australia, and that experience broadened his perspective on the world, at the price of much sleep as they negotiated time differences. Now twenty-one, he has gone through his normal share of other romantic entanglements, some online, more face-to-face (with many of the latter conducted, at least in part, online to endure the summer vacation separation).

We've read more than a decade of press coverage about online relationships—much of it written since my son and I made this trip together. Journalists love to talk about the aberrant qualities of virtual sex. Yet, many of us embraced the Internet because it has fit into the most personal and banal spaces of our lives. Focusing on the revolutionary aspects of online courtship blinds us to the continuities in courtship rituals across generations and across media. Indeed, the power of physical artifacts (the imprint of lips on paper, the faded petals of a rose), of photographs, of the voice on the telephone, gain new poignancy in the context of these new relationships. Moreover, focusing on the online aspects of these relationships blinds us to the agility with which teens move back and forth across media. Their daily lives require constant decisions about what to say on the phone, what to write by hand, what to communicate in chat rooms, what to send by e-mail. They juggle multiple identities—the fictional personas of electronic wrestling, the constructed ideals of romantic love, and the realities of real bodies and real emotions.

<Cathy Davidson>

we can't ignore the influence of digital technologies

Originally published in *The Chronicle of Higher Education* (March 19, 2007).

CATHY DAVIDSON is the John Hope Franklin Humanities Institute Professor of Interdisciplinary Studies and Ruth F. DeVarney Professor of English at Duke University. She is the codirector of the $2 million annual HASTAC/John D. and Catherine T. MacArthur Foundation Digital Media and Learning Competition. Her books include *Revolution and the Word: The Rise of the Novel in America* (1986) and *The Future of Thinking: Learning Institutions in a Digital Age* (with HASTAC cofounder David Theo Goldberg in 2010). She blogs on new media and learning at www.hastac.org as "Cat in the Stack."

WHEN I READ the other day that the history department at Middlebury College had "banned Wikipedia," I immediately wrote to the college's president, Ronald D. Liebowitz, to express my concern that such a decision would lead to a national trend, one that would not be good for higher education. "Banning" has connotations of evil or heresy. Is Wikipedia really that bad?

I learned from Mr. Liebowitz that the news media had exaggerated the real story. The history department's policy that students not cite Wikipedia in papers or examinations is consistent with an existing policy on not citing sources such as *Encyclopaedia Britannica*. It is hardly a "ban." It is a definition of what constitutes credible scholarly or archival sources.

Even granting that the news media exaggerated, it is useful to think about why this was a story at all and what we can learn from it. The coverage echoed the most Luddite reactions to Wikipedia and other ventures in creating knowledge in a collaborative, digital environment. In fact, soon after the Middlebury story was reported, one of my colleagues harrumphed, "Thank goodness someone is maintaining standards!" I asked what he meant, and he said that Wikipedia was prone to error. So are encyclopedias, I countered. So are refereed scholarly books. (*Gasp!*) He was surprised when I noted that several comparative studies have shown that errors in Wikipedia are not more frequent than those in comparable print sources. More to the point, in Wikipedia, errors can be corrected. The specific one cited by the Middlebury history department—an erroneous statement that Jesuits had supported a rebellion in seventeenth-century Japan—was amended in a matter of hours.

That brings us to a second point. Wikipedia is not just an encyclopedia. It is a knowledge community, uniting anonymous readers all over the world who edit and correct grammar, style, interpretations, and facts. It is a community devoted to a common good—the life of the intellect. Isn't that what we educators want to model for our students?

Rather than banning Wikipedia, why not make studying what it does and does not do part of the research-and-methods portion of our courses? Instead of resorting to the "Delete" button for new forms of collaborative knowledge made possible by the Internet, why not make the practice of research in the digital age the object of study? That is already happening, of course, but we could do more. For example, some professors already ask students to pursue archival research for a paper and then to post their writing on a class wiki. It's just another step to ask them to post their labors on Wikipedia, where they can learn to participate in a community of lifelong learners. That's not as much a reach for students as it is for some of their professors.

Most of the students who entered Middlebury last fall were born around 1988. They have grown up with new technology skills, new ways of finding information, and new modes of informal learning that are also intimately connected to their social lives. I recently spent time with a five-year-old who was consumed by Pokémon. His parents were alarmed by his obsession, although his father reluctantly admitted that, at the same age, he had known every dinosaur and could recite their names with the same passion that his son now has for the almost five hundred (and growing) Pokémon characters. I also was able to assure the parents that by mastering the game at the level he had, their son was actually mastering a nine-year-old's reading vocabulary. He was also customizing his games with editing tools that I can only begin to manipulate, and doing so with creativity and remarkable manual dexterity. The students at Middlebury have grown up honing those skills. Don't we want them to both mine the potential of such tools in their formal education and think critically about them? That would be far more productive than a knee-jerk "Delete."

I must admit I have an investment in this issue. A passionate one. I am on the advisory board of the John D. and Catherine T. MacArthur Foundation's Digital Media and Learning initiative, a five-year, $50 million project started last year to study how digital technologies are changing all forms of learning, play, and social interaction. One focus of the initiative is research on ways that schools and colleges can be as lively and inspiring intellectually as are the Internet imaginations of our children. Grantees are working on such projects as learning games where young children create their own Frankensteins, then consider the ethics and science of

their creations; other researchers are helping students develop a
new civic awareness as they use three-dimensional virtual environments to create new worlds with new social rules. In the spirit of
collaboration, the MacArthur program sponsors a blog, *Spotlight*,
where visitors can interact with grantees (http://spotlight.mac-
found.org). In all the projects, the knowledge is shared, collaborative, cumulative. Like Wikipedia.

I am also co-founder of a voluntary network of academics called
HASTAC (http://www.hastac.org)—an unwieldy acronym that
stands for Humanities, Arts, Science, and Technology Advanced
Collaboratory, but everyone just calls it "haystack." With my co-
founder, David Theo Goldberg, I have recently posted the first draft
of a paper, written for the MacArthur program, on "The Future of
Learning Institutions in a Digital Age." That paper is on a collaborative website (http://www.futureofthebook.org/HASTAC/learning
report/about) that allows anyone to edit it, make comments, and
contribute examples of innovative work. The site is sponsored by the
Institute for the Future of the Book, a group dedicated to investigat-
ing how intellectual discourse changes as it shifts from printed
pages to networked screens. We are holding a series of public forums
and, in the end, will synthesize responses and include, in a "Hall of
Vision," examples of the most inventive learning we have found in
the country, learning that is collaborative and forward-looking. We
will also include a "Hall of Shame," for retrograde and unthinking
reactions to new technologies. (I was delighted to learn that, despite
media reports, Middlebury College won't have to go there.)

As a cultural historian and historian of technology, I find that
I often go to Wikipedia for a quick and easy reference before head-
ing into more scholarly depths. I'm often surprised at how sound
and good a first source it is. Its problems have been well rehearsed
in the media—to take a case that came recently to light, the way
someone can create a persona as a scholar and contribute information under false pretenses. Some entries are bogged down in con-

troversies, and some controversial figures (including scholars whose work I admire) are discussed in essays that are a mess of point and counterpoint. But I just looked up two well-known literary critics, Judith Butler and Fredric Jameson, on Wikipedia. Two months ago, when I first looked, the entries I found amounted to "idea assassinations" (if not outright character assassinations). But someone has been busy. The entries on both figures are much improved. I clicked on the editing history to see who had added what and why. I looked up a half hour later and realized I'd gotten lost in a trail of ideas about postmodernism and the Frankfurt School—when I had a deadline to meet. Isn't that the fantasy of what the educated life is like?

I also find that my book purchasing has probably increased threefold because of Wikipedia. I am often engaged by an entry, then I go to the discussion pages, and then I find myself caught up in debate among contributors. Pretty soon I am locating articles via Project Muse and 1-Click shopping for books on Amazon. Why not teach that way of using the resource to our students? Why rush to ban the single most impressive collaborative intellectual tool produced at least since the *Oxford English Dictionary,* which started when a nonacademic organization, the Philological Society, decided to enlist hundreds of volunteer readers to copy down unusual usages of so-called unregistered words?

I urge readers to take the hubbub around Middlebury's decision as an opportunity to engage students—and the country—in a substantive discussion of how we learn today, of how we make arguments from evidence, of how we extrapolate from discrete facts to theories and interpretations, and on what basis. Knowledge isn't just information, and it isn't just opinion. There are better and worse ways to reach conclusions, and complex reasons for how we arrive at them. The "discussion" section of Wikipedia is a great place to begin to consider some of the processes involved.

When he responded to my letter of concern, Middlebury's president also noted that "the history department's stance is not shared by all Middlebury faculty, and in fact last night we held an open forum on the topic, in which a junior faculty member in the history department and a junior faculty member in our program in film and media culture presented opposing views and invited questions and comments from a large and interested audience." He added that "the continuing evolution of new ways of sharing ideas and information will require that the academy continue to evolve as well in its understanding of how these technologies fit into our conception of scholarly discourse. We are pleased that Middlebury can take part in this important debate."

The Middlebury debate, by the way, already has a place on Wikipedia. Maybe that's the right place for high schools and colleges to begin as they hold their own forums on the learning opportunities of our moment, and the best ways to use new tools, critically, conscientiously, and creatively.

<Christine Rosen>

virtual friendship and the new narcissism

Originally published in *The New Atlantis*
(Summer 2007).

CHRISTINE ROSEN is senior editor of *The New Atlantis: A Journal of Technology & Society*. She is the author of *Preaching Eugenics: Religious Leaders and the American Eugenics Movement* (2004) and *My Fundamentalist Education: A Memoir of a Divine Girlhood* (2005). Since 1999, Mrs. Rosen has been an adjunct scholar at the American Enterprise Institute for Public Policy Research, where she has written about women and the economy, feminism, and women's studies. Her commentaries and essays have appeared in *The New York Times Magazine, The Wall Street Journal, The New Republic, Washington Post, The Weekly Standard, Commentary, Wilson Quarterly,* and *Policy Review.* She earned a Ph.D. in history from Emory University in 1999.

FOR CENTURIES, the rich and the powerful documented their existence and their status through painted portraits. A marker of wealth and a bid for immortality, portraits offer intriguing hints about the daily life of their subjects—professions, ambitions, attitudes, and, most important, social standing. Such portraits, as German art historian Hans Belting has argued, can be understood as "painted anthropology," with much to teach us, both intentionally and unintentionally, about the culture in which they were created.

Self-portraits can be especially instructive. By showing the artist both as he sees his true self and as he wishes to be seen, self-portraits can at once expose and obscure, clarify and distort. They offer opportunities for both self-expression and self-seeking. They can display egotism and modesty, self-aggrandizement and self-mockery.

Today, our self-portraits are democratic and digital; they are crafted from pixels rather than paints. On social networking websites like MySpace and Facebook, our modern self-portraits feature background music, carefully manipulated photographs, stream-of-consciousness musings, and lists of our hobbies and friends. They are interactive, inviting viewers not merely to look at, but also to respond to, the life portrayed online. We create them to find friendship, love, and that ambiguous modern thing called connection. Like painters constantly retouching their work, we alter, update, and tweak our online self-portraits; but as digital objects they are far more ephemeral than oil on canvas. Vital statistics, glimpses of bare flesh, lists of favorite bands and favorite poems all clamor for our attention—and it is the timeless human desire for attention that emerges as the dominant theme of these vast virtual galleries.

Although social networking sites are in their infancy, we are seeing their impact culturally: in language (where "to friend" is now a verb), in politics (where it is de rigueur for presidential aspirants to catalogue their virtues on MySpace), and on college campuses (where *not* using Facebook can be a social handicap). But we are only beginning to come to grips with the consequences of our use of these sites: for friendship, and for our notions of privacy, authenticity, community, and identity. As with any new technological advance, we must consider what type of behavior online social networking encourages. Does this technology, with its constant demands to collect (friends and status) and perform (by marketing ourselves), in some ways undermine our ability to attain what it promises—a surer sense of who we are and where we belong? The Delphic oracle's guidance was *know thyself.* Today, in the world of online social networks, the oracle's advice might be *show thyself.*

>>> making connections

The earliest online social networks were arguably the Bulletin Board Systems of the 1980s that let users post public messages, send and receive private messages, play games, and exchange software. Some of those BBSs, like The WELL (Whole Earth 'Lectronic Link) that technologist Larry Brilliant and futurist Stewart Brand started in 1985, made the transition to the World Wide Web in the mid-1990s. (Now owned by Salon.com, The WELL boasts that it was "the primordial ooze where the online community movement was born.") Other websites for community and connection emerged in the 1990s, including Classmates.com (1995), where users register by high school and year of graduation; Company of Friends, a business-oriented site founded in 1997; and Epinions, founded in 1999 to allow users to give their opinions about various consumer products.

A new generation of social networking websites appeared in 2002 with the launch of Friendster, whose founder, Jonathan Abrams, admitted that his main motivation for creating the site was to meet attractive women. Unlike previous online communities, which brought together anonymous strangers with shared interests, Friendster uses a model of social networking known as the "Circle of Friends" (developed by British computer scientist Jonathan Bishop), in which users invite friends and acquaintances—that is, people they already know and like—to join their network.

Friendster was an immediate success, with millions of registered users by mid-2003. But technological glitches and poor management at the company allowed a new social networking site, MySpace, launched in 2003, quickly to surpass it. Originally started by musicians, MySpace has become a major venue for sharing music as well as videos and photos. It is now the behemoth of online social networking, with over 100 million registered users. Connection has become big business: In 2005, Rupert Murdoch's News Corporation bought MySpace for $580 million.

Besides MySpace and Friendster, the best-known social networking site is Facebook, launched in 2004. Originally restricted to college students, Facebook—which takes its name from the small photo albums that colleges once gave to incoming freshmen and faculty to help them cope with meeting so many new people—soon extended membership to high schoolers and is now open to anyone. Still, it is most popular among college students and recent college graduates, many of whom use the site as their primary method of communicating with one another. Millions of college students check their Facebook pages several times every day and spend hours sending and receiving messages, making appointments, getting updates on their friends' activities, and learning about people they might recently have met or heard about.

There are dozens of other social networking sites, including Orkut, Bebo, and Yahoo 360°. Microsoft recently announced its own plans for a social networking site called Wallop; the company boasts that the site will offer "an entirely new way for consumers to express their individuality online." (It is noteworthy that Microsoft refers to social networkers as "consumers" rather than merely "users" or, say, "people.") Niche social networking sites are also flourishing: there are sites offering forums and fellowship for photographers, music lovers, and sports fans. There are professional networking sites, such as LinkedIn, that keep people connected with present and former colleagues and other business acquaintances. There are sites specifically for younger children, such as Club Penguin, which lets kids pretend to be chubby, colored penguins who waddle around, chatting, playing games, earning virtual money, and buy-ing virtual clothes. Other niche social networking sites connect like-minded self-improvers; the site 43things.com encourages peo-ple to share their personal goals. Click on "watch less TV," one of the goals listed on the site, and you can see the profiles of the 1,300 other people in the network who want to do the same thing. And for people who want to join a social network but don't know which niche site is right for them, there are sites that help users locate the proper online social networking community for their particular (or peculiar) interests.

Social networking sites are also fertile ground for those who make it their lives' work to get your attention—namely, spammers, marketers, and politicians. Incidents of spamming and spyware on MySpace and other social networking sites are legion. Legitimate advertisers such as record labels and film studios have also set up pages for their products. In some cases, fictional characters from books and movies are given their own official MySpace pages. Some sports mascots and brand icons have them, too. Procter & Gamble has a Crest toothpaste page on MySpace featuring a sultry-looking model called "Miss Irresistible." As of this summer, she had about 50,000 users linked as friends, whom she urged to "spice it up by sending a naughty (or nice) e-card." The e-cards are emblazoned with Crest or Scope logos, of course, and include messages such as "I wanna get fresh with you" or "Pucker up baby—I'm getting fresh." A P & G marketing officer recently told the *Wall Street Jour-nal* that from a business perspective social networking sites are "going to be one giant living dynamic learning experience about consumers."

As for politicians, with the presidential primary season now underway, candidates have embraced a no-website-left-behind pol-icy. Senator Hillary Clinton has official pages on social networking sites MySpace, Flickr, LiveJournal, Facebook, Friendster, and Orkut. As of July 1, 2007, she had a mere 52,472 friends on MySpace (a bit more than Miss Irresistible); her Democratic rival Senator Barack Obama had an impressive 128,859. Former Senator John Edwards has profiles on twenty-three different sites. Republican contenders for the White House are poorer social networkers than their Democratic counterparts; as of this writing, none of the GOP candidates has as many MySpace friends as Hillary, and some of the leading Republican candidates have no social networking presence at all.

Despite the increasingly diverse range of social networking sites, the most popular sites share certain features. On MySpace and Facebook, for example, the process of setting up one's online identity is relatively simple: Provide your name, address, e-mail address, and a few other pieces of information and you're up and running and ready to create your online persona. MySpace includes a section, "About Me," where you can post your name, age, where you live, and other personal details such as your zodiac sign, religion, sexual orientation, and relationship status. There is also a "Who I'd Like to Meet" section, which on most MySpace profiles is filled with images of celebrities. Users can also list their favorite music, movies, and television shows, as well as their personal heroes; MySpace users can also blog on their pages. A user "friends" people—that is, invites them by e-mail to appear on the user's "Friend Space," where they are listed, linked, and ranked. Below the Friends space is a Comments section where friends can post notes. MySpace allows users to personalize their pages by uploading images and music and videos; indeed, one of the defining features of most MySpace pages is the ubiquity of visual and audio clutter. With silly, hyper flashing graphics in neon colors and clip-art-style images of kittens and cartoons, MySpace pages often resemble an overdecorated high school yearbook.

By contrast, Facebook limits what its users can do to their profiles. Besides general personal information, Facebook users have a "Wall" where people can leave them brief notes, as well as a Messages feature that functions like an in-house Facebook e-mail account. You list your friends on Facebook as well, but in general, unlike MySpace friends, which are often complete strangers (or spammers), Facebook friends tend to be part of one's offline social circle. (This might change, however, now that Facebook has opened its site to anyone rather than restricting it to college and high school students.) Facebook (and MySpace) allow users to form groups based on mutual interests. Facebook users can also send "pokes" to friends; these little digital nudges are meant to let someone know you are thinking about him or her. But they can also be interpreted as not-so-subtle come-ons; one Facebook group with over 200,000 members is called "Enough with the Poking, Let's Just Have Sex."

>>> degrees of separation

It is worth pausing for a moment to reflect on the curious use of the word *networking* to describe this new form of human interaction. Social networking websites "connect" users with a network—literally, a computer network. But the verb *to network* has long been used to describe an act of intentional social connecting, especially for professionals seeking career-boosting contacts. When the word first came into circulation in the 1970s, computer networks were rare and mysterious. Back then, "network" usually referred to television. But social scientists were already using the notion of networks and nodes to map out human relations and calculate just how closely we are connected.

In 1967, Harvard sociologist and psychologist Stanley Milgram, best known for his earlier Yale experiments on obedience to authority, published the results of a study about social connection that he called the "small world experiment." "Given any two people in the world, person X and person Z," he asked, "how many intermediate acquaintance links are needed before X and Z are connected?" Milgram's research, which involved sending out a kind of chain letter and tracing its journey to a particular target person, yielded an average number of 5.5 connections. The idea that we are all connected by "six degrees of separation" (a phrase later popularized by playwright John Guare) is now conventional wisdom.

But is it true? Duncan J. Watts, a professor at Columbia University and author of *Six Degrees: The Science of a Connected Age*, has embarked on a new small world project to test Milgram's theory. Similar in spirit to Milgram's work, it relies on e-mail to determine whether "any two people in the world can be connected via 'six degrees of separation.'" Unlike Milgram's experiment, which was restricted to the United States, Watts's project is global; as he and his colleagues reported in *Science*, "Targets included a professor at an Ivy League university, an archival inspector in Estonia, a technology consultant in India, a policeman in Australia, and a veterinarian in the Norwegian army." Their early results suggest that Milgram might have been right: messages reached their targets in five to seven steps, on average. Other social networking theorists are equally optimistic about the smallness of our wireless world. In *Linked: The New Science of Networks*, Albert-László Barabási enthuses, "The world is shrinking because social links that would have died out a hundred years ago are kept alive and can be easily activated. The number of social links an individual can actively maintain has increased dramatically, bringing down the degrees of separation. Milgram estimated six," Barabási writes. "We could be much closer these days to three."

What kind of "links" are these? In a 1973 essay, "The Strength of Weak Ties," sociologist Mark Granovetter argued that weaker relationships, such as those we form with colleagues at work or minor acquaintances, were more useful in spreading certain kinds of information than networks of close friends and family. Watts found a similar phenomenon in his online small world experiment: weak ties (largely professional ones) were more useful than strong ties for locating far-flung individuals, for example.

Today's online social networks are congeries of mostly weak

ties—no one who lists thousands of "friends" on MySpace thinks of those people in the same way as he does his flesh-and-blood acquaintances, for example. It is surely no coincidence, then, that the activities social networking sites promote are precisely the ones weak ties foster, like rumor-mongering, gossip, finding people, and tracking the ever-shifting movements of popular culture and fad. If this is our small world, it is one that gives its greatest attention to small things.

Even more intriguing than the actual results of Milgram's small world experiment—our supposed closeness to each other—was the swiftness and credulity of the public in embracing those results. But as psychologist Judith Kleinfeld found when she delved into Milgram's research (much of which was methodologically flawed and never adequately replicated), entrenched barriers of race and social class undermine the idea that we live in a small world. Computer networks have not removed those barriers. As Watts and his colleagues conceded in describing their own digital small world experiment, "more than half of all participants resided in North America and were middle class, professional, college educated, and Christian."

Nevertheless, our need to believe in the possibility of a small world and in the power of connection is strong, as evidenced by the popularity and proliferation of contemporary online social networks. Perhaps the question we should be asking isn't how closely are we connected, but rather what kinds of communities and friendships are we creating?

>>> won't you be my digital neighbor

According to a survey recently conducted by the Pew Internet and American Life Project, more than half of all Americans between the ages of twelve and seventeen use some online social networking site. Indeed, media coverage of social networking sites usually describes them as vast teenage playgrounds—or wastelands, depending on one's perspective. Central to this narrative is a nearly unbridgeable generational divide, with tech-savvy youngsters redefining friendship while their doddering elders look on with bafflement and increasing anxiety. This seems anecdotally correct; I can't count how many times I have mentioned social networking websites to someone over the age of forty and received the reply, "Oh yes, I've heard about that MyFace! All the kids are doing that these days. Very interesting!"

Numerous articles have chronicled adults' attempts to navigate the world of social networking, such as the recent *New York Times* essay in which columnist Michelle Slatalla described the incredible embarrassment she caused her teenage daughter when she joined Facebook: "everyone in the whole world thinks its super creepy when adults have facebooks," her daughter instant-messaged her. "unfriend paige right now. im serious. . . . i will be soo mad if you dont unfriend paige right now. actually." In fact, social networking sites are not only for the young. More than half of the visitors to MySpace claim to be over the age of thirty-five. And now that the first generation of college Facebook users have graduated, and the site is open to all, more than half of Facebook users are no longer students. What's more, the proliferation of niche social networking sites, including those aimed at adults, suggests that it is not only teenagers who will nurture relationships in virtual space for the foreseeable future.

What characterizes these online communities in which an increasing number of us are spending our time? Social networking sites have a peculiar psychogeography. As researchers at the Pew project have noted, the proto–social networking sites of a decade ago used metaphors of *place* to organize their members: people were linked through virtual cities, communities, and home pages. In 1997, GeoCities boasted thirty virtual "neighborhoods" in which "homesteaders" or "GeoCitizens" could gather—"Heartland" for family and parenting tips, "SouthBeach" for socializing, "Vienna" for classical music aficionados, "Broadway" for theater buffs, and so on. By contrast, today's social networking sites organize themselves around metaphors of the *person*, with individual profiles that list hobbies and interests. As a result, one's entrée into this world generally isn't through a virtual neighborhood or community but through the revelation of personal information. And unlike a neighborhood, where one usually has a general knowledge of others who live in the area, social networking sites are gatherings of deracinated individuals, none of whose personal boastings and musings are necessarily trustworthy. Here, the old arbiters of community— geographic location, family, role, or occupation—have little effect on relationships.

Also, in the offline world, communities typically are responsible for enforcing norms of privacy and general etiquette. In the online world, which is unfettered by the boundaries of real-world communities, new etiquette challenges abound. For example, what do you do with a "friend" who posts inappropriate comments on your Wall? What recourse do you have if someone posts an embarrassing picture of you on his MySpace page? What happens when a friend breaks up with someone—do you defriend the ex? If someone "friends" you and you don't accept the overture, how serious a rejection is it? Some of these scenarios can be resolved with split-second snap judgments; others can provoke days of agonizing.

Enthusiasts of social networking argue that these sites are not merely entertaining; they also edify by teaching users about the rules of social space. As Danah Boyd, a graduate student studying social networks at the University of California, Berkeley, told the authors of *MySpace Unraveled*, social networking promotes "informal learning. . . . It's where you learn social norms, rules, how to interact with others, narrative, personal and group history, and media literacy." This is more a hopeful assertion than a proven fact,

however. The question that isn't asked is how the technology itself—
the way it encourages us to present ourselves and interact—limits
or imposes on that process of informal learning. All communities
expect their members to internalize certain norms. Even individuals in the transient communities that form in public spaces obey
these rules, for the most part; for example, patrons of libraries are
expected to keep noise to a minimum. New technologies are challenging such norms—cell phones ring during church sermons; blaring televisions in doctors' waiting rooms make it difficult to talk
quietly—and new norms must develop to replace the old. What cues
are young, avid social networkers learning about social space? What
unspoken rules and communal norms have the millions of participants in these online social networks internalized, and how have
these new norms influenced their behavior in the offline world?

Social rules and norms are not merely the straitlaced conceits
of a bygone era; they serve a protective function. I know a young
woman—attractive, intelligent, and well-spoken—who, like many
other people in their twenties, joined Facebook as a college student
when it launched. When she and her boyfriend got engaged, they
both updated their relationship status to "Engaged" on their profiles and friends posted congratulatory messages on her Wall.

But then they broke off the engagement. And a funny thing happened. Although she had already told a few friends and family
members that the relationship was over, her ex decided to make it
official in a very twenty-first-century way: he changed his status on
his profile from "Engaged" to "Single." Facebook immediately sent
out a feed to every one of their mutual "friends" announcing the
news, "Mr. X and Ms. Y are no longer in a relationship," complete
with an icon of a broken heart. When I asked the young woman how
she felt about this, she said that although she assumed her friends
and acquaintances would eventually hear the news, there was
something disconcerting about the fact that everyone found out
about it instantaneously; and since the message came from Face-

book, rather than in a face-to-face exchange initiated by her, it was devoid of context—save for a helpful notation of the time and that tacky little heart.

>>> indecent exposure

Enthusiasts praise social networking for presenting chances for identity-play; they see opportunities for all of us to be little Van Goghs and Warhols, rendering quixotic and ever-changing versions of ourselves for others to enjoy. Instead of a palette of oils, we can employ services such as PimpMySpace.org, which offers "layouts, graphics, background, and more!" to gussy up an online presentation of self, albeit in a decidedly raunchy fashion. Among the most popular graphics used by PimpMySpace clients on a given day in June 2007 were short video clips of two women kissing and another of a man and an obese woman having sex; a picture of a gleaming pink handgun; and an image of the cartoon character SpongeBob SquarePants, looking alarmed and uttering a profanity.

This kind of coarseness and vulgarity is commonplace on social networking sites for a reason: it's an easy way to set oneself apart. Pharaohs and kings once celebrated themselves by erecting towering statues or, like the emperor Augustus, placing their own visages on coins. But now, as the insightful technology observer Jaron Lanier has written, "Since there are only a few archetypes, ideals, or icons to strive for in comparison to the vastness of instances of everything online, quirks and idiosyncrasies stand out better than grandeur in this new domain. I imagine Augustus' MySpace page would have pictured him picking his nose." And he wouldn't be alone. Indeed, this is one of the characteristics of MySpace most striking to anyone who spends a few hours trolling its millions of pages: it is an overwhelmingly dull sea of monotonous uniqueness, of conventional individuality, of distinctive sameness.

The world of online social networking is practically homogenous in one other sense, however diverse it might at first appear: its users are committed to self-exposure. The creation and conspicuous consumption of intimate details and images of one's own and others' lives is the main activity in the online social networking world. There is no room for reticence; there is only revelation. Quickly peruse a profile and you know more about a potential acquaintance in a moment than you might have learned about a flesh-and-blood friend in a month. As one college student recently described to the *New York Times Magazine*: "You might run into someone at a party, and then you Facebook them: what are their interests? Are they crazy-religious, is their favorite quote from the Bible? Everyone takes great pains over presenting themselves. It's like an embodiment of your personality."

It seems that in our headlong rush to join social networking sites, many of us give up one of the Internet's supposed charms: the promise of anonymity. As Michael Kinsley noted in *Slate*, in order to "stake their claims as unique individuals," users enumerate personal information: "Here is a list of my friends. Here are all the CDs in my collection. Here is a picture of my dog." Kinsley is not impressed; he judges these sites "vast celebrations of solipsism."

Social networkers, particularly younger users, are often naive or ill-informed about the amount of information they are making publicly available. "One cannot help but marvel at the amount, detail, and nature of the personal information some users provide, and ponder how informed this information sharing can be," Carnegie Mellon researchers Alessandro Acquisti and Ralph Gross wrote in 2006. In a survey of Facebook users at their university, Acquisti and Gross "detected little or no relation between participants' reported privacy attitudes and their likelihood" of publishing personal information online. Even among the students in the survey who claimed to be most concerned about their privacy—the ones who worried about "the scenario in which a stranger knew their schedule of classes and where they lived"—about 40 percent provided their class schedule on Facebook, about 22 percent put their address on Facebook, and almost 16 percent published both.

This kind of carelessness has provided fodder for many sensationalist news stories. To cite just one: In 2006, NBC's *Dateline* featured a police officer posing as a nineteen-year-old boy who was new in town. Although not grounded in any particular local community, the impostor quickly gathered more than 100 friends for his MySpace profile and began corresponding with several teenage girls. Although the girls claimed to be careful about the kind of information they posted online, when *Dateline* revealed that their new friend was actually an adult male who had figured out their names and where they lived, they were surprised. The danger posed by strangers who use social networking sites to prey on children is real; there have been several such cases. This danger was highlighted in July 2007 when MySpace booted from its system 29,000 sex offenders who had signed up for memberships using their real names. There is no way of knowing how many sex offenders have MySpace accounts registered under fake names.

There are also professional risks to putting too much information on social networking sites, just as for several years there have been career risks associated with personal home pages and blogs. A survey conducted in 2006 by researchers at the University of Dayton found that "40 percent of employers say they would consider the Facebook profile of a potential employee as part of their hiring decision, and several reported rescinding offers after checking out Facebook." Yet college students' reaction to this fact suggests that they have a different understanding of privacy than potential employers: 42 percent thought it was a violation of privacy for employers to peruse their profiles, and "64 percent of students said employers should not consider Facebook profiles during the hiring process."

This is a quaintly Victorian notion of privacy, embracing the idea that individuals should be able to compartmentalize and parcel out parts of their personalities in different settings. It suggests that even behavior of a decidedly questionable or hypocritical bent (the Victorian patriarch who also cavorts with prostitutes, for example, or the straight-A business major who posts picture of himself funneling beer on his MySpace page) should be tolerated if appropriately segregated. But when one's darker side finds expression in a virtual space, privacy becomes more difficult and true compartmentalization nearly impossible; on the Internet, private misbehavior becomes public exhibitionism.

In many ways, the manners and mores that have already developed in the world of online social networking suggest that these sites promote gatherings of what psychiatrist Robert Jay Lifton has called "protean selves." Named after Proteus, the Greek sea god of many forms, the protean self evinces "mockery and self-mockery, irony, absurdity, and humor." (Indeed, the University of Dayton survey found that "23 percent [of students] said they intentionally misrepresented themselves [on Facebook] to be funny or as a joke.") Also, Lifton argues, "the emotions of the protean self tend to be free-floating, not clearly tied to cause or target." So, too, with protean communities: "Not just individual emotions but communities as well may be free-floating," Lifton writes, "removed geographically and embraced temporarily and selectively, with no promise of permanence." This is precisely the appeal of online social networking. These sites make certain kinds of connections easier, but because they are governed not by geography or community mores but by personal whim, they free users from the responsibilities that tend to come with membership in a community. This fundamentally changes the tenor of the relationships that form there, something best observed in the way social networks treat friendship. . . .

We should also take note of the trend toward giving up face-to-face for virtual contact—and, in some cases, a preference for the latter. Today, many of our cultural, social, and political interactions take place through eminently convenient technological surrogates—why go to the bank if you can use the ATM? Why browse in a bookstore when you can simply peruse the personalized selections Amazon.com has made for you? In the same vein, social networking sites are often convenient surrogates for offline friendship and community. In this context it is worth considering an observation that Stanley Milgram made in 1974, regarding his experiments with obedience: "The social psychology of this century reveals a major lesson," he wrote. "Often it is not so much the kind of person a man is as the kind of situation in which he finds himself that determines how he will act." To an increasing degree, we find and form our friendships and communities in the virtual world as well as the real world. These virtual networks greatly expand our opportunities to meet others, but they might also result in our valuing less the capacity for genuine connection. As the young woman writing in the *Times* admitted, "I consistently trade actual human contact for the more reliable high of smiles on MySpace, winks on Match.com, and pokes on Facebook." That she finds these online relationships more *reliable* is telling: it shows a desire to avoid the vulnerability and uncertainty that true friendship entails. Real intimacy requires risk—the risk of disapproval, of heartache, of being thought a fool. Social networking websites may make relationships more reliable, but whether those relationships can be humanly satisfying remains to be seen.

<John Palfrey>

<Urs Gasser>

activists

Excerpted from *Born Digital* (pp. 255–67)

JOHN PALFREY is Henry N. Ess Professor of Law and Vice
Dean for Library and Information Resources at Harvard Law
School. Along with coauthoring with Urs Gasser *Born Digi-
tal: Understanding the First Generation of Digital Natives* (2008),
Palfrey is the coeditor of *Access Denied: The Practice and
Politics of Internet Filtering* (2008). He is a graduate of Harvard
College, the University of Cambridge, and Harvard Law
School.

URS GASSER is executive director of the Berkman Center
for Internet and Society at Harvard University. He has published and edited many books and has written more than
sixty articles in books, law reviews, and professional journals. Recent publications have included a study on ICT inter-
operability and eInnovation, an article on search engine
regulation, and an extensive comparative legal study on anti-
circumvention legislation.

I MAGINE A DEVELOPING country that is starting to get some
economic traction, with a growth rate of 6 or 7 percent per year.
The president, up for reelection, faces a stiff challenge from a
popular opposition leader. The challenger, a charismatic tribesman

with a wide following, campaigns hard. The election is extremely close. After the vote, the president arranges for a quick swearing-in and abruptly declares himself the winner. Supporters of his opponent cry foul. Violence erupts across the country. The major city is thrown into turmoil. The country's main port shuts down.

During the election, a group of citizens used the Internet and their cell phones to tell the story of what was going on through firsthand accounts. These activists, some of them Digital Natives, took photographs of events as they broke and posted them to the Web. They critiqued the formal accounts coming from the government and from the mainstream press. They organized their opposition over cell phones and in e-mail, in the process connecting people who never before would have found one another and orchestrating meetings and rallies in far more efficient ways than they could have without the technology.

In the aftermath of the election, activists on both sides of the dispute continue to chronicle the violence and to tell the story of what is taking place for a global audience. The world's press relies, in no small part, on the most reliable of these firsthand accounts for the articles that people outside of the country read in their local papers in London, Tokyo, and Washington, D.C.

This story is no mere hypothetical. In Kenya in early 2008, a period of violent political unrest followed a contested election.[1] Skilled political activists, taking advantage of Kenya's partially networked environment, provided firsthand accounts of the election and its aftermath that helped to shape what people in Kenya and others around the world came to know about what happened in those heady days.

In Kenya, Internet and cell-phone penetration is relatively low by global standards, but the country's elites are online. Just as important, there is a large diaspora community of Kenyans who use the Internet as a primary means of communication. Within the wired subpopulace of Kenyans, there is a growing, vibrant community of people who are writing and posting digital media to the

Web in highly sophisticated ways, geared toward having a political impact. Young people played a leading role in the election narrative. But Kenya is not the only developing country where the Web, and young people, are beginning to influence the course of important events.[2]

The new mode of activism, made possible by the use of networked digital tools, leads to benefits for citizens of established democracies, countries in transition, and authoritarian regimes alike. First, as the Kenyan example demonstrates, it is possible to harness the Internet's power to render more transparent the actions of a specific government. This transparency matters both in times of crisis—in an unruly election, for example—and in times of orderly governance. Second, the Internet can provide a means for ordinary citizens to participate in the way that public events are told to others, set into context, understood by people far and near, and remembered for posterity. The traditional hierarchies of control of news and information are crumbling, with new dynamics replacing the old. These new dynamics will lead to a more responsive politics.

The ability of networked activists to transform politics in some countries could prove to be the single most important trend in the global Internet culture. The early signs of a culture of civic activism among young people, joined by networked technologies, are cropping up around the world. If these early signs turn into a bigger movement, politics as we know it is in for big changes.

Presidential campaigns have drawn a lot of attention to the role of Digital Natives in politics, but these campaigns are only the very beginning of the story. Howard Dean's presidential primary run in 2004 is the paradigmatic example. Led by campaign manager Joe Trippi and visionary organizers like Zephyr Teachout and Jim Moore, the Dean campaign used the Internet to harness grassroots energy, to pull new people into the campaign, and to raise a great deal of money online. Barack Obama's 2008 campaign has done all that the Dean campaign did, and more, online. Participation in electoral affairs is a starting point and has led to a lot of hype, but it is also not the most important aspect of how Digital Natives are participating in civic life.

The Internet has not fundamentally changed the nature of political action, nor has it brought millions of new people into civic life. The Internet provides tools that empower people, young and old, to have a greater level of direct, personal participation in the formal political process—if they want to. No new technology is going to make someone have a conversion experience. What the Net provides is an increasingly useful, attractive platform for those who are predisposed to be active in civic life. The Internet makes possible new and occasionally astonishing things for a set of highly empowered individuals. Young people can gain access to far more information than ever before. They can reach out to other people far more efficiently. With huge ambition, one or two people can establish a news operation that can put huge pressure on mainstream news providers, offer alternative viewpoints, and reach a global audience on a modest budget.

That said, we must acknowledge up front that our argument about the political potentialities of the Internet is not data driven. The data do not support the argument that Digital Natives, or anyone else, are, in large percentages, using new technologies for purposes of civic activism. The story of the effect of Internet use on politics is just now breaking; these issues are playing themselves out, right now, in different contexts around the world. The terrain is unsettled. The scholarly field studying these issues is nascent. Empirical evidence is more or less nonexistent. Our interviews and focus groups suggest that the percentage of Digital Natives doing new things online in the activist realm is modest, at best. Most studies that others have conducted regarding the levels of participation have confirmed what we found. The fault lines in the relevant debates are becoming clear, but there's no consensus as to the likely outcome or impact. Though our instinct is to be hopeful, our frame of reference needs to be skeptical.

It is also important to recognize that the story of civic engagement online is not solely about Digital Natives. It can be, and should be, a story about people of all ages. The single best thing that could be accomplished online would be a connection across generations, especially one that is geared toward taking advantage of the networked public sphere in the public interest.

New technologies are transforming certain aspects of politics. The fundamental rules still apply, but the way the game is played is changing. Digital Natives are, in many cases, leading the way. The big impact will occur if the rest of their generation around the world follows suit.

Digital Natives have been at the forefront of the movement to change politics through use of digital tools. Though the Internet doesn't change everything when it comes to politics, in a few instances use of new technologies has made a notable difference in terms of *how* campaigns are conducted. Examples where the netroots have made a difference include South Korea in 2002, Ukraine's Orange Revolution in 2004 and 2005, and the presidential primary elections in 2004 and 2008 in the United States.

The use of the Internet to deepen the participation of individuals in formal political campaigns comes at a welcome moment in history. Over the past twenty years, there's been a lot of hand-wringing about the purported decline in voting among young people in the United States. At the same time, there has been a recent increase in other kinds of civic involvement that point to opportunities that Internet-based activism could exploit. This divergence suggests that it isn't that kids are apathetic. It's just that they are interested in changing the world through ways other than voting. During the last thirty years of the twentieth century the youth vote fell precipitously. In 1972, fully half (50.3 percent) of all eligible Americans aged eighteen to twenty-four voted in the election that gave Richard Nixon his landslide victory over George McGovern (the percentage for all age groups combined was 55.2).[3] In 2000, only about one-third (37.3 percent) of eligible young Americans voted in the excruciatingly close general election between George W. Bush and Al Gore (this time, the percentage for all age groups was 51.3).[4] The decline among young voters occurred even though the voter-registration process had become dramatically easier— through motor-voter, same-day registration, aggressive registration drives, and ubiquitous registration forms. This is not just an American phenomenon. Youth in the United Kingdom were also less likely to vote in elections than older citizens.[5]

But by other accounts, many young people demonstrated that they are more engaged than ever—just in ways other than voting. During this same period, young people got involved in public service outside the political sphere more extensively than ever before. Young volunteers stepped up the time they spent helping out in AIDS hospices and homeless shelters, teaching in Head Start centers, providing disaster relief in developing countries, and doing other good works. So while the number of young Americans voting in the presidential elections declined between 1972 and 2000, increasing numbers of young people were participating in public service before they graduated from college.[6]

Although these trends were emerging even prior to 9/11, that event—and the consequent outbreak of war—meant that a lot of people, particularly young people, were galvanized in ways that the Internet was poised to take advantage of. Some were nudged into political activism by a sense that America was increasingly becoming isolated in a post-9/11 world at precisely the moment when we should be drawing closer to other cultures.[7] Others—particularly youth outside the United States—were stirred to action by the reaction of the world's lone superpower to the terrorist crisis. The polarizing effect of a world divided between sharply differing ideologies at the start of the new millennium created an environment that drew people into the debate, including youth.

The decline in the youth vote and the concurrent rise in youth participation in other civic activities set up a dynamic that those promoting use of the Internet could exploit. The Internet offers a way for young people to be engaged in civic affairs that combines the political with the cultural, social, and technological. It also provides a medium through which the creativity of Digital Natives can affect politics. For some young people, interest in politics on the Net offered a path that would lead them back to the polls, too.

Politicians didn't see this potential to engage young people in campaigns right away. Most got off to a slow start in using the Internet as part of their campaigns, but the most savvy among them have caught on quickly of late. American political campaigning on the Internet began in earnest in the 1996 presidential election in the United States and has been surging ever since. Candidates, particularly Republicans in the early days, established their own websites during the campaign cycle. Little more than virtual billboards, these websites offered campaign material that would ordinarily be printed on leaflets, but in an electronic form. In the 2000 presidential election, candidates' Internet presences began to develop beyond just a Web page, a photo, and a list of issues. Internet users in the 2000 election cycle could further connect with politicians through making online donations, seeing a candidate's speaking calendar, and viewing photos of political events.[8]

The 2004 presidential election cycle in the United States marked a watershed in participation in online politics, which continues to this day.[9] New participants, many of them young people, entered the political process, and campaigns deployed new information technology tools with vast potential. A fresh crop of young, wired leaders joined the political fray. For many of the young new politicos, faith in the grassroots organizing potential of the Internet—also called the "Net roots"—is an essential motivating force. They didn't get involved in politics because of the technology, but the technology became the medium that drew them together. The Internet became the common network, both literally and figuratively, of a new generation of activists who came of age in the 2004, 2006, and 2008 election cycles. In 2004, the percentage of young voters surged (to 47.7 percent). This percentage still lagged behind the percentage for all age groups combined (55.3 percent), but it signaled the possibility of a new trend.[10] By 2008, candidates didn't just have their own websites; they had entire Web strategies, Web teams, and multiple points of presence online, including Facebook and MySpace accounts and YouTube videos of speeches.

The Internet enables traditional political campaigns to be more efficient and to increase online participation, but it does not change campaigning altogether. Big-time political campaigns are still largely about fund-raising (both online and off), which in turn pays the bill for copious amounts of television advertising. The political process hasn't changed fundamentally just because more money is being raised online. But the Internet has become an essential component of the all-important fund-raising process, largely through small donations. In 2000, Senator John McCain's campaign made headlines when it raised nearly $7 million online.[11] Senator John Kerry's campaign raised $45 million online in the first five months of 2004 alone, with an average contribution of just over $100.[12] Kerry's total online fund-raising during the primary topped $80 million.[13] Barack Obama eclipsed records yet again in 2008, raising a total of more than $235 million by May 2008, the vast majority of it online—in the primary alone.[14] Internet fund-raising works primarily because it makes donating easy—no checks, stamps, or envelopes. Many campaigns take donations via PayPal, which means it takes only a single click of the mouse to donate to a favorite candidate. In turn, the new technologies enable candidates and their organizers to reach out to donors and likely donors more easily and less expensively than in the past. The Internet helps motivated organizers to develop relationships with those who are inclined to help, but who are too busy, too shy, or otherwise disinclined to reach out to others themselves. It's much easier to send someone an e-mail to ask for money than it is to call someone up or knock on doors, and it's easier for the average voter to click on a link to donate instead of having to go write out and mail a check.

Fund-raising is only one of the ways that technology has changed the campaign process; online organizing is in fact the area where the greatest, most lasting transformation can occur. A volunteer for the Ron Paul campaign, for instance, can manage an outreach effort, coordinating thousands of volunteers, from a home computer and an ordinary network connection. These new tools haven't changed the fundamental machinery of a campaign, by any means, but they have increased flexibility and autonomy. A Web-savvy volunteer ran the entire Texas operation for the Obama campaign until the campaign leadership determined that they might have a shot at winning the prized state. At that point, the campaign swooped in to establish a formal presence a few weeks ahead of the primary—while retaining many of the structures that the all-volunteer team had set in place. Similarly, all the classic aspects of campaigning—going door-to-door using detailed walk-lists, arranging for speeches by surrogates, managing get-out-the-vote (GOTV) efforts—allow for forms of participation mediated by new information technologies. The use of these technologies may draw young people into the campaigns, but the participatory acts are not fundamentally altered in the process. It's much the same activity, perhaps done more efficiently or more attractively, but it can draw some young people, particularly Digital Natives, into the political process in a fresh way.

Just as in social networks and in gaming environments, the Internet makes it possible for young people with common interests to find one another and to connect; in politics it enables young people to connect who are on the same page politically and who want to work for the same cause or candidate. In a previous era, these young people might never have found one another; the Internet makes heretofore impossible connections possible, and these connections can lead to collective action around shared ideas at much faster speeds than ever before. They are facilitated by the powerful search tools and social networking features of the Internet. All of this has had a multiplying effect when it comes to enabling young people to engage in political activity in democratic societies.

The formal political sphere is only the most obvious context in which young people are getting involved in civic life. Digital Natives are using new technologies to participate in civic life outside of campaigns in ways that are potentially more constructive to societies on an enduring basis. One of the bigger stories is how young people are using these new technologies to jump-start their own work in social causes. The networked environment is conducive to getting the word out to friends about a topic of public interest. Participation is not different, just more connected. As one student told us, she uses a MySpace page and a Facebook group to coordinate a growing network of young people interested in peer-education work on teen-dating violence. When students are working on issues of political engagement, such as raising awareness about the humanitarian crisis in Darfur or the interests of Latino/as in a given American city, they told us that their first outreach is through e-mail, instant messaging, and social networks from Facebook and MySpace.

Critics argue that the highly visible activism in social networks doesn't add up to much. It doesn't really mean much, these critics say, when a Digital Native joins a "cause" on Facebook. Often, that's true. It is nothing more than a convenient way to make a statement, the digital equivalent of a "Save the Whales" bumper sticker. Viewed from this angle, it can be a relatively cheap way to speak out by a simple mouse-click, but it doesn't accomplish much. As one college student put it: "Today it's more like people writing their names on a big list . . . [T]he effect is lower when it's not face-to-face, when it's not physical. . . . You can let millions of people know with just one click what's happening. But it's hard to get all the million people involved just because of that click."

It's true that it doesn't always mean much when a Digital Native "friends" a politician in MySpace or Facebook. The "friendships" between young people and politicians online are more like style choices—accessories on a social network profile—than like knocking on doors or phone-banking for a favorite cause. But neither are these acts the important parts of the story; they're just some of the most visible. The act of joining a Facebook group may lead to participation that is bigger and better than merely clicking on "accept" in an online invitation. Some Digital Natives venture outside of Facebook to use specially designed applications such as TakingITGlobal, YouthNoise, Zaadz, or UNICEF Voices of Youth, all of which promote civic engagement and community involvement. These sites are the starting place, for something bigger than a personal statement about a public issue, and once young people do get started, they are more likely to begin to engage in some sort of *action*.

The medium is not the message when it comes to the political lives of Digital Natives. Internet engagement sites are usually only facilitators, rather than places of action; the civic engagement activities that result from online interactions often happen in the *offline* space. That said, the relevant online tools make activism less daunting and anonymous for those Digital Natives who already have an interest in civic engagement. These online tools simply make it easier for them to connect with like-minded people, or to share information and get organized.[15]

Digital Natives are shifting many of their core social activities from the offline space to the hybrid online-offline world. These social activities include, for some, political activism. Sometimes this activism expresses itself through traditional political campaigns. More often, and more important over the long term, this activism is expressed through a wide range of civic activities. This is not an apathetic bunch; it's just a group of young people getting engaged in civic life on their own terms, in their own ways.

* * *

THE SECOND BIG SHIFT in participation online is the move away
from a broadcast media model and toward a more diverse, participatory media model. In the new media environment, Digital
Natives (and many other users, too) are no longer mere readers,
listeners, or passive viewers. Instead, affordable Internet technology and highly interactive, easy-to-use applications have enabled
individuals to become active users and participants in public conversations. As a consequence, it's no longer a few professional journalists or powerful media conglomerates with strong commercial
interests who define what we as a society talk and care about.
Rather, the public agenda in the digital age is increasingly influenced by the observations, experiences, and concerns of all of us in
our roles as citizens. Many Digital Natives are at the forefront of
this trend; they take participation for granted as part of their
media environment.

Without owning a press or having the capital to rent one, an
individual activist can bring a topic into the public discourse by
breaking an important story through a credible, firsthand account.
The activist can shed light on issues that would otherwise have
remained covered up, or that had emerged but been purposely buried again. These activists can get word out to others who need it
fast, on devices that are cheap and ubiquitous. With the right command of these services, people who have traditionally been outside
the mainstream of civic life can today command greater authority,
and have far greater impact, than they could in an environment
where the news media were tightly controlled.

Digital activists are chipping away at the corporate control of
the media infrastructure.[16] In the television era, people heard from
the candidates but rarely met them. The conversation was mediated primarily by the TV stations. It is still true that few people
meet the candidates, compared to those who experience their words
through electronic media. TV remains the primary battleground on

which campaigns are waged, both through advertising and news coverage. During the 2004 election, presidential candidates spent $2.66 million on Internet ads versus $330 million on traditional television ads.[17] But nonetheless, the Internet has allowed citizens to sneak past the editorial cordon that has separated them from candidates in the past. In this sense, the Internet represents a continuation of a trend begun with the introduction of television into politics in the 1960s. Prior to that time, party bosses controlled access to and the message of the candidates. Both television and the Internet are part of a broader trend toward a more direct relationship between candidates and individual voters. The major political parties, along with labor unions, are part of the hierarchical framework of American politics that is under great pressure in the digital era.

Even as traditional hierarchies are breaking apart, powerful, consolidated interests still play a disproportionate role in politics, especially in America. Strong brands still have it in their power to make or break candidates. As in the commercial space, the Internet often causes first disintermediation, then *re*intermediation. The forums are slightly different in the digital age and modestly more diverse. Cable networks like Fox and CNN have expanded the group of networks with the power to influence elections; people like Glenn Reynolds of *Instapundit*, Markos Moulitsas Zúniga of the *Daily Kos*, Matt Drudge of the *Drudge Report*, Charles Johnson of *Little Green Footballs*, and Arianna Huffington and her colleagues at the *Huffington Post* are giving the mainstream newspapers a run for their money in the online text media world; and even small bloggers and video creators can become stars with the power to move discussions in elections.

It's not just the relationship with the candidates that is changing in a digital age, but also the relationship of citizens to mainstream media—and to one another. Digital technologies make possible a more interactive relationship between people and media.[18] Thanks to Internet technologies, Digital Natives and others are presented with near-constant opportunities to take on a more active relationship with information—not just passively accepting what is fed through the broadcast medium, but rather engaging with it and re-creating it in intriguing, creative ways. The result might be a more energized citizenry with closer ties to the public discussion about politics.

This phenomenon of citizens telling the stories of politics themselves, through digital media, could have a profound and lasting impact on democracies. Instead of thinking in terms of classical participatory politics, we should expand our frame to include the kinds of political involvement in which Digital Natives specialize. One aspect of this broader conception of participation is the making and remaking of narratives of a campaign or of other important public events. This broader frame encompasses notions of semiotic democracy. In a semiotic democracy, a greater number of people are able to tell the stories of their times. This broader group of people participates in the "recoding" and "reworking" of cultural meaning.[19] For example, instead of just receiving a newscast of the day's events in politics from one of three mainstream news channels, citizens can themselves take the video clip of a candidate's speech, interpret it themselves, and remix it into a video that they share with friends—or with the rest of the world on YouTube. In a semiotic democracy, the story can be reinterpreted and reshaped by any citizen with the skills, time, and access to digital technologies to do so. The idea of semiotic democracy sounds academic, but it might just be the most profound difference made possible by the Internet for our time.

The fact that Digital Natives and others have this opportunity to participate actively in the news, information, and entertainment creation and dissemination process doesn't mean that they will avail themselves of it. The Internet isn't going to solve the problem of civic disengagement. Not everyone will be taking advantage of these opportunities—indeed, the data suggest that most of them are not at present. But as events around the world in recent years have shown, when a lot of people care passionately about something, the Internet can become an extraordinarily powerful tool of organization, recruitment, and participation in the telling of the narratives of our society.

notes

1. See Joshua Goldstein, "Blogs, SMS, and the Kenyan Election," Internet and Democracy blog, http://blogs.law.harvard.edu/idblog/2008/01/03/blogs-sms-and-the-kenyan-election/.
2. See http://www.kenyanpundit.com; http://www.mzalendo.com/2007/08/03/outrageousrt-mp-performance-continues/.
3. See http://www.census.gov/population/socdemo/voting/tabA-1.pdf.
4. Ibid. See also http://www.census.gov/population/socdemo/voting/p20-542/tab01.pdf; http://www.statemaster.com/graph/gov_201_ele_you_vot_tur-2000-election-youth-voter-turnout; and http://www.infoplease.com/Vipa/A0781453.html.
5. Sonia Livingstone, Nick Couldry, and Tim Markham, "Youthful Steps towards Civic Participation," in Brian Loader, ed., *Young Citizens in the Digital Age* (Routledge, 2007).
6. See http://www.compact.org/newscc/2003_Statistics.pdf.
7. One of the most interesting of the Net-driven 527 organizations, Win Back Respect, got traction by joining young activists from the United States with those from other countries with a distaste for the foreign policy of the Bush administration.
8. Steven Schneider and Kirsten Foot, "Web Campaigning by U.S. Presidential Candidates in 2000 and 2004," in Andrew P. Williams and John C. Tedesco, eds., *The Internet Election* (Rowman & Littlefield, 2006).

9. Matt Bai's book, *The Argument: Billionaires, Bloggers, and the Battle to Remake Democratic Politics* (Penguin, 2007), includes an excellent discussion of the role of the bloggers in the 2004 election cycle. Bai comes at the topic from the slant of a Democrat; a similar, though distinct, story could be told from the slant of a Republican.

10. See www.statemaster.com/graph/gov_200_ele_you_vot_tur-2004-election-youth-voter-turnout; http://www.infoplease.com/ipa/A07 81453.html.

11. Becki Donatelli of Hockaday Donatelli, McCain campaign consultant, interview of March 10, 2000.

12. See http://www.johnkerry.com/pressroom/releases/pr_2004_061 6a.html.

13. See http://www.gwu.edu/~action/2004/kerry/kerrfin.html.

14. See http://www.opensecrets.org/pres08/summary.asp?id=N00009 638.

15. Kate Raynes-Goldie and Luke Walker, "Our Space: Online Civic Engagement Tools for Youth," in W. Lance Bennett, ed., *Civic Life Online: Learning How Digital Media Can Engage Youth*, The John D. and Catherine T. MacArthur Foundation Series on Digital Media and Learning (MIT Press, 2008), pp. 161–188.

16. See Dan Gillmor, *We the Media: Grassroots Journalism by the People, for the People* (O'Reilly Media, 2004), and Yochai Benkler, *The Wealth of Networks: How Social Production Transforms Markets and Freedom* (Yale University Press, 2006) for two variants of this story.

17. Michael Cornfield, *Presidential Campaign Advertising on the Internet*, Pew Internet and American Life Project.

18. Terry Fisher, Lawrence Lessig, and Yochai Benkler, among others, have made the case for this trend from consumers to creators of digital media.

19. See Terry Fisher, "Semiotic Democracy," http://www.lawharvard .edu/faculty/tfisher/music/Semiotic.html.

section three

the fate of
culture

———————>>>

<Todd Gitlin>

nomadicity

Excerpted from *Media Unlimited* (pp. 53–60).

TODD GITLIN is the author of fourteen books, including
(with Liel Leibovitz) *The Chosen Peoples: America, Israel, and
the Ordeals of Divine Election* (2010). Other titles include *The
Intellectuals and the Flag* (2006), *Media Unlimited: How the
Torrent of Images and Sounds Overwhelms Our Lives* (2002),
and *The Sixties: Years of Hope, Days of Rage* (1987). He has
published in general periodicals (*The New York Times, The Los
Angeles Times, The Washington Post, Dissent, The New Republic, The Nation, Wilson Quarterly, Harper's*) and scholarly journals. He is now a professor of journalism and sociology and
chair of the Ph.D. program in communications at Columbia
University. His website is http://toddgitlin.net.

INCREASINGLY, YOU COULD CARRY your private current anywhere. The home entertainment center was, after all, a luxury
for which you had to confine yourself. Images and manufac-
tured sounds came home, but you had to be home to greet them. So
why not render your private amusements portable? Why not, like
Pascal's well-served if pitiable monarch, have it all wherever and
whenever you like?

Self-sufficiency, that most tempting and expansive of modern
motifs, feels like a sort of liberation—until it becomes banal and we

have need of the next liberation. People gravitate toward portability and miniaturization—each a kind of freedom—in everyday life. The mountaineer's backpack evolved into the hippie traveler's aluminum-framed pack, which in turn evolved into the contemporary frameless version, which in turn gave rise to the utilitarian but waistline-disturbing fanny pack, the bulky monster sticking out horizontally, and the trim designer variety that is, in effect, a purse that leaves the hands free. Portable nourishment is another sign of the nomadic thrust toward self-sufficiency: the Hershey bar (1894), the ice-cream cone (1904), Life Savers (1913), trail mix (1970s), the portable water bottle (1990s). The tendency has been toward performing as many functions as possible in the course of one's movements—"multitasking"—so that as we move, new accessories become mandatory. The indented tray inside the glove compartment and the cup holder next to the front seat have become standard equipment.

Not only must material provisions be available on demand; so must sustenance for the senses, not least the ears. After the portable battery-powered radio, the car radio, and the transistorized radio, the logic of individualism pointed toward that exemplary little machine for musical transport, Sony's Walkman. The theme is well enunciated in a London billboard of 2001 that does not even bother to indicate any particular product: "Give today a soundtrack."

The Walkman story shows how the convenience of a single powerful man could generate a marketing triumph. Before a transoceanic flight in 1979, Sony chairman Masaru Ibuka asked company engineers to create a stereo music player so he could hear classical favorites of his choice. Airlines already provided passengers with earphones and canned musical loops, but Ibuka did not want anyone overriding his personal taste, so Sony engineers connected headphones to an advanced tape recorder for him. Ibuka was delighted with the results, and his partner Akio Morita realized that this jury-rigged contraption might have sales potential among teenagers, who were already accustomed to carrying portable radios. The Walkman was born. What had begun as a toy for Ibuka was promptly sold to consumers less accustomed to indulging their personal whims. Supply proceeded to trigger demand. By the end of 1998, without much advertising, Sony had sold almost 250 million Walkmen worldwide, not to mention the Discmen and all the specialized spinoff players for joggers, swimmers, and skiers.

Throughout the twentieth century, supply and demand looped together in an unceasing Möbius strip, technology always increasing the radius of contact: the pay phone, car radio, battery-powered radio, transistor radio, remote-accessible answering machine, fax machine, car phone, laptop computer, Walkman, airplane and train phone, portable CD player, beeper, mobile phone, Palm Pilot, Internet access, PCD, GPD, and so on ad acronym. Once "interactivity" by machine became feasible, the hallmark of so many communication inventions was *nomadicity*, which, according to the Internet pioneer who coined the term, "means that wherever and whenever we move around, the underlying system always knows who we are, where we are, and what services we need." Actually, not we so much as *I,* for more and more often the contemporary nomad travels alone, detribalized—or rather, in the company of that curious modern tribe each of whose members seeks to travel alone while being technologically connected to others. Equipped for accessibility, he may encroach upon the right of others to control their own private space: the battery-powered boom box blaring music or narrating a ball game (even the one taking place before one's eyes in the stadium itself); the cell phone trilling during the play or the concert; the caller shouting into his phone on the train, in the restaurant, at the park, or on the street.

Charles Baudelaire once lamented: "They left one right out of the Declaration of the Rights of Man and Citizen: the right to leave." Now, for hours each day, the right to leave is secure, though doubtless not in the way Baudelaire had in mind. In fact, the right to leave has merged with the right to be *somewhere else*. For a growing proportion of the population, and for a growing number of hours per day, you can, after a fashion, break the limits of space, choosing from your private menu of activities, amusements, and contacts. You are not exactly alone, because you are with others, their music, their games, their voices. Commuting or washing the floors, you are a movable node, never wholly abandoned. Even in extremis—but who could have imagined such extremity?—your voice can reach out to a loved one from the inferno of the World Trade Center about to collapse or the cabin of a hijacked plane. The horrific emergencies of September 11, 2001, put to extraordinary ends what have become the ordinary means to overcome distance.

How shall we understand the appeal of these ordinary means? Consider the humdrum experience of waiting for a bus, which Jean-Paul Sartre took as a metaphor for modern alienation. Sartre called this ordinary condition *serialization*, by which he meant losing one's individuality and being reduced to a function—waiting. The immobilized man on line cannot pursue his own ends because he has lost control of his time in favor of the bus company's schedule, the pileup of fellow travelers, the traffic that has delayed the bus. He is the creature of a routine that demands self-suppression. Now imagine this man in line equipped with a personal stereo. His ears project him, at least partially, elsewhere—or rather, elsewhere enters him, corporeal, immediate, intimate. He stands in the line but leaves it behind for a chosen communion. He blocks out unwanted contact. Now he is, paradoxically, an individual because he has company— music, familiar music at that. He feels little spurts of emotion. Music rubs up against him, gets inside him. He nods along with the beat. Against the pressures of work and environment—even against his own unpleasant obsessions—he has a compensation: he has enveloped himself in a sort of mobile bubble. He has—to quote from Walkmanned Londoners interviewed in one study—"shut everything out" and "squashed thoughts." The music, turned up loud enough to drown out ambient noise, "takes over his senses." "It's like living in a movie." Availing himself of "a life-support machine," he has taken charge of his mood.

Now imagine this man still in line or trapped in some other serialized reality—in an elevator, on the train, or stuck in a traffic jam—equip him with escape implements in the form of today's proliferating mobile equipment: the cellular phone, the Game Boy, the personal communication system with text messaging and Internet access, feeding him sports scores and stock quotes, eventually cartoons, jokes, slot machines, card games, and pornographic images, asking him at all hours: "Where would you like to go?" Take charge of your mood! Possessing an "arsenal of mobile technology," he comes to feel that he has the right to them. He is, to some degree, shielded from urban fear.

Some admirers of our present-day electronic efflorescence are carried away with promises of the technological sublime. One recent enthusiast heralds *techgnosis*. But nomadic access raised to the level of gods and angels rings sublimely ridiculous. Usually, the very point of dot-communion is banality. Through the most mundane act of e-mailing about the weather or instant-messaging a "buddy" about nothing at all except that you're stuck in a boring lecture, or that you exist and affirm the other's existence ("Whassup?" "Not much"), or phoning your loved one from the air to report that your plane is late or from the street to report that you are just now emerging from the subway, you have, in a sense, spun off a filament of yourself to conduct your business, secure your network, greet your friend, discharge your duty, arrange your pleasure. Intellectuals may scoff, but it is this relatively trivial mercy that most people in a consumerist culture seek much of the time.

But the freedom to be even incidentally connected is not uncomplicated. It goes with being incidentally accessible, which amounts to being on call and interruptible everywhere by your boss, your nurse, your patient, your anxious parent, your client, your stockbroker, your babysitter, as well as your friend whose voice, even electronically, you welcome even if you have just seen each other face-to-face. Friendship makes intrusion welcome—perhaps that is part of its definition—and nomadicity, no question, is a boon to certain kinds of friendship. In a suburb where nothing seems to happen, *something* can happen—again and again. You can send along jokes, photos, shopping recommendations, references smart and dumb. It was probably America Online's "buddy lists" for instant messaging that made that huge Internet portal so popular.

Wireless handheld devices with Internet access carry the instantaneous buddy principle out into public space. Having been launched in Japan with considerable success, they are galloping through the United States and Europe. Sony's mobile Internet device, no doubt to be called Webman, is set to go into American circulation shortly. "We believe that the mobile terminal will be a very . . . strategic product for Sony," the company's president, Kunitake Ando, told the *Asian Wall Street Journal.* "Just like we created a Walkman culture, we'll have a sort of mobile culture," he said, adding that sooner or later Sony was planning to pipe online music and even movies through a new generation of mobile phones. Such prognostications may be hype, but Sony's have a way of turning out accurate.

At this writing, though, the principle of instantaneous access is most firmly at work with nomad-friendly mobile phones. In the year 2000, 53 percent of Americans owned mobile phones, up from 24 percent in 1995. So did 63 percent of British adults, about as many as in Japan though not so many as in Italy, Sweden, and Finland. Their diffusion rate is tremendous, comparable to television's, exceeding that of telephones, radios, and VCRs, and more visible in public, of course, than any of those.

The mobile phone radically transforms the soundscape. Like the servant's bell, its chime or ditty is a summons, but also a claim that you have the right to conduct your business willy-nilly wherever you are, whether you're a day trader in New York or a Hong Kong youngster chatting away in a subway car (that city has wired its tunnels). Private practices open out into public spaces. So if the Webbed-up, wired, or wireless nomad rarely gets to relish full-bodied freedom, there is still the pleasure of knowing one is wanted right now.

The new technonomadicity comes with this paradox: the fully equipped nomad, seeking freedom of access at will, becomes freely accessible to other people's wills. The sender also receives. The potential for being intruded upon spurs technological fixes; with caller ID, for example, you can block calls from old boyfriends, or screen calls to see who wants contact, or defer contact by dumping a call into voice mail. As in a military arms race, the dialectic of offense and defense ratchets up. There is a second paradox: those who hope to control their moods when they go out in public find themselves invaded by alien noises. In theaters, concerts, conferences, parks, and churches, the trill of the cell phone is not an angelic visitation. The commons explodes with private signals. Again, the defense also improves. Theaters announce, before the curtain goes up, that ringers should be turned off—with uneven success. Devices to block mobile phones are already being marketed to restaurants and theater owners.

So communication comes at a price—not just the monetary price, which falls year after year; not just the invasion of solitude; no, the third inevitable price of nomadicity is surveillance. This is not just the risk of being overheard in a public place. After all, the mobile phoner who wishes to preserve privacy in the face of proximity can still do so, for the new devices amplify the lowered human voice with wondrous fidelity. But cellular conversations are peculiarly capable of being intercepted, not only by public agencies but by interested private parties, whether by accident or deliberately.

Still, the new nomad, intent on living out a dream of personal power, seems willing to pay the price. The omnicommunicative

utopia appeals to a centuries-old passion to control one's circumstances without renouncing social bonds. This is the version of freedom that drives the civilization that American (but not only
American) enterprise and power carry to the ends of the earth. It
is an omnivorous freedom, freedom to behold, to seek distraction,
to seek distraction *from* distraction (in T. S. Eliot's words), to enjoy
one's rootlessness, to relish the evanescent. But as the Canadian
songwriter Leonard Cohen once wrote, "Where do all these high-
ways go now that we are free?"

<Tim O'Reilly>

what is web 2.0: design patterns and business models for the next generation of software

By Tim O'Reilly. Originally published in 2005
at www.oreilly.com.

TIM O'REILLY is the CEO of O'Reilly Media, Inc. In addition to Foo Camps ("Friends of O'Reilly" Camps, which gave rise to the "un-conference" movement), O'Reilly Media hosts conferences on technology topics, including the Web 2.0 Summit, the Web 2.0 Expo, and the Gov 2.0 Expo. O'Reilly's blog, the *O'Reilly Radar*, "watches the alpha geeks" to determine emerging technology trends. O'Reilly is a founder of Safari Books Online, a pioneering subscription service for accessing books online, and O'Reilly AlphaTech Ventures, an early-stage venture firm.

THE BURSTING OF the dot-com bubble in the fall of 2001 marked a turning point for the Web. Many people concluded that the Web was overhyped, when in fact bubbles and consequent shakeouts appear to be a common feature of all technological revolutions. Shakeouts typically mark the point at which an ascendant technology is ready to take its place at center stage. The pretenders are given the bum's rush, the real success stories show their strength, and there begins to be an understanding of what separates one from the other.

The concept of "Web 2.0" began with a conference brainstorming session between O'Reilly and MediaLive International. Dale Dougherty, Web pioneer and O'Reilly VP, noted that far from having "crashed," the Web was more important than ever, with exciting new applications and sites popping up with surprising regularity. What's more, the companies that had survived the collapse seemed to have some things in common. Could it be that the dot-com collapse marked some kind of turning point for the Web, such that a call to action such as "Web 2.0" might make sense? We agreed that it did, and so the Web 2.0 Conference was born.

In the year and a half since, the term "Web 2.0" has clearly taken hold, with more than 9.5 million citations in Google. But there's still a huge amount of disagreement about just what Web 2.0 means, with some people decrying it as a meaningless marketing buzzword, and others accepting it as the new conventional wisdom.

This article is an attempt to clarify just what we mean by Web 2.0.

In our initial brainstorming, we formulated our sense of Web 2.0 by example:

Web 1.0		Web 2.0
DoubleClick	⟶	Google AdSense
Ofoto	⟶	Flickr
Akamai	⟶	BitTorrent
mp3.com	⟶	Napster
Britannica Online	⟶	Wikipedia
personal websites	⟶	blogging
evite	⟶	upcoming.org and EVDB
domain name speculation	⟶	search engine optimization
page views	⟶	cost per click
screen scraping	⟶	Web services
publishing	⟶	participation
content management systems	⟶	wikis
directories (taxonomy)	⟶	tagging ("folksonomy")
stickiness	⟶	syndication

The list went on and on. But what was it that made us identify one application or approach as "Web 1.0" and another as "Web 2.0"? (The question is particularly urgent because the Web 2.0 meme has become so widespread that companies are now pasting it on as a marketing buzzword, with no real understanding of just what it means. The question is particularly difficult because many of those buzzword-addicted start–ups are definitely *not* Web 2.0, while some of the applications we identified as Web 2.0, like Napster and Bit-Torrent, are not even properly Web applications!) We began trying to tease out the principles that are demonstrated in one way or another by the success stories of Web 1.0 and by the most interesting of the new applications.

1 > the web as platform

Like many important concepts, Web 2.0 doesn't have a hard boundary, but rather, a gravitational core. You can visualize Web 2.0 as a set of principles and practices that tie together a veritable solar system of sites that demonstrate some or all of those principles, at a varying distance from that core.

For example, at the first Web 2.0 conference, in October 2004, John Battelle and I listed a preliminary set of principles in our opening talk. The first of those principles was "The Web as platform." Yet that was also a rallying cry of Web 1.0 darling Netscape, which went down in flames after a heated battle with Microsoft. What's more, two of our initial Web 1.0 exemplars, DoubleClick and Akamai, were both pioneers in treating the Web as a platform. People don't often think of it as "Web services," but in fact, ad serving was the first widely deployed Web service, and the first widely deployed "mashup" (to use another term that has gained currency of late). Every banner ad is served as a seamless cooperation between two websites, delivering an integrated page to a reader on yet another computer. Akamai also treats the network as the platform, and at a deeper level of the stack, building a transparent caching and content delivery network that eases bandwidth congestion.

Nonetheless, these pioneers provided useful contrasts because later entrants have taken their solution to the same problem even further, understanding something deeper about the nature of the new platform. Both DoubleClick and Akamai were Web 2.0 pioneers,

---

FACING PAGE: Figure I shows a "meme map" of Web 2.0 that was developed at a brainstorming session during Foo Camp, a conference at O'Reilly Media. It's very much a work in progress, but shows the many ideas that radiate out from the Web 2.0 core.

WEB 2.0 MEME MAP

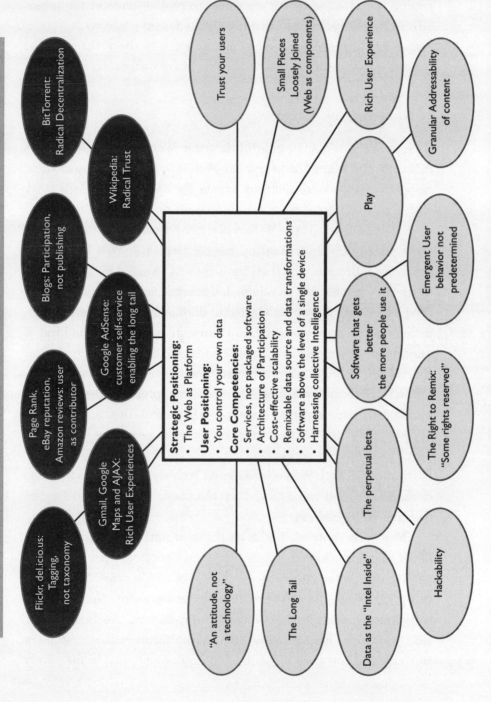

BitTorrent:
Radical Decentralization

Wikipedia:
Radical Trust

Blogs: Participation,
not publishing

Page Rank,
eBay reputation,
Amazon reviews: user
as contributor

Google AdSense:
customer self-service
enabling the long tail

Flickr, del.icio.us:
Tagging,
not taxonomy

**Gmail, Google
Maps and AJAX:**
Rich User Experiences

Strategic Positioning:
• The Web as Platform
User Positioning:
• You control your own data
Core Competencies:
• Services, not packaged software
• Architecture of Participation
• Cost-effective scalability
• Remixable data source and data transformations
• Software above the level of a single device
• Harnessing collective Intelligence

Trust your users

Small Pieces
Loosely Joined
(Web as components)

Rich User Experience

Granular Addressability
of content

Play

Emergent User
behavior not
predetermined

Software that gets
better
the more people use it

The Right to Remix:
"Some rights reserved"

The perpetual beta

Hackability

Data as the "Intel Inside"

The Long Tail

"An attitude, not
a technology"

yet we can also see how it's possible to realize more of the possibilities by embracing additional Web 2.0 design patterns.

Let's drill down for a moment into each of these three cases, teasing out some of the essential elements of difference.

Netscape vs. Google

If Netscape was the standard-bearer for Web 1.0, Google is most certainly the standard-bearer for Web 2.0, if only because their respective IPOs were defining events for each era. So let's start with a comparison of these two companies and their positioning.

Netscape framed "the Web as platform" in terms of the old software paradigm: their flagship product was the Web browser, a desktop application, and their strategy was to use their dominance in the browser market to establish a market for high-priced server products. Control over standards for displaying content and applications in the browser would, in theory, give Netscape the kind of market power enjoyed by Microsoft in the PC market. Much like the "horseless carriage" framed the automobile as an extension of the familiar, Netscape promoted a "webtop" to replace the desktop, and planned to populate that webtop with information updates and applets pushed to the webtop by information providers who would purchase Netscape servers.

In the end, both Web browsers and Web servers turned out to be commodities, and value moved "up the stack" to services delivered over the Web platform.

Google, by contrast, began its life as a native Web application, never sold or packaged, but delivered as a service, with customers paying, directly or indirectly, for the use of that service. None of the trappings of the old software industry are present. No scheduled software releases, just continuous improvement. No licensing or sale, just usage. No porting to different platforms so that customers can run the software on their own equipment, just a massively scalable collection of commodity PCs running open-source operating systems plus homegrown applications and utilities that no one outside the company ever gets to see.

At bottom, Google requires a competency that Netscape never needed: database management. Google isn't just a collection of software tools; it's a specialized database. Without the data, the tools are useless; without the software, the data is unmanageable. Software licensing and control over APIs—the lever of power in the previous era—is irrelevant because the software never need be distributed but only performed, and also because without the ability to collect and manage the data, the software is of little use. In fact, *the value of the software is proportional to the scale and dynamism of the data it helps to manage.*

Google's service is not a server—though it is delivered by a massive collection of Internet servers—nor a browser—though it is experienced by the user within the browser. Nor does its flagship search service even host the content that it enables users to find. Much like a phone call, which happens not just on the phones at either end of the call, but on the network in between, Google happens in the space between browser and search engine and destination content server, as an enabler or middleman between the user and his or her online experience.

While both Netscape and Google could be described as software companies, it's clear that Netscape belonged to the same software world as Lotus, Microsoft, Oracle, SAP, and other companies that got their start in the 1980s software revolution, while Google's fellows are other Internet applications like eBay, Amazon, Napster, and, yes, DoubleClick and Akamai.

DoubleClick vs. Overture and AdSense

Like Google, DoubleClick is a true child of the Internet era. It harnesses software as a service, has a core competency in data management, and, as noted above, was a pioneer in Web services long before Web services even had a name. However, DoubleClick was ultimately limited by its business model. It bought into the '90s notion that the Web was about publishing, not participation; that advertisers, not consumers, ought to call the shots; that size mattered; and that the Internet was increasingly being dominated by the top websites as measured by MediaMetrix and other Web ad scoring companies.

As a result, DoubleClick proudly cites on its website "over 2,000 successful implementations" of its software. Yahoo! Search Marketing (formerly Overture) and Google AdSense, by contrast, already serve hundreds of thousands of advertisers apiece.

Overture and Google's success came from an understanding of what Chris Anderson refers to as "the long tail," the collective power of the small sites that make up the bulk of the Web's content. DoubleClick's offerings require a formal sales contract, limiting their market to the few thousand largest websites. Overture and Google figured out how to enable ad placement on virtually any Web page. What's more, they eschewed publisher/ad-agency-friendly advertising formats such as banner ads and pop-ups in favor of minimally intrusive, context-sensitive, consumer-friendly text advertising.

The Web 2.0 lesson: *leverage customer-self service and algorithmic data management to reach out to the entire Web, to the edges and not just the center, to the long tail and not just the head.*

Not surprisingly, other Web 2.0 success stories demonstrate this same behavior. eBay enables occasional transactions of only a few dollars between single individuals, acting as an automated intermediary. Napster (though shut down for legal reasons) built its network not by building a centralized song database, but by architecting a system in such a way that every downloader also became a server, and thus grew the network.

Akamai vs. BitTorrent

Like DoubleClick, Akamai is optimized to do business with the head, not the tail, with the center, not the edges. While it serves the benefit of the individuals at the edge of the Web by smoothing their access to the high-demand sites at the center, it collects its revenue from those central sites.

BitTorrent, like other pioneers in the P2P movement, takes a radical approach to Internet decentralization. Every client is also a server; files are broken up into fragments that can be served from multiple locations, transparently harnessing the network of down-loaders to provide both bandwidth and data to other users. The more popular the file, in fact, the faster it can be served, as there are more users providing bandwidth and fragments of the complete file.

BitTorrent thus demonstrates a key Web 2.0 principle: *the service automatically gets better the more people use it*. While Akamai must add servers to improve service, every BitTorrent consumer brings his own resources to the party. There's an implicit "architecture of participation," a built-in ethic of cooperation, in which the service acts primarily as an intelligent broker, connecting the edges to each other and harnessing the power of the users themselves.

2 > harnessing collective intelligence

The central principle behind the success of the giants born in the Web 1.0 era who have survived to lead the Web 2.0 era appears to be that they have embraced the power of the Web to harness collective intelligence:

- Hyperlinking is the foundation of the Web. As users add new content, and new sites, it is bound in to the structure of the Web by other users discovering the content and linking to it. Much as synapses form in the brain, with associations becoming stronger through repetition or intensity, the web of connections grows organically as an output of the collective activity of all Web users.

- Yahoo!, the first great Internet success story, was born as a catalog, or directory of links, an aggregation of the best work of thousands, then millions of Web users. While Yahoo! has since moved into the business of creating many types of content, its role as a portal to the collective work of the Net's users remains the core of its value.

- Google's breakthrough in search, which quickly made it the undisputed search market leader, was PageRank, a method of using the link structure of the Web rather than just the characteristics of documents to provide better search results.

- eBay's product is the collective activity of all its users; like the Web itself, eBay grows organically in response to user activity, and the company's role is as an enabler of a context in which that user activity can happen. What's more, eBay's competitive advantage comes almost entirely from the critical mass of buyers and sellers, which makes any new entrant offering similar services significantly less attractive.

- Amazon sells the same products as competitors such as Barnesandnoble.com, and they receive the same product descriptions, cover images, and editorial content from their vendors. But Amazon has made a science of user engagement. They have an order of magnitude more user reviews, invitations to participate in varied ways on virtually every page—and even more important, they use user activity to produce better search results. While a Barnesandnoble.com search is likely to lead with the company's own products, or sponsored results, Amazon always leads with "most popular," a real-time computation based not only on sales but other factors that Amazon insiders call the "flow" around products. With an order of magnitude more user participation, it's no surprise that Amazon's sales also outpace competitors'.

Now, innovative companies that pick up on this insight and perhaps extend it even further are making their mark on the Web:

- Wikipedia, an online encyclopedia based on the unlikely notion that an entry can be added by any Web user, and edited by any other, is a radical experiment in trust, applying Eric Raymond's dictum (originally coined in the context of open source software) that "with enough eyeballs, all bugs are shallow" to content creation. Wikipedia is already in the top 100 websites, and many think it will be in the top ten before long. This is a profound change in the dynamics of content creation!

- Sites like del.icio.us and Flickr, two companies that have received a great deal of attention of late, have pioneered a concept that some people call "folksonomy" (in contrast to taxonomy), a style of collaborative categorization of sites using freely chosen keywords, often referred to as tags. Tagging allows for the kind of multiple, overlapping associations that the brain itself uses, rather than rigid categories. In the canonical example, a Flickr photo of a puppy might be tagged both "puppy" and "cute"—allowing for retrieval along natural axes-generated user activity.

- Collaborative spam-filtering products like Cloudmark aggregate the individual decisions of e-mail users about what is and is not spam, outperforming systems that rely on analysis of the messages themselves.

- It is a truism that the greatest Internet success stories don't advertise their products. Their adoption is driven by "viral marketing"—that is, recommendations propagating directly from one user to another. You can almost make the case that if a site or product relies on advertising to get the word out, it isn't Web 2.0.

- Even much of the infrastructure of the Web—including the Linux, Apache, MySQL, and Perl, PHP, or Python code involved in most Web servers—relies on the peer-production methods of open source, in themselves an instance of collective, Net-enabled intelligence. There are more than 100,000 open source software projects listed on SourceForge.net. Anyone can add a project, anyone can download and use the code, and new projects migrate from the edges to the center as a result of users putting them to work, an organic software adoption process relying almost entirely on viral marketing.

The lesson: *Network effects from user contributions are the key to market dominance in the Web 2.0 era.*

Blogging and the Wisdom of Crowds

One of the most highly touted features of the Web 2.0 era is the rise of blogging. Personal home pages have been around since the early days of the Web, and the personal diary and daily opinion column around much longer than that, so just what is the fuss all about?

At its most basic, a blog is just a personal home page in diary format. But as Rich Skrenta notes, the chronological organization of a blog "seems like a trivial difference, but it drives an entirely different delivery, advertising and value chain."

One of the things that has made a difference is a technology called RSS. RSS is the most significant advance in the fundamental architecture of the Web since early hackers realized that CGI could be used to create database-backed websites. RSS allows someone to link not just to a page, but to subscribe to it, with notification every time that page changes. Skrenta calls this "the incremental Web." Others call it the "live Web."

Now, of course, "dynamic websites" (i.e., database-backed sites with dynamically generated content) replaced static Web pages well over ten years ago. What's dynamic about the live Web are not just the pages, but the links. A link to a weblog is expected to point to a perennially changing page, with "permalinks" for any individual entry, and notification for each change. An RSS feed is thus a much stronger link than, say, a bookmark or a link to a single page.

RSS also means that the Web browser is not the only means of viewing a Web page. While some RSS aggregators, such as Bloglines, are Web-based, others are desktop clients, and still others allow users of portable devices to subscribe to constantly updated content.

RSS is now being used to push not just notices of new blog entries, but also all kinds of data updates, including stock quotes, weather data, and photo availability. This use is actually a return to one of its roots: RSS was born in 1997 out of the confluence of Dave Winer's "Really Simple Syndication" technology, used to push out blog updates, and Netscape's "Rich Site Summary," which allowed users to create custom Netscape home pages with regularly updated data flows. Netscape lost interest, and the technology was carried forward by blogging pioneer Userland, Winer's company. In the current crop of applications, we see, though, the heritage of both parents.

But RSS is only part of what makes a weblog different from an ordinary Web page. Tom Coates remarks on the significance of the permalink:

> It may seem like a trivial piece of functionality now, but it was effectively the device that turned weblogs from an ease-of-publishing phenomenon into a conversational mess of overlapping communities. For the first time it became relatively easy to gesture directly at a highly specific post on someone else's site and talk about it. Discussion emerged. Chat emerged. And—as a result—friendships emerged or became more entrenched. The permalink was the first—and most successful—attempt to build bridges between weblogs.

In many ways, the combination of RSS and permalinks adds many of the features of NNTP, the Network News Protocol of the Usenet, onto HTTP, the Web protocol. The "blogosphere" can be thought of as a new, peer-to-peer equivalent to Usenet and bulletin boards, the conversational watering holes of the early Internet. Not only can people subscribe to each other's sites, and easily link to individual comments on a page, but also, via a mechanism known as track-backs, they can see when anyone else links to their pages, and can respond, either with reciprocal links or by adding comments.

Interestingly, two-way links were the goal of early hypertext systems like Xanadu. Hypertext purists have celebrated trackbacks as a step towards two-way links. But note that trackbacks are not properly two-way—rather, they are really (potentially) symmetrical one-way links that create the effect of two-way links. The difference may seem subtle, but in practice it is enormous. Social networking systems like Friendster, Orkut, and LinkedIn, which require acknowledgment by the recipient in order to establish a connection, lack the same scalability as the Web. As noted by Caterina Fake,

cofounder of the Flickr photo-sharing service, attention is only coin-
cidentally reciprocal. (Flickr thus allows users to set watch lists—
any user can subscribe to any other user's photostream via RSS.
The object of attention is notified, but does not have to approve the
connection.)

If an essential part of Web 2.0 is harnessing collective intelligence, turning the Web into a kind of global brain, the blogosphere
is the equivalent of constant mental chatter in the forebrain, the
voice we hear in all of our heads. It may not reflect the deep structure of the brain, which is often unconscious, but is instead the
equivalent of conscious thought. And as a reflection of conscious
thought and attention, the blogosphere has begun to have a powerful effect.

First, because search engines use link structure to help predict
useful pages, bloggers, as the most prolific and timely linkers, have
a disproportionate role in shaping search engine results. Second,
because the blogging community is so highly self-referential, bloggers paying attention to other bloggers magnify their visibility and
power. The "echo chamber" that critics decry is also an amplifier.

If it were merely an amplifier, blogging would be uninteresting.
But like Wikipedia, blogging harnesses collective intelligence as a
kind of filter. What James Suriowecki calls "the wisdom of crowds"
comes into play, and much as PageRank produces better results
than analysis of any individual document, the collective attention
of the blogosphere selects for value.

While mainstream media may see individual blogs as competitors, what is really unnerving is that the competition is with the
blogosphere as a whole. This is not just a competition between sites,
but a competition between business models. The world of Web 2.0
is also the world of what Dan Gillmor calls "we, the media," a world
in which "the former audience," not a few people in a back room,
decides what's important.

<Tim O'Reilly>
<John Battelle>

web squared:
web 2.0 five years on

By Tim O'Reilly and John Battelle.
Originally published in 2009 at www.oreilly.com.

JOHN BATTELLE is founder and executive chairman of Federated Media Publishing. He has been a visiting professor of journalism at the University of California, Berkeley, and also maintains *Searchblog*, a weblog covering technology, culture, and media. Battelle is one of the original founders of *Wired* magazine, the founder of *The Industry Standard* magazine and website, and "band manager" of the weblog *Boing Boing*. In 2005, he published *The Search: How Google and Its Rivals Rewrote the Rules of Business and Transformed Our Culture*.

FIVE YEARS AGO, we launched a conference based on a simple idea, and that idea grew into a movement. The original Web 2.0 Conference (now the Web 2.0 Summit) was designed to restore confidence in an industry that had lost its way after the dot-com bust. The Web was far from done, we argued. In fact, it was on its way to becoming a robust platform for a culture-changing generation of computer applications and services.

In our first program, we asked why some companies survived the dot-com bust while others had failed so miserably. We also studied a burgeoning group of start–ups and asked why they were growing so quickly. The answers helped us understand the rules of business on this new platform.

Chief among our insights was that "the network as platform" means far more than just offering old applications via the network ("software as a service"); it means building applications that literally get better the more people use them, harnessing network effects not only to acquire users, but also to learn from them and build on their contributions.

From Google and Amazon to Wikipedia, eBay, and craigslist, we saw that the value was facilitated by the software, but was co-created by and for the community of connected users. Since then, powerful new platforms like YouTube, Facebook, and Twitter have demonstrated that same insight in new ways. Web 2.0 is all about harnessing collective intelligence.

Collective intelligence applications depend on managing, understanding, and responding to massive amounts of user-generated data in real time. The "subsystems" of the emerging Internet operating system are increasingly data subsystems: location, identity (of people, products, and places), and the skeins of meaning that tie them together. This leads to new levers of competitive advantage: Data is the "Intel Inside" of the next generation of computer applications.

Today, we realize that these insights were not only directionally right, but are being applied in areas we only imagined in 2004. The smartphone revolution has moved the Web from our desks to our pockets. Collective intelligence applications are no longer being driven solely by humans typing on keyboards but, increasingly, by sensors. Our phones and cameras are being turned into eyes and ears for applications; motion and location sensors tell where we are, what we're looking at, and how fast we're moving. Data is being collected, presented, and acted upon in real time. The scale of participation has increased by orders of magnitude.

With more users and sensors feeding more applications and platforms, developers are able to tackle serious real-world problems. As a result, the Web opportunity is no longer growing arithmetically; it's growing exponentially. Hence our theme for this year: Web Squared. 1990–2004 was the match being struck; 2005–2009 was the fuse; and 2010 will be the explosion.

Ever since we first introduced the term "Web 2.0," people have been asking, "What's next?" Assuming that Web 2.0 was meant to be a kind of software version number (rather than a statement about the second coming of the Web after the dot-com bust), we're constantly asked about "Web 3.0." Is it the semantic web? The sentient web? Is it the social web? The mobile web? Is it some form of virtual reality?

It is all of those, and more.

The Web is no longer a collection of static pages of HTML that describe something in the world. Increasingly, the Web is the world—everything and everyone in the world casts an "information shadow," an aura of data which, when captured and processed intelligently, offers extraordinary opportunity and mind-bending implications. Web Squared is our way of exploring this phenomenon and giving it a name.

>>> redefining collective intelligence: new sensory input

To understand where the Web is going, it helps to return to one of the fundamental ideas underlying Web 2.0, namely that successful network applications are systems for harnessing collective intelligence.

Many people now understand this idea in the sense of "crowdsourcing"—namely, that a large group of people can create a collective work whose value far exceeds that provided by any of the individual participants. The Web as a whole is a marvel of crowd-sourcing, as are marketplaces such as those on eBay and craigslist, mixed media collections such as YouTube and Flickr, and the vast personal lifestream collections on Twitter, MySpace, and Facebook.

Many people also understand that applications can be constructed in such a way as to direct their users to perform specific tasks, like building an online encyclopedia (Wikipedia), annotating an online catalog (Amazon), adding data points onto a map (the many Web-mapping applications), or finding the most popular news stories (Digg, Twine). Amazon's Mechanical Turk has gone so far as to provide a generalized platform for harnessing people to do tasks that are difficult for computers to perform on their own.

But is this really what we mean by collective intelligence? Isn't one definition of intelligence, after all, that characteristic that allows an organism to learn from and respond to its environment? (Please note that we're leaving aside entirely the question of self-awareness. For now, anyway.)

Imagine the Web (broadly defined as the network of all connected devices and applications, not just the PC-based application formally known as the World Wide Web) as a newborn baby. She sees, but at first she can't focus. She can feel, but she has no idea of size till she puts something in her mouth. She hears the words of her smiling parents, but she can't understand them. She is awash in sensations, few of which she understands. She has little or no control over her environment.

Gradually, the world begins to make sense. The baby coordinates the input from multiple senses, filters signal from noise, learns new skills, and once-difficult tasks become automatic.

The question before us is this: Is the Web getting smarter as it grows up?

Consider search—currently the lingua franca of the Web. The first search engines, starting with Brian Pinkerton's webcrawler, put everything in their mouth, so to speak. They hungrily followed links, consuming everything they found. Ranking was by brute-force keyword matching.

In 1998, Larry Page and Sergey Brin had a breakthrough, realizing that links were not merely a way of finding new content, but of ranking it and connecting it to a more sophisticated natural language grammar. In essence, every link became a vote, and votes from knowledgeable people (as measured by the number and quality of people who in turn vote for them) count more than others.

Modern search engines now use complex algorithms and hundreds of different ranking criteria to produce their results. Among the data sources is the feedback loop generated by the frequency of search terms, the number of user clicks on search results, and our own personal search and browsing history. For example, if a majority of users start clicking on the fifth item on a particular search results page more often than the first, Google's algorithms take this as a signal that the fifth result may well be better than the first, and eventually adjust the results accordingly.

Now consider an even more current search application, the Google Mobile Application for the iPhone. The application detects the movement of the phone to your ear, and automatically goes into speech recognition mode. It uses its microphone to listen to your voice, and decodes what you are saying by referencing not only its speech recognition database and algorithms, but also the correlation to the most frequent search terms in its search database. The phone uses GPS or cell-tower triangulation to detect its location, and uses that information as well. A search for "pizza" returns the result you most likely want: the name, location, and contact information for the three nearest pizza restaurants.

All of a sudden, we're not using search via a keyboard and a stilted search grammar, we're talking to and with the Web. It's getting smart enough to understand some things (such as where we are) without us having to tell it explicitly. And that's just the beginning.

And while some of the databases referenced by the application—such as the mapping of GPS coordinates to addresses—are "taught" to the application, others, such as the recognition of speech, are "learned" by processing large, crowdsourced data sets.

Clearly, this is a "smarter" system than what we saw even a few years ago. Coordinating speech recognition and search, search results and location, is similar to the "hand-eye" coordination the baby gradually acquires. The Web is growing up, and we are all its collective parents.

>>> cooperating data subsystems

In our original Web 2.0 analysis, we posited that the future "Internet operating system" would consist of a series of interoperating data subsystems. The Google Mobile Application provides one example of how such a data-driven operating system might work.

In this case, all of the data subsystems are owned by one vendor—Google. In other cases, as with Apple's iPhoto '09, which integrates Flickr and Google Maps as well as Apple's own cloud services, an application uses cloud database services from multiple vendors.

As we first noted back in 2003, "data is the Intel Inside" of the next generation of computer applications. That is, if a company has control over a unique source of data that is required for applications to function, they will be able to extract monopoly rents from the use of that data. In particular, if a database is generated by user contribution, market leaders will see increasing returns as the size and value of their database grows more quickly than that of any new entrants.

We see the era of Web 2.0, therefore, as a race to acquire and control data assets. Some of these assets—the critical mass of seller listings on eBay, or the critical mass of classified advertising on craigslist—are application-specific. But others have already taken on the characteristic of fundamental system services.

Take for example the domain registries of the DNS, which are a backbone service of the Internet. Or consider CDDB, used by virtually every music application to look up the metadata for songs and albums. Mapping data from providers like Navteq and TeleAtlas is used by virtually all online mapping applications.

There is a race on right now to own the social graph. But we must ask whether this service is so fundamental that it needs to be open to all.

It's easy to forget that only fifteen years ago, e-mail was as fragmented as social networking is today, with hundreds of incompatible e-mail systems joined by fragile and congested gateways. One of those systems—Internet RFC 822 e-mail—became the gold standard for interchange.

We expect to see similar standardization in key Internet utilities and subsystems. Vendors who are competing with a winner-takes-all mind-set would be advised to join together to enable systems built from the best-of-breed data subsystems of cooperating companies.

>>> how the web learns: explicit vs. implicit meaning

But how does the Web learn? Some people imagine that for computer programs to understand and react to meaning, meaning needs to be encoded in some special taxonomy. What we see in practice is that meaning is learned "inferentially" from a body of data.

Speech recognition and computer vision are both excellent examples of this kind of machine learning. But it's important to realize that machine learning techniques apply to far more than just sensor data. For example, Google's ad auction is a learning system, in which optimal ad placement and pricing are generated in real time by machine learning algorithms.

In other cases, meaning is "taught" to the computer. That is, the application is given a mapping between one structured data set and another. For example, the association between street addresses and GPS coordinates is taught rather than learned. Both data sets are structured, but need a gateway to connect them.

It's also possible to give structure to what appears to be unstructured data by teaching an application how to recognize the connection between the two. For example, You R Here, an iPhone app, neatly combines these two approaches. You use your iPhone camera to take a photo of a map that contains details not found on generic mapping applications such as Google maps—say, a trailhead map in a park, or another hiking map. Use the phone's GPS to set your current location on the map. Walk a distance away, and set a second point. Now your iPhone can track your position on that custom map image as easily as it can on Google maps.

Some of the most fundamental and useful services on the Web have been constructed in this way, by recognizing and then teaching the overlooked regularity of what at first appears to be unstructured data.

Ti Kan, Steve Scherf, and Graham Toal, the creators of CDDB, realized that the sequence of track lengths on a CD formed a unique signature that could be correlated with artist, album, and song names. Larry Page and Sergey Brin realized that a link is a vote. Marc Hedlund at Wesabe realized that every credit card swipe is also a vote, that there is hidden meaning in repeated visits to the same merchant. Mark Zuckerberg at Facebook realized that friend relationships online actually constitute a generalized social graph. They thus turn what at first appeared to be unstructured into structured data. And all of them used both machines and humans to do it. . . .

>>> the rise of real time: a collective mind

As it becomes more conversational, search has also gotten faster. Blogging added tens of millions of sites that needed to be crawled daily or even hourly, but microblogging requires instantaneous update—which means a significant shift in both infrastructure and approach. Anyone who searches Twitter on a trending topic has to be struck by the message: "See what's happening right now" followed, a few moments later, by "42 more results since you started searching. Refresh to see them."

What's more, users are continuing to co-evolve with our search systems. Take hashtags on Twitter: a human convention that facilitates real-time search on shared events. Once again, you see how human participation adds a layer of structure—rough and inconsistent as it is—to the raw data stream.

Real-time search encourages real-time response. Retweeted "information cascades" spread breaking news across Twitter in moments, making it the earliest source for many people to learn about what's just happened. And again, this is just the beginning. With services like Twitter and Facebook's status updates, a new data source has been added to the Web—real-time indications of what is on our collective mind.

Guatemala and Iran have both recently felt the Twitter effect, as political protests have been kicked off and coordinated via Twitter.

Which leads us to a timely debate: There are many who worry about the dehumanizing effect of technology. We share that worry, but also see the countertrend, that communication binds us together, gives us shared context, and ultimately shared identity.

Twitter also teaches us something important about how applications adapt to devices. Tweets are limited to 140 characters; the very limits of Twitter have led to an outpouring of innovation. Twitter users developed shorthand (@username, #hashtag, $stock-ticker), which Twitter clients soon turned into clickable links. URL shorteners for traditional Web links became popular, and soon realized that the database of clicked links enable new real-time analytics. Bit.ly, for example, shows the number of clicks your links generate in real time.

As a result, there's a new information layer being built around Twitter that could grow up to rival the services that have become so central to the Web: search, analytics, and social networks. Twitter also provides an object lesson to mobile providers about what can happen when you provide APIs. Lessons from the Twitter application ecosystem could show opportunities for SMS and other mobile services, or it could grow up to replace them.

Real-time is not limited to social media or mobile. Much as Google realized that a link is a vote, Walmart realized that a customer purchasing an item is a vote, and the cash register is a sensor counting that vote. Real-time feedback loops drive inventory. Walmart may not be a Web 2.0 company, but they are without doubt a Web Squared company: one whose operations are so infused with IT, so innately driven by data from their customers, that it provides them immense competitive advantage. One of the great Web Squared opportunities is providing this kind of real-time intelligence to smaller retailers without monolithic supply chains.

As explained so eloquently by Vivek Ranadive, founder and CEO of Tibco, in Malcolm Gladwell's recent *New Yorker* profile:

> Everything in the world is now real time. So when a certain type of shoe isn't selling at your corner shop, it's not six months before the guy in China finds out. It's almost instantaneous, thanks to my software.

Even without sensor-driven purchasing, real-time information is having a huge impact on business. When your customers are declaring their intent all over the Web (and on Twitter)—either through their actions or their words, companies must both listen and join the conversation. Comcast has changed its customer service approach using Twitter; other companies are following suit.

Another striking story we've recently heard about a real-time feedback loop is the Houdini system used by the Obama campaign to remove voters from the Get Out the Vote calling list as soon as they had actually voted. Poll watchers in key districts reported in as they saw names crossed off the voter lists; these were then made to "disappear" from the calling lists that were being provided to volunteers. (Hence the name Houdini.)

Houdini is Amazon's Mechanical Turk writ large: one group of volunteers acting as sensors, multiple real-time data queues being synchronized and used to affect the instructions for another group of volunteers being used as actuators in that same system.

Businesses must learn to harness real-time data as key signals that inform a far more efficient feedback loop for product development, customer service, and resource allocation.

>>> in conclusion: the stuff that matters

All of this is in many ways a preamble to what may be the most important part of the Web Squared opportunity.

The new direction for the Web, its collision course with the physical world, opens enormous new possibilities for business, and enormous new possibilities to make a difference on the world's most pressing problems.

There are already hundreds of examples of this happening. But there are many other areas in which we need to see a lot more progress—from our energy ecosystem to our approach to health care. Not to mention our financial system, which is in disarray.

Even in a pro-regulatory environment, the regulators in government are hopelessly outclassed by real-time automated financial systems. What have we learned from the consumer Internet that could become the basis for a new twenty-first-century financial regulatory system? We need machine learning to be applied here, algorithms to detect anomalies, transparency that allows auditing by anyone who cares, not just by overworked understaffed regulators.

When we started the Web 2.0 events, we stated that "the Web is a platform." Since then, thousands of businesses and millions of lives have been changed by the products and services built on that platform.

But 2009 marks a pivot point in the history of the Web. It's time to leverage the true power of the platform we've built. The Web is no longer an industry unto itself—the Web is now the world.

And the world needs our help.

If we are going to solve the world's most pressing problems, we must put the power of the Web to work—its technologies, its business models, and perhaps most important, its philosophies of openness, collective intelligence, and transparency. And to do that, we must take the Web to another level. We can't afford incremental evolution anymore.

It's time for the Web to engage the real world. Web meets World—that's Web Squared.

<Andrew Keen>

web 2.0: the second generation of the internet has arrived and it's worse than you think

**Originally published in *The Weekly Standard*
(February 14, 2006).**

Writer and entrepreneur **ANDREW KEEN** is the author of
The Cult of the Amateur: How the Internet Is Killing Our Culture
(2007). Keen founded Audiocafe.com in 1995 and is currently the host of the "Keen On" show on Techcrunch.tv.
His new book about the social media revolution, *Digital Vertigo: An Anti-Social Manifesto*, will be published by St. Martin's
Press in 2012. You can follow him on Twitter at twitter.com/
ajkeen.

THE ANCIENTS were good at resisting seduction. Odysseus
fought the seductive song of the Sirens by having his men
tie him to the mast of his ship as it sailed past the Sirens'
Isle. Socrates was so intent on protecting citizens from the seductive opinions of artists and writers that he outlawed them from his
imaginary republic.

We moderns are less nimble at resisting great seductions, particularly those utopian visions that promise grand political or cultural salvation. From the French and Russian revolutions to the countercultural upheavals of the '60s and the digital revolution of the '90s, we have been seduced, time after time and text after text, by the vision of a political or economic utopia.

Rather than Paris, Moscow, or Berkeley, the grand utopian movement of our contemporary age is headquartered in Silicon Valley, whose great seduction is actually a fusion of two historical movements: the countercultural utopianism of the '60s and the techno-economic utopianism of the '90s. Here in Silicon Valley, this seduction has announced itself to the world as the "Web 2.0" movement.

Last week, I was treated to lunch at a fashionable Japanese restaurant in Palo Alto by a serial Silicon Valley entrepreneur who, back in the dot-com boom, had invested in my start–up Audiocafe .com. The entrepreneur, like me a Silicon Valley veteran, was pitching me his latest start-up: a technology platform that creates easy-to-use software tools for online communities to publish weblogs, digital movies, and music. It is technology that enables anyone with a computer to become an author, a film director, or a musician. This Web 2.0 dream is Socrates' nightmare: technology that arms every citizen with the means to be an opinionated artist or writer.

"This is historic," my friend promised me. "We are enabling Internet users to author their own content. Think of it as empowering citizen media. We can help smash the elitism of the Hollywood studios and the big record labels. Our technology platform will radically democratize culture, build authentic community, create citizen media." Welcome to Web 2.0.

Buzzwords from the old dot-com era—like "cool," "eyeballs," or "burn-rate"—have been replaced in Web 2.0 by language which is simultaneously more militant and absurd: Empowering citizen media, radically democratize, smash elitism, content redistribution, authentic community. . . . This sociological jargon, once the preserve of the hippie counterculture, has now become the lexicon of new media capitalism.

Yet this entrepreneur owns a $4 million house a few blocks from Steve Jobs's house. He vacations in the South Pacific. His children attend the most exclusive private academy on the peninsula. But for all of this he sounds more like a cultural Marxist—a disciple of Gramsci or Herbert Marcuse—than a capitalist with an MBA from Stanford.

In his mind, "big media"—the Hollywood studios, the major record labels and international publishing houses—really did represent the enemy. The promised land was user-generated online content. In Marxist terms, the traditional media had become the exploitative "bourgeoisie," and citizen media, those heroic bloggers and podcasters, were the "proletariat."

This outlook is typical of the Web 2.0 movement, which fuses '60s radicalism with the utopian eschatology of digital technology. The ideological outcome may be trouble for all of us.

So what, exactly, is the Web 2.0 movement? As an ideology, it is based upon a series of ethical assumptions about media, culture, and technology. It worships the creative amateur: the self-taught filmmaker, the dorm-room musician, the unpublished writer. It suggests that everyone—even the most poorly educated and inarticulate amongst us—can and should use digital media to express and realize themselves. Web 2.0 "empowers" our creativity, it "democratizes" media, it "levels the playing field" between experts and amateurs. The enemy of Web 2.0 is "elitist" traditional media.

Empowered by Web 2.0 technology, we can all become citizen journalists, citizen videographers, citizen musicians. Empowered by this technology, we will be able to write in the morning, direct movies in the afternoon, and make music in the evening.

Sounds familiar? It's eerily similar to Marx's seductive promise about individual self-realization in his *German Ideology*:

> Whereas in communist society, where nobody has one
> exclusive sphere of activity but each can become accom-
> plished in any branch he wishes, society regulates the gen-
> eral production and thus makes it possible for me to do
> one thing today and another tomorrow, to hunt in the
> morning, fish in the afternoon, rear cattle in the evening,
> criticise after dinner, just as I have a mind, without ever
> becoming hunter, fisherman, shepherd or critic.

Just as Marx seduced a generation of European idealists with his fantasy of self-realization in a communist utopia, so the Web 2.0 cult of creative self-realization has seduced everyone in Silicon Valley. The movement bridges countercultural radicals of the '60s such as Steve Jobs with the contemporary geek culture of Google's Larry Page. Between the bookends of Jobs and Page lies the rest of Silicon Valley, including radical communitarians like Craig Newmark (of Craigslist.com), intellectual property communists such as Stanford Law professor Larry Lessig, economic cornucopians like *Wired* magazine editor Chris "Long Tail" Anderson, and new media moguls Tim O'Reilly and John Battelle.

The ideology of the Web 2.0 movement was perfectly summarized at the Technology Education and Design (TED) show in Monterey last year, when Kevin Kelly, Silicon Valley's über-idealist and author of the Web 1.0 Internet utopia *New Rules for the New Economy*, said:

> Imagine Mozart before the technology of the piano. Imag-
> ine Van Gogh before the technology of affordable oil paints.
> Imagine Hitchcock before the technology of film. We have
> a moral obligation to develop technology.

But where Kelly sees a moral obligation to develop technology, we should actually have—if we really care about Mozart, Van Gogh, and Hitchcock—a moral obligation to question the development of technology.

The consequences of Web 2.0 are inherently dangerous for the vitality of culture and the arts. Its empowering promises play upon that legacy of the '60s—the creeping narcissism that Christopher Lasch described so presciently, with its obsessive focus on the realization of the self.

Another word for narcissism is "personalization." Web 2.0 technology personalizes culture so that it reflects ourselves rather than the world around us. Blogs personalize media content so that all we read are our own thoughts. Online stores personalize our preferences, thus feeding back to us our own taste. Google personalizes searches so that all we see are advertisements for products and services we already use.

Instead of Mozart, Van Gogh, or Hitchcock, all we get with the Web 2.0 revolution is more of ourselves.

Still, the idea of inevitable technological progress has become so seductive that it has been transformed into "laws." In Silicon Valley, the most quoted of these laws, Moore's Law, states that the number of transistors on a chip doubles every two years, thus doubling the memory capacity of the personal computer every two years. On one level, of course, Moore's Law is real and it has driven the Silicon Valley economy. But there is an unspoken ethical dimension to Moore's Law. It presumes that each advance in technology is accompanied by an equivalent improvement in the condition of man.

But as Max Weber so convincingly demonstrated, the only really reliable law of history is the Law of Unintended Consequences.

We know what happened first time around, in the dot-com boom of the '90s. At first there was irrational exuberance. Then the dot-com bubble popped; some people lost a lot of money and a lot of people lost some money. But nothing really changed. Big media remained big media and almost everything else—with the exception of Amazon.com and eBay—withered away.

This time, however, the consequences of the digital media revolution are much more profound. Apple and Google and craigslist really are revolutionizing our cultural habits, our ways of entertaining ourselves, our ways of defining who we are. Traditional "elitist" media is being destroyed by digital technologies. Newspapers are in free fall. Network television, the modern equivalent of the dinosaur, is being shaken by TiVo's overnight annihilation of the thirty-second commercial. The iPod is undermining the multi-billion-dollar music industry. Meanwhile, digital piracy, enabled by Silicon Valley hardware and justified by Silicon Valley intellectual property communists such as Larry Lessig, is draining revenue from established artists, movie studios, newspapers, record labels, and songwriters.

Is this a bad thing? The purpose of our media and culture industries—beyond the obvious need to make money and entertain people—is to discover, nurture, and reward elite talent. Our traditional mainstream media has done this with great success over the last century. Consider Alfred Hitchcock's masterpiece *Vertigo*, and a couple of other brilliantly talented works of the same name: the 1999 book called *Vertigo*, by Anglo-German writer W. G. Sebald, and the 2004 song "Vertigo," by Irish rock star Bono. Hitchcock could never have made his expensive, complex movies outside the Hollywood studio system. Bono would never have become Bono without the music industry's super-heavyweight marketing muscle. And W. G. Sebald, the most obscure of this trinity of talent, would have remained an unknown university professor had a high-end publishing house not had the good taste to discover and distribute his work. Elite artists and an elite media industry are symbiotic. If you democratize media, then you end up democratizing talent. The unintended consequence of all this democratization, to misquote Web 2.0 apologist Thomas Friedman, is cultural "flattening." No more Hitchcocks, Bonos, or Sebalds. Just the flat noise of opinion—Socrates's nightmare.

While Socrates correctly gave warning about the dangers of a society infatuated by opinion in Plato's *Republic*, more modern dystopian writers—Huxley, Bradbury, and Orwell—got the Web 2.0 future exactly wrong. Much has been made, for example, of the associations between the all-seeing, all-knowing qualities of Google's search engine and the Big Brother in *1984*. But Orwell's fear was the disappearance of the individual right to self-expression. Thus Winston Smith's great act of rebellion in *1984* was his decision to pick up a rusty pen and express his own thoughts:

> The thing that he was about to do was open a diary. This was not illegal, but if detected it was reasonably certain that it would be punished by death . . . Winston fitted a nib into the penholder and sucked it to get the grease off . . . He dipped the pen into the ink and then faltered for just a second. A tremor had gone through his bowels. To mark the paper was the decisive act.

In the Web 2.0 world, however, the nightmare is not the scarcity, but the overabundance of authors. Since everyone will use digital media to express themselves, the only decisive act will be to not mark the paper. Not writing as rebellion sounds bizarre—like a piece of fiction authored by Franz Kafka. But one of the unintended consequences of the Web 2.0 future may well be that everyone is an author, while there is no longer any audience.

Speaking of Kafka, on the back cover of the January 2006 issue of *Poets and Writers* magazine, there is a seductive Web 2.0 style advertisement that reads:

> Kafka toiled in obscurity and died penniless. If only he'd had a website . . .

Presumably, if Kafka had had a website, it would be located at kafka.com, which is today an address owned by a mad left-wing blog called *The Biscuit Report*. The front page of this site quotes some words written by Kafka in his diary:

> I have no memory for things I have learned, nor things I have read, nor things experienced or heard, neither for people nor events; I feel that I have experienced nothing, learned nothing, that I actually know less than the average schoolboy, and that what I do know is superficial, and that every second question is beyond me. I am incapable of thinking deliberately; my thoughts run into a wall. I can grasp the essence of things in isolation, but I am quite incapable of coherent, unbroken thinking. I can't even tell a story properly; in fact, I can scarcely talk. . . .

One of the unintended consequences of the Web 2.0 movement may well be that we fall, collectively, into the amnesia that Kafka describes. Without an elite mainstream media, we will lose our memory for things learned, read, experienced, or heard. The cultural consequences of this are dire, requiring the authoritative voice of at least an Allan Bloom, if not an Oswald Spengler. But here in Silicon Valley, on the brink of the Web 2.0 epoch, there no longer are any Blooms or Spenglers. All we have is the great seduction of citizen media, democratized content and authentic online communities. And weblogs, course. Millions and millions of blogs.

<Katherine Mangu-Ward>

wikipedia and beyond: jimmy wales's sprawling vision

Originally published in *Reason* magazine (June 2007).

KATHERINE MANGU-WARD is a senior editor at *Reason* magazine. Previously, Mangu-Ward worked as a reporter for *The Weekly Standard* magazine and as a researcher on *The New York Times* op-ed page. Her work has appeared in *The Wall Street Journal*, *Washington Post*, *The Los Angeles Times*, *New York Times* online, and numerous other publications. She blogs at reason.com.

JIMMY WALES, the founder of Wikipedia, lives in a house fit for a grandmother. The progenitor and public face of one of the ten most popular websites in the world beds down in a one-story bungalow on a cul-de-sac near St. Petersburg, Florida. The neighborhood, with its scrubby vegetation and plastic lawn furniture, screams "Bingo Night." Inside the house, the décor is minimal, and the stucco and cool tile floors make the place echo. A few potted plants bravely attempt domesticity. Out front sits a cherry red Hyundai.

I arrive at Wales's house on a gray, humid day in December. It's 11 a.m., and after wrapping up some e-mails on his white Mac iBook, Wales proposes lunch. We hit the mean streets of Gulf Coast Florida in the Hyundai, in search of "this really great Indian place that's part of a motel," and wind up cruising for hours—stopping at Starbucks, hitting the mall, and generally duplicating the average day of millions of suburban teenagers. Walmarts and Olive Gardens slip past as Wales, often taciturn and abrupt in public statements, lets loose a flood of words about his past, his politics, the future of the Internet, and why he's optimistic about pretty much everything.

Despite his modest digs, Wales is an Internet rock star. He was included on *Time*'s list of the 100 most influential people of 2006. Pages from Wikipedia dominate Google search results, making the operation, which dubs itself "the free encyclopedia that anyone can edit," a primary source of information for millions of people. (Do a Google search for "monkeys," "Azerbaijan," "mass spectrometry," or "Jesus," and the first hit will be from Wikipedia.) Although he insists he isn't a "rich guy" and doesn't have "rich guy hobbies," when pressed Wales admits to hobnobbing with other geek elites, such as Amazon founder Jeff Bezos, and hanging out on Virgin CEO Richard Branson's private island. (The only available estimate of Wales's net worth comes from a now-removed section of his own Wikipedia entry, pinning his fortune at less than $1 million.) Scruffy in a gray mock turtleneck and a closely cropped beard, the forty-year-old Wales plays it low-key. But he is well aware that he is a strangely powerful man. He has utterly changed the way people extract information from the chaos of the World Wide Web, and he is the master of a huge, robust online community of writers, editors, and users. Asked about the secret to Wikipedia's success, Wales says simply, "We make the Internet not suck."

On other occasions, Wales has offered a more erudite account of the site's origins and purpose. In 1945, in his famous essay "The

Use of Knowledge in Society," the libertarian economist F. A. Hayek argued that market mechanisms serve "to share and synchronize local and personal knowledge, allowing society's members to achieve diverse, complicated ends through a principle of spontaneous self-organization." (These are the words not of the Nobel Prize winner himself but of Wikipedia's entry on him.) "Hayek's work on price theory is central to my own thinking about how to manage the Wikipedia project," Wales wrote on the blog of the Internet law guru Lawrence Lessig. "One can't understand my ideas about Wikipedia without understanding Hayek." Long before socialism crumbled, Hayek saw the perils of centralization. When information is dispersed (as it always is), decisions are best left to those with the most local knowledge. This insight, which undergirds contemporary libertarianism, earned Hayek plaudits from fellow libertarian economist and Nobel Prize winner Milton Friedman as the "most important social thinker of the twentieth century." The question: Will traditional reference works like *Encyclopaedia Britannica*, that great centralizer of knowledge, fall before Wikipedia the way the Soviet Union fell before the West?

When Wales founded the site in 2001, his plan was simple yet seemingly insane: "Imagine a world in which every single person on the planet is given free access to the sum of all human knowledge. That's what we're doing." In case that plan didn't sound nutty enough on its own, he went on to let every Tom, Dick, and Friedrich write and edit articles for that mystical encyclopedia. "Now it's obvious that it works," says Wales, "but then most people couldn't get it." And not everyone gets it yet. Wales has his share of enemies, detractors, and doubters. But he also has a growing fan club. Wikipedia, which is run by Wales's nonprofit Wikimedia Foundation, is now almost fully supported by small donations (in addition to a few grants and gifts of servers and hosting), and many of its savviest users consider it the search of first resort, bypassing Google entirely.

Wikipedia was born as an experiment in aggregating information. But the reason it works isn't that the world was clamoring for a new kind of encyclopedia. It took off because of the robust, self-policing community it created. Despite its critics, it is transforming our everyday lives; as with Amazon, Google, and eBay, it is almost impossible to remember how much more circumscribed our world was before it existed.

Hayek's arguments inspired Wales to take on traditional encyclopedias, and now they're inspiring Wales's next big project: Wikia, a for-profit venture that hopes to expand the idea beyond encyclopedias into all kinds of Internet-based communities and collaborative projects. If Wikia succeeds, it will open up this spontaneously ordered, self-governing world to millions more people. Encyclopedias aren't the only places to gather knowledge, and by making tools available to create other kinds of collaborative communities, Wales is fleshing out and bringing to life Hayek's insights about the power of decentralized knowledge gathering, the surprising strength of communities bound only by reputation, and the fluidity of self-governance.

>>> jimbo

Wales was born in Huntsville, Alabama, in 1966, the son of a grocery store manager. He was educated at a tiny private school run by his mother, Doris, and grandmother, Erma. His education, which he has described as "a one-room schoolhouse or Abe Lincoln type of thing," was fairly unstructured. He "spent many, many hours just poring over the World Book Encyclopedia." Wales received his B.A. in finance from Auburn University, a hotbed of free-market economists, and got his master's degree in finance from the University of Alabama. He did coursework and taught at Indiana University, but he failed to complete a Ph.D. dissertation—largely, he says, because he "got bored."

Wales moved to Chicago and became a futures and options trader. After six years of betting on interest rates and currency fluctuations, he made enough money to pay the mortgage for the rest of his life. In 1998 he moved to San Diego and started a Web portal, Bomis, which featured, among other things, a "guy-oriented search engine" and pictures of scantily clad women. The *en désha-billé* ladies have since caused trouble for Wales, who regularly fields questions about his former life as a "porn king." In a typically blunt move, Wales often responds to criticism of his Bomis days by sending reporters links to Yahoo's midget porn category page. If he was a porn king, he suggests, so is the head of the biggest Web portal in the world.

Bomis didn't make it big—it was no Yahoo—but in March 2000 the site hosted Nupedia, Wales's first attempt to build a free online encyclopedia. Wales hired Larry Sanger, at the time a doctoral candidate in philosophy at Ohio State, to edit encyclopedia articles submitted voluntarily by scholars, and to manage a multistage peer review process. After a slow start, Wales and Sanger decided to try something more radical. In 2001 they bracketed the Nupedia project and started a new venture built on the same foundations. The twist: It would be an open-source encyclopedia. Any user could exercise editorial control, and no one person or group would have ultimate authority.

Sanger resigned from the project in 2002 and since then has been in an ongoing low-grade war with Wales over who founded Wikipedia. Everyone agrees that Sanger came up with the name while Wales wrote the checks and provided the underlying open-source philosophy. But who thought of powering the site with a wiki?

Wikis are simple software that allow anyone to create or edit a Web page. The first wikis were developed by Ward Cunningham, a programmer who created the WikiWikiWeb, a collaborative software guide, in 1995. ("Wiki wiki" means "quick" in Hawaiian.)

Gradually adopted by a variety of companies to facilitate internal collaboration (IBM and Google, for instance, use wikis for project management and document version control), wikis were spreading under the radar until Wikipedia started using the software.

Wales characterizes the dispute with Sanger as a fight over the "project's radically open nature" and the question of "whether there was a role for an editor in chief" in the new project. Sanger says he wanted to implement the "commonsense" rules that "experts and specialists should be given some particular respect when writing in their areas of expertise." (Sanger has since launched a competitor to Wikipedia called Citizendium, with stricter rules about editors' credentials.) They also differed over whether advertising should be permitted on the site. Not only does Wikipedia allow anyone to write or edit any article, but the site contains no ads. Yet it allows others to use its content to make money. The site Answers. com, for example, is composed almost entirely of Wikipedia content reposted with ads.

When Nupedia finally shut down for good in 2003, only twenty-four articles had completed its onerous scholarly review process. In contrast, Wikipedia was flourishing, with 20,000 articles by the end of its first year. It now has six million articles, 1.7 million of which are in English. It has become a verb ("What exactly is a quark?" "I don't know. Did you Wikipedia it?"), a sure sign of Internet success.

>>> the troublemaker

An obvious question troubled, and continues to trouble, many: How could an "encyclopedia that anyone can edit" possibly be reliable? Can truth be reached by a consensus of amateurs? Can a community of volunteers aggregate and assimilate knowledge the way a market assimilates price information? Can it do so with consistent accuracy? If markets fail sometimes, shouldn't the same be true of market-based systems?

Wikipedia does fail sometimes. The most famous controversy over its accuracy boiled over when John Seigenthaler Sr., a former assistant to Attorney General Robert F. Kennedy, wrote about his own Wikipedia entry in a November 2005 *USA Today* op-ed. The entry on Seigenthaler included a claim that he had been involved in both Kennedy assassinations. "We live in a universe of new media," wrote Seigenthaler, "with phenomenal opportunities for worldwide communications and research—but populated by volunteer vandals with poison-pen intellects."

The false claim had been added to the entry as a prank in May 2005. When Seigenthaler contacted Wikipedia about the error in October, Wales personally took the unusual step of removing the false allegations from the editing history on the page, wiping out the publicly accessible records of the error. After the *USA Today* story ran, dozens of the site's contributors (who call themselves "Wikipedians") visited the page, vastly improving the short blurb that had been put in place after the prank entry was removed. As in a market, when a failure was detected, people rushed in to take advantage of the gap and, in doing so, made things better than they were before. Print outlets couldn't hope to compete with Wikipedians' speed in correcting, expanding, and footnoting the new Seigenthaler entry. At best, a traditional encyclopedia would have pasted a correction into a little-consulted annual, mailed out to some users many months after the fact. And even then, it would have been little more than a correction blurb, not a dramatic rethinking and rewriting of the whole entry.

But well-intentioned Wikipedians weren't the only ones attracted to Seigenthaler's Wikipedia entry. Since the article appeared, Seigenthaler says, he has been a constant target for vandals—people whose only goal is to deface an entry. He has been struck by the "vulgarity and mean-spiritedness of the attacks," which included replacing his picture with photos of Hitler, Himmler, and "an unattractive cross-dresser in a big red wig and a short skirt," Seigenthaler tells me. "I don't care what the hell they put up. When you're eighty years old, there's not much they can say that hasn't been said before. But my, they've been creative over the last months."

Seigenthaler's primary concern these days is about the history page that accompanies each Wikipedia article. Even though various allegations against Seigenthaler have been removed promptly from the main encyclopedia entry, a record of each change and reversion is stored on the site. Many of the comments, says Seigenthaler, are things he would not want his nine-year-old grandson to see.

Seigenthaler says he never intended to sue (surprisingly, the site has never been sued), but he worries that Wales will eventually find himself in legal trouble unless he takes more action to control what appears on the site: "I said to Jimmy Wales, 'You're going to offend enough members of Congress that you're going to get more regulation.' I don't want more regulation of the media, but once the Congress starts regulating they never stop." Coverage of the scandal was largely anti-Wikipedia, focusing on the system's lack of ethical editorial oversight. Sample headline: "There's No Wikipedia Entry for 'Moral Responsibility.'"

Wikipedia's flexibility allows anyone who stumbles on an error to correct it quickly. But that's not enough for some detractors. "There is little evidence to suggest that simply having a lot of people freely editing encyclopedia articles produces more balanced coverage," the editor in chief of *Encyclopaedia Britannica* said last year in an online debate hosted by *The Wall Street Journal*. "On the contrary, it opens the gates to propaganda and seesaw fights between writers." Another *Britannica* editor dissed Wikipedia by comparing it to a toilet seat (you don't know who used it last). A host of academics charged Wikipedia with having too casual a relationship with authority and objectivity. Michael Gorman, former president of the American Library Association, told the *San Francisco Chronicle* in 2006, "The problem with an online encyclopedia created by anybody is that you have no idea whether you are reading an established person in the field or someone with an ax to grind." Last summer at Wikimania 2006, a gathering of Wikipedians and various hangers-on at the Harvard Law School's Berkman Center for Internet and Society, university professors expressed concern that their students were treating Wikipedia as an authoritative source. In January the history faculty at Vermont's Middlebury College voted to ban the use of Wikipedia in bibliographies. Wales has issued statements telling kids to use Wikipedia as a starting point, but not to include it in their bibliographies as a final source. Good Wikipedia articles have links to authoritative sources, he explains; students should take advantage of them.

Referring to the Seigenthaler controversy during his opening remarks at Wikimania 2006, Wales got one of the biggest laughs of the weekend when he said: "Apparently there was an error in Wikipedia. Who knew?" Wales and the hundreds of Wikipedians could afford a giggle or two because the entry had long since been corrected. This wasn't a traumatic incident to Wikipedians because they admit error hundreds of times a day. There is no pretense of infallibility at Wikipedia, an attitude that sets it apart from traditional reference works, or even *The New York Times*; when an error is found it doesn't undermine the project. Readers who know better than the people who made the error just fix it and move on.

Wikipedia's other major scandal hasn't been quite as easy for Wales to laugh off, because he was the culprit. In 2005 he was caught with his hand on the edit button, taking advantage of Wikipedia's open editing policy to remove Larry Sanger from the encyclopedia's official history of itself. There has been an ongoing controversy about Wales's attempts to edit his own Wikipedia entry, which is permitted but considered extremely bad form. After a round of negative publicity when the edits were discovered, Wales stopped editing his own profile. But in the site's discussion pages, using the handle "Jimbo Wales," he can be found trying to persuade others to make changes on this and other topics. If he wanted to, Wales could make these and other changes by fiat, then lock out other editors. But he doesn't. If the individuals that people Wales's experiment in free association choose to ignore his pleas, as they occasionally do, he takes a deep breath and lets it happen.

Wales isn't the only one who has tried to use Wikipedia to rewrite history. In January 2006, all edits originating with the House of Representatives were briefly blocked after staffers for Rep. Martin Meehan (D-Mass.) were caught systematically replacing unflattering facts in his entry with campaign material; among other things, they removed a reference to his broken promise not to serve more than four terms. In the fall of 2006, officials from the National Institute on Drug Abuse dramatically edited their own entry to remove criticism of the agency. In both cases, the editors got more than they bargained for: Not only was the original material quickly restored, but a section describing the editing scandal was tacked on to each entry.

Then there are edits that are less ideological but still troublesome. Wales has adopted Hayek's view that change is handled more smoothly by an interlocking network of diverse individuals than by a central planning authority. One test of the rapid response to change in Wikipedia is how the site deals with vandalism. Fairly often, says Wales, someone comes along and replaces an entry on, say, George W. Bush with a "giant picture of a penis." Such vandalism tends to be corrected in less than five minutes, and a 2002 study by IBM found that even subtler vandalism rarely lasts more than a few hours. This, Wales argues, is only possible because responsibility for the content of Wikipedia is so widely distributed. Even hundreds of professional editors would struggle to keep six million articles clean day in and day out, but Wikipedia manages it fairly easily by relying on its thousands of volunteer contributors.

The delicate compromise wording of the entry about abortion is an example of how collaborative editing can succeed. One passage reads: "Most often those in favor of legal prohibition of abortion describe themselves as pro-life while those against legal restrictions on abortion describe themselves as pro-choice." Imagine the fighting that went into producing these simple words. But the article, as it stands, is not disputed. Discussants have found a middle ground. "It's fabulous," says Wales, citing another example, "that our article about Taiwan was written by Mainlanders and Taiwanese who don't agree." That said, other entries—such as the page on the Iraq War—host ongoing battles that have not reached equilibrium.

Skeptics of Wikipedia's model emphasize that the writers have no authority; there is no way to verify credentials on the site. But Wikipedia seems to be doing okay without letters after its name. In 2005 the journal *Nature* compared the accuracy of scientific articles in Wikipedia with that of *Encyclopaedia Britannica*. Articles were sent to panels of experts in the appropriate field for review. Reviewers found an average of four errors in Wikipedia entries, only slightly higher than *Britannica*'s average of three errors per entry.

>>> the federalist

One way to understand what makes Wikipedia unique is its reaction to the threat of blackout by the Chinese government. When government censors in China blocked the Chinese-language Wikipedia page and demanded that the content be heavily censored before it was unblocked, the site's Chinese contributors chose to lie low and wait. Wales agreed to let them handle it. Eventually the site was unblocked, although its status is always precarious.

Wikipedia's decision not to censor its content selectively in order to meet the demands of the Chinese government was easy, since it would be almost impossible to do, anyway. The "encyclopedia that anyone can edit" would have to employ a full-time staff just to remove objectionable content, which could be added back moments later by anyone, anywhere. The diffuse responsibility for the content of Wikipedia protects it from censorship.

By leaving such a big decision to the community of Chinese Wikipedia users, Wales made good on his boast that he's "a big supporter of federalism," not just in politics but in the governance of Wikipedia. Wales tries to let communities of users make their own decisions in every possible case. "It's not healthy for us if there are certain decisions that are simply removed from the democratic realm and are just 'the Supreme Court says so,'" he argues. "I would even say this about abortion, although I'm a big pro-choice guy. It's not clear to me that it's such a great thing to have removed it completely from politics."

Politically, Wales cops to various libertarian positions but prefers to call his views "center-right." By that he means that he sees himself as part of a silent majority of socially liberal, fiscally conservative people who value liberty—"people who vote Republican but who worry about right-wingers." The Libertarian Party, he says, is full of "lunatics." But even as he outlines all the reasons why he prefers to stay close to the American political mainstream, Wales delicately parses the various libertarian positions on intellectual property and other points of dispute without breaking a sweat. He swears to have actually read Ludwig von Mises's ten-pound tome *Human Action* (which he ultimately found "bombastic and wrong in many ways"). And of course, he credits Hayek with the central insight that made Wikipedia possible.

Wales's political philosophy isn't confined to books. Pulling onto yet another seemingly identical Florida highway during our day-long road trip, Wales blows past the Knight Shooting Sports Indoor Range, lamenting that he hasn't made it to the range in a long time. "When I lived in San Diego," he says, "the range was on my way home from work." Wales used to be preoccupied with gun rights, or the lack thereof. "In California," he says, "the gun laws irritated me so much that I cared, but then I moved to Florida and I stopped caring because everything is fine here."

Wales, whose wife Christine teaches their five-year-old daughter Kira at home, says he is disappointed by the "factory nature" of American education: "There's something significantly broken about the whole concept of school." A longtime opponent of mandatory public school attendance, Wales says that part of the allure of Florida, where his Wikimedia Foundation is based, is its relatively laissez-faire attitude toward homeschoolers. This makes it easier for Wales and his wife to let Kira (a tiny genius in her father's eyes) follow her own interests and travel with her parents when Wales gives one of his many speeches abroad.

Kira has recently become interested in Ancient Egypt, and a few books on the subject lie on the kitchen counter of their sparse house. When she was younger, Kira was transfixed by digital clocks, staring at one minute after minute, trying to guess which number would be next. "She just needed time to do that," says Wales. "Once she figured it out, she stopped. Christine and I were a little worried, but we let her do her thing, and it turned out fine."

Likewise, Wales says he prefers the users of his encyclopedia to make their own decisions about governance and follow their own peculiar interests wherever possible; things usually turn out fine. "Simply having rules does not change the things that people want to do," he says. "You have to change incentives."

One of the most powerful forces on Wikipedia is reputation. Users rarely identify themselves by their real names, but regular users maintain consistent identities. When a particularly obnoxious edit or egregious error is found, it's easy to check all of the other changes made by the same user; you just click on his name. Users who catch others at misdeeds are praised, and frequent abusers are abused. Because it's so easy to get caught in one stupid mistake or prank, every user has an incentive to do the best he can with each entry. The evolution of a praise/shame economy within Wikipedia has been far more effective at keeping most users in line than the addition of formal rules to deal with specific conflicts.

"It's always better not to have a rule," Wales says. "But sometimes you have to say, 'Don't be a dick.'" On the English Wikipedia, there is a rule that you can't undo someone else's changes more than three times. It is formalized, a part of the system. But Wikipedias in other languages have a more casual approach to the same problem. Wales himself sometimes talks to troublemakers. "I try to talk jerks into adopting a three-revert rule as a principle for themselves," he says.

Wikipedias in different languages have developed their own policies about practically everything. Only one point is "not negotiable": the maintenance of a "neutral point of view" in Wikipedia encyclopedia entries. Wikipedia has been uniquely successful in maintaining the neutrality ethos, says Wales, because "text is so flexible and fluid that you can find amongst reasonable people with different perspectives something that is functional." ("Most people assume the fights are going to be the left vs. the right," Wales has said, "but it always is the reasonable versus the jerks.")

The jerks range from the Chinese government to the giant penis guy. But mostly they're regular contributors who get upset about some hobbyhorse and have to be talked down or even shamed by their communities.

Although he professes to hate phrases like "swarm intelligence" and "the wisdom of crowds," Wales's phenomenal success springs largely from his willingness to trust large aggregations of human beings to produce good outcomes through decentralized, market-like mechanisms. He is suspicious of a priori planning and centralization, and he places a high value on freedom and independence for individuals. He is also suspicious of mob rule. Most Wikipedia entries, Wales notes, are actually written by two or three people, or reflect decisions made by small groups in the discussion forums on the site. Wales calls himself an "anti-credentialist" but adds that doesn't mean he's anti-elitist. He likes elites, he says; they just have to duke it out with the rest of us on Wikipedia and his other projects.

"Jimmy Wales is a very open person," says his friend Irene McGee, the host of the radio show *No One's Listening* and a former *Real World* cast member. "He has very genuine intentions and faith in people. He'll come to San Francisco and come to little Meetups that don't have anything to do with anything, just to find out what's going on. He'll go to meet the kid in this town who writes articles and then meet with people who run countries. He can meet somebody really fancy and he could meet somebody who nobody would recognize and tell the story as if it's the same."

>>> the individualist communitarian

Rock star status can be fleeting, of course. Whether Jimmy Wales will still be meeting fancy people who run countries five years from now may depend on the success of his new venture, Wikia. Wikipedia is here to stay, but the public has an annoying habit of demanding that its heroes achieve ever more heroic feats. Wikia is an attempt to take the open-source, community-based model to profitability and broader public acceptance.

Consider, for instance, the astonishing growth and readership at the Wikia site devoted to Muppets. At a little over one year old, the Muppet Wiki has 13,700 articles. Every single one is about Muppets. Interested in an in-depth look at the use of gorilla suits in the Muppet movies? No problem. Just type in "gorilla suits" and enjoy a well-illustrated article that documents, among other things, the names of actors who have worn an ape outfit for Jim Henson. There is a timeline of all things Muppet-related. An entry on China details Big Bird's reception in the People's Republic. The site is astonishingly comprehensive and, perhaps more impressive, comprehensible to a Muppet novice.

This ever-expanding encyclopedia of Muppetry is just a tiny part of Wikia. It is an arguably trivial but hugely telling example of the power of open publishing systems to enable professionals and amateurs to work together to aggregate vast amounts of data and conversation on topics and areas ranging from the serious to the sublime. Founded in November 2004, Wikia communities use the same editing and writing structure as Wikipedia. The site provides free bandwidth, storage, blogging software, and other tools to anyone who wants to start an online community or collaborative project. If you don't care for Kermit the Frog, you can try the Your Subculture Soundtrack, an "interconnecting database of the music scene" with more than 5,600 articles. Many of them are just enormous lists of discographies, lyrics, or guitar tabs. The topics of other Wikis range from *Star Wars* to polyamory to transhumanism. Wikia also includes collaborative online projects such as the Search Wiki, an effort to create an open-source competitor to Google where a Wikipedia-style universe of users rates websites and sorts the search results instead of relying solely on an algorithm.

In December, Wikia announced that its first corporate partner, Amazon, had committed $10 million to further development of the project. Amazon's money added to the $4 million kicked in by angel investors earlier in the year. Amazon and Wikia have not integrated their services, but Wales has not ruled out the possibility of cooperation at a later date, spurring not entirely tongue-in-cheek rumors of a joint Wikipedia-Amazon takeover of the Web. The site plans to make money by showing a few well-targeted, well-placed ads to massive numbers of community members and users.

Amazon founder Jeff Bezos (a supporter of Reason Foundation, the nonprofit that publishes this magazine) has spoken enviously of Wikipedia's collaborative model, expressed his regret that Amazon's user reviews aren't more like wikis, and credited Wikipedia with having "cracked the code for user-generated content." Bezos "really drove this deal personally," Wales says, adding that he was in the enviable position of vetting potential investors.

Wales is reluctant to get into more precise detail about what exactly Wikia will do, or what the communities or collaborative projects will produce, since that will be up to the users. This reticence turns out to be, in part, philosophical. Wikia is radically devoted to the idea that if you provide free, flexible tools, people will build interesting things. It's the same concept that drives Wikipedia, but expanded to nonencyclopedic functions. Like the rest of the cohort sometimes dubbed "Web 2.0"—YouTube, MySpace, Blogger, and other services that emphasize collaboration and user-generated content—Wales is relying on users to make his sites interesting. It isn't always easy to explain this to investors. "Before Wikipedia, the idea of an encyclopedia on a wiki seemed completely insane," says Wales. "It's obvious that it works now, but at the time no one was sure. Now we're going through the same moment with Wikia."

Perhaps because of the indeterminate nature of the final product, Wales has opted for the '90s approach of "build the site now, make money later." Industry analyst Peter Cohan thinks Wikia isn't likely to fall into the same trap as the busted Internet companies of the dot-com era. "Wikia is getting two and a half million page views a day," he says, "and it's growing steadily. There are people who are willing to pay for those eyeballs." (It has been growing at about the same rate as Wikipedia did at this stage of its development.) Still, says Cohan, there will be some hurdles for Wales, who is known only for his nonprofit work. "When you bring money into the picture it might change the incentives for people to participate in this thing," he says. "When people know that there is no money involved, then ego gets involved and it's a matter of pride."

Wales is banking on strong communities to give Wikia the staying power that flash-in-the-pan Internet sensations or more loosely knit social networking sites lack. Wales is plugged into social networking sites (and has more than a few online friends/fans), but he says he finds the exhibitionism and technical precocity of MySpace somewhat creepy.

It might sound strange, but Wales's interest in community dovetails nicely with his interest in individualism. No one is born into the Muppet Wiki community. Everyone who is there chooses to be there, and everyone who participates has a chance to shape its rules and content. People naturally form communities with their own delicate etiquette and expectations, and they jealously guard their own protocols. Each one is different, making Wikia communities fertile ground where thousands of experimental social arrangements can be tried—some with millions of members and some with just two or three. Like the "framework for utopia" described in the libertarian philosopher Robert Nozick's *Anarchy, State, and Utopia*, Wikia maximizes the chance that people can work together to get exactly what they want, while still being part of a meaningful community by maximizing freedom and opportunities for voluntary cooperation.

Wikia boosters contend that many existing online communities would benefit from the kind of curb appeal a wiki offers. The firm hopes to co-opt, buy, or duplicate them. Wikia CEO Gil Penchina, formerly of eBay, is a frequent-flier-miles enthusiast, for example. But most of the sites now haunted by airfare obsessives deal in nitty-gritty details and are useless to the outsider hoping to figure out the best way to get a free ticket by gaming various frequent-flier plans, or by finding fares listed erroneously as $3.75 instead of $375. "This makes it hard to monetize that content," says Wales. "People just come and look around and don't find what they want and leave." Incorporating those same geeks into a wiki community could make their considerable knowledge available to outsiders and make the page more welcoming to advertisers. If lots of outsiders looking for a good price on a specific product can use the site, advertisers will compete (and pay) to grab their attention.

For now, Wikia makes money solely from Google ads running on its community pages. Wales says this is because they're "lazy" and because Google ads are a good way to generate a little revenue while they "build communities." Since its 2004 launch, Wikia has spent exactly $5.74 on advertising—a small fee for Google analytics to track stats on the site. "That makes our ad budget about 25 cents per month," Wales grins. It's early yet to expect a big push to generate revenue, but this charming laziness could be troublesome if it persists much longer.

Wikia now has forty employees, including a handful of Polish programmers—a huge staff compared with the three people it takes to run Wikipedia. With 500,000 articles on 2,000 topics produced by 60,000 registered users in forty-five languages, the network of websites is growing fast. The biggest wikis are dedicated to *Star Trek* and *Star Wars*. Wales is partial to the wiki devoted to the TV show *Lost*. He also admires the Campaign Wiki, which among other projects has neutral voter guides for elections.

Even as Wikia relies on Google ads for its only revenue at the moment, Wales recently has started to talk publicly about building a search engine using open-source tools, a project Wales casually calls "The Google Killer." Wales hopes the transparency and flexibility of an open-source model will discourage the gaming of the system that plagues Google. A search for "hotels in Tampa" on Google, a search I tried before my trip into town to interview Wales, yields nothing useful, just a jumble of defunct ratings sites and some ads that aren't tailored to my needs. By using a community of volunteers who will rerank results and tweak algorithms, Wales hopes to get useful results in categories that are particularly subject to gaming.

>>> the pathological optimist

Later that December afternoon, after an excellent Indian lunch in a Florida strip mall, Wales proposes that we hop back into the Hyundai for a stop at the "fancy mall" in the Tampa area. En route to the Apple store, he surveys the bright lights and luxury goods for sale and announces that he is generally pretty pleased with how things are going in the world. In fact, he calls himself a "pathological optimist." On issue after issue, he pronounces some version of "things aren't that bad" or "things are getting better." People are more connected than they used to be (thanks, in part, to Internet communities), the wide availability of ethnic food has made the American diet more interesting, bookstore mega-chains are increasing the diversity of media available in America, entertainment is increasing in quality, gun rights are expanding, and so on. Tempted to get involved with free-speech activists, Wales, a self-declared "First Amendment extremist," says he drew back because real repression doesn't seem likely. "There's a lot of hysteria around this," he says—concerns about censorship that aren't supported by the facts.

Wales is optimistic about the Internet, too. "There's a certain kind of dire anti-market person," he says, "who assumes that no matter what happens, it's all driving toward one monopoly—the ominous view that all of these companies are going to consolidate into the Matrix." His own view is that radical decentralization will win out, to good effect: "If everybody has a gigabit [broadband Internet connection] to their home as their basic $40-a-month connection, anybody can write Wikipedia."

Wales's optimism isn't without perspective. After reading Tom Standage's book about the impact of the telegraph, *The Victorian Internet*, he was "struck by how much of the semi-utopian rhetoric that comes out of people like me sounds just like what people like them said back then."

Among Wikipedians, there is constant squabbling about how to characterize Wales's role in the project. He is often called a "benevolent dictator," or a "God-King," or sometimes a "tyrant." While the 200,000 mere mortals who have contributed articles and edits to the site are circumscribed by rules and elaborate community-enforced norms, Wales has amorphous and wide-ranging powers to block users, delete pages, and lock entries outside of the usual processes. But if Wales is a god, he is like the gods of ancient times (though his is a flat, suburban Olympus), periodically making his presence and preferences known through interventions large and small, but primarily leaving the world he created to chug along according to rules of its own devising.

After spending a day cruising the greater Tampa Bay area, I find myself back at the Wales homestead, sitting with the family as they watch a video of Wales's daughter delivering a presentation on Germany for a first-grade enrichment class. Wales is learning German, in part because the German Wikipedia is the second largest after English, in part because "I'm a geek." Daughter Kira stands in front of a board, wearing a dirndl and reciting facts about Germany. Asked where she did her research, she cops to using Wikipedia for part of the project. Wales smiles sheepishly; the Wikipedia revolution has penetrated even his own small bungalow.

People who don't "get" Wikipedia, or who get it and recoil in horror, tend to be from an older generation literally and figuratively: the Seigenthalers and *Britannica* editors of the world. People who get it are younger and hipper: the Irene McGees and Jeff Bezoses. But the people who really matter are the Kiras, who will never remember a time without Wikipedia (or perhaps Wikia), the people for whom open-source, self-governed, spontaneously ordered online community projects don't seem insane, scary, or even particularly remarkable. If Wales has his way—and if Wikipedia is any indication, he will—such projects will just be another reason the Internet doesn't suck.

<Maggie Jackson>

judgment: of molly's gaze and taylor's watch

why more is less in a split-screen world

Excerpted from *Distracted* (pp. 71–95). This is an abridged version of the original chapter.

Columnist and author **MAGGIE JACKSON'S** recent book is *Distracted: The Erosion of Attention and the Coming Dark Age* (2008). Jackson has published in *The Boston Globe*, *The New York Times*, *BusinessWeek*, *Utne*, and *Gastronomica*. She is a graduate of Yale University and the London School of Economics. For more information, see www.maggie-jackson .com.

MOLLY WAS BUSY. A cherubic, dark-haired fourteen-month-old still unsteady on her feet, she hung on to a bookcase with one hand and doggedly yanked toys off the shelves. One, two, three brightly colored plastic blocks dropped to the floor. A teddy bear got a fierce hug before being hurled aside. Then abruptly, she stood stock-still and swiveled her head toward a big television set at one end of the room, entranced by the image of a singing, swaying Baby Elmo. "She's being pulled away," whispered Dan Anderson, a psychology professor who was videotaping Molly and her mother from an adjoining room of his laboratory. "What's happening is that she's being pulled away by the TV all the time, rather than making a behavioral decision to watch TV."[1] As Anderson and two graduate students observed through an enormous one-way wall mirror and two video monitors, Molly stood entranced for a few seconds, took a step toward the screen and tumbled over. Her young mother, sitting on the floor nearby, turned her attention from the television in time to catch Molly before her head hit the floor. Anderson didn't react. He was tuned to the back-and-forth in the room: Molly turning from the toy to the TV to her mother; her mother watching her baby, but mostly the video, which was being developed by *Sesame Street* for the exploding under-two market. This was rich fodder for a man who's spent his life studying children's attention to television.

A congenial University of Massachusetts professor with a melodic voice, Anderson resembles a character in a fairy tale—perhaps the gentle wizard who shows the lost child the way home. First in viewers' homes and now in his lab in a working-class neighborhood of Springfield, Massachusetts, he studies heart rate, eye tracking, and an array of other measures to understand what happens when we watch television. People aren't as glued to the tube as they might think, Anderson has found. On average, both children and adults look at and away from a set up to one hundred and fifty times an hour.[2] Only if a look lasts fifteen seconds or longer are we likely to watch for up to ten minutes at a stretch—a phenomenon called "attentional inertia."[3] When a show is either too fast and stimulating or too calm and slow, our attention slips away. Television attracts us because its content can challenge our cognition. But foremost, its quick cuts and rapid imagery are designed to keep tugging at our natural inclination to orient toward the shiny, the bright, the mobile—whatever's eye-catching in our environment.

It's ingenious: entertainment that hooks us by appealing to our very instincts for survival. This is why very young viewers like Molly are entranced by the plethora of new "educational" shows and DVDs aimed at them, even though they understand little and likely learn little from this fare.[4] Push and pull, back and forth, television is in essence an interruption machine, the most powerful attention slicer yet invented. Just step into the room with the enticing glow, and life changes.

This was the intriguing discovery that Anderson made while exploring the gaze of the tiniest watchers, the final frontier of TV viewership. In all the years that he and others sought to probe the question of how much we attend to television, no one thought to ask how television changed off-screen life during an on-air moment. (The point of most such research, after all, was to measure the watching, the more of it the better, in the industry's view.) But Anderson and his research team recently discovered that television influences family life even when kids don't seem to be watching. When a game show is on, children ages one to three play with toys for half the amount of time and show up to 25 percent less focus in their play than they do when the TV is off.[5] In other words, they exhibit key characteristics—abbreviated and less focused play—of attention-deficient children.[6] They begin to look like junior multi-taskers, moving from toy to toy, forgetting what they were doing when they were interrupted by an interesting snippet of the show. Not surprisingly, parents in turn are distracted, interacting 20 percent less with their kids and relating passively—"That's nice, dear," or "Don't bother me, I'm watching TV"—when they do. Consider that more than half of children ages eight to eighteen live in homes where the TV is on most of the time.[7] Factor in the screens in the doctor's office, airport, elevator, classroom, backseat—and don't forget that many, if not most, are splintered by the wiggling, blinking crawl. Then, zoom out and remember that television is just one element in a daily deluge of split focus. Wherever Molly's gaze falls, wherever she turns, whomever she talks to, she'll likely experience divided attention. She's being groomed for a multitasking, interrupt-driven world. And she doesn't need Elmo to teach her that.

If the virtual gives us a limitless array of alternative spaces to inhabit, then multitasking seems to hand us a new way to reap time. Cyberspace allowed us to conquer distance and, seemingly, the limitations of our earthly selves. It has broken down the doors of perception. Now, we're adopting split focus as a cognitive booster rocket, the upgrade we need to survive in our multilayered new spaces. How else can we cope with an era of unprecedented simul-taneity, a place we've hurtled into without any "way of getting our bearings," as Marshall McLuhan noted in 1967.[8] Multitasking is the answer, the sword in the stone. Why not do two (or more) things per moment when before you would have done one? "It's a multitask-ing world out there. Your news should be the same. CNN Pipeline—multiple simultaneous news streams straight to your desktop." I am watching this ad on a huge screen at the Detroit airport one May evening after my flight home is canceled. Travelers all around me move restlessly between PDA, iPod, laptop, cell phone, and ubiq-uitous TV screens. "CNN Pipeline," the ad concludes. "Ride your world." Rev up your engines, Molly, it's a big universe out there.

Now working parents spend a quarter of their waking hours multitasking.[9] Grafted to our cell phones, we drive like drunks; even if it kills us, we get in that call. Instant messaging's disjointed, pause-button flavor makes it the perfect multitasking communica-tions medium. More than half of instant-message users say they always Web surf, watch TV, talk on the phone, or play computer games while IM'ing.[10] Teens say, duh, *that's* the attraction: face-to-face is better, but with IM, you get more done![11] Joichi Ito's "heck-lebot," which publicly displays the "back-channel chat" or wireless banter of conference attendees, may be just the pipe dream of a subversive venture capitalist for now, but it captures the tenor of the attentional turf wars erupting in meeting rooms, conference symposia, and college classes.[12] "Did he really say that?" instant-messages an audience member to fellow IM'ers in the room. "Wow? He did," someone responds.[13] This parallel channel adds a new layer to the surfing and e-mail checking already rife at live-time events . . . Bosses, speakers, and professors respond with threats and electronic blackouts to wrest people's primary focus back to the front of the room. Audiences ignore them, asserting the right to split their focus. Are these just bumps along the road to progress? Can we time-splice our way to unlimited productivity? Certainly, the disjunction between TV news anchors and the crawl "captures the way we live now: faster than ever, wishing we had eyes in the back of our heads," notes media critic Caryn James.[14] The inventor of the Kaiserpanorama, a nineteenth-century slide show, put it more simply. In an age of technological wonders, merely traveling to far-off places won't be enough, wrote August Fuhrmann. Next, we'll want to penetrate the unknown, do the impossible—instantaneously. "The more we have, the more we want," he wrote.[15]

ANOTHER DAY IN THE LAB, and this time I was the baby. Sitting in a cramped booth in a basement laboratory at the University of Michigan in Ann Arbor, my head was cradled in a chin rest and capped by a headset. My right hand rested on a set of four metal keys. On the table in front of me, two eyeball-shaped video cams sat atop a computer screen, monitoring me as I struggled to correctly respond to beeps, squeaks, and colored words—red, blue, yellow, green—appearing on the screen. "Beep," I heard and tried to recall if that was supposed to be sound one, two, or three. The lone word *red* appeared on the screen, and I thankfully remembered to press the corresponding pinkie finger key. Two practice rounds and then paired tones and colors flew at me simultaneously, even though I seemed to sense just one and then, after a long pause, the other. The colors I could handle, but sometimes I didn't

even hear the tones. I pictured Adam and Jonathan, the two graduate students in the next booth, rolling their eyes as they ran this
test taker through her paces. I pressed on, trying to concentrate. It
felt like gritting my teeth, except in my brain.

David Meyer, head of the University of Michigan's Brain, Cognition, and Action Lab, was my guide that day to the burgeoning
realm of cognitive neuroscience research into multitasking.[16] Considered by many of his peers to be one of the greatest experimental
psychologists of our time, Meyer looks more like an outdoorsman
than a brilliant scientist. Lanky and tall, he has a chiseled face and
a down-home way of talking, with faint traces of a Kentucky accent.
Blessed with the ability to translate brain science into plain English, he's become a media darling in recent years, the one to call for
a quote on the latest multitasking research. He's more than generous with his time and willing to endure the interruptions of press
calls. He's also a driven man.

Dressed in a faded T-shirt and blue jeans, he'd dragged himself
into the lab this stifling May morning despite a painful stomach
ailment. Now sixty-four, he's made it a point in recent years, even
at a cost to his time for other research, of warning anyone who will
listen about the dangers of multitasking. It's an unrecognized
scourge, he believes, akin to cigarette smoking a generation ago. Is
he riding a hobbyhorse, perhaps overreacting a trifle? Certainly, his
"call a spade a spade" demeanor has raised eyebrows in the button-
down scientific community. He writes lengthy scientific papers and
speeches when snappy four-page reports are increasingly in fashion. He refuses to lard his work with superficial pandering citations
to big names in the field. At the same time, Meyer is a renaissance
scientist, respected for his achievements in areas from computa-
tional modeling of the brain to "semantic priming"—or the automatic spread of mental and neural activity in response to processing
the meaning of words. Is he a provocative maverick devoted to a
peripheral pet cause or a prophetic visionary who can help save us
from ourselves?

Certainly, it's ironic that Meyer is best known in the public sphere for his work in an area of study that long was a backwater in attention research. By the time Wilhelm Wundt established the first psychology lab at the University of Leipzig in 1879, a generation of scientists had spent years studying how humans perceive the world, especially visually.[17] The discovery that we *interpret* daily life via our senses, not just digest it objectively, paved the way for endless attempts to rigorously measure how a human responds to environmental stimuli and to what extent the waters of perception are influenced by the forces of "memory, desire, will, anticipation and immediate experience," as delineated by art historian Jonathan Crary.[18] Part of the vision of William James stems from the fact that he never underestimated the complexity of such processes. Yet however crucial and enigmatic, the "input-output" transactions that fascinated early psychological researchers entail only one slice of the pie of cognition.

It wasn't until after World War II that scientists began to see that studying how we switch mental gears, especially under pressure, can illuminate the higher workings of the mind. Arthur T. Jersild had carried out the first systematic study of task-switching in 1927 for his dissertation by timing students solving long lists of similar or differing math problems. Then he abandoned the topic, never to return.[19] Later, postwar British scientists began tackling task switching as part of their groundbreaking research into higher cognitive processing. A parallel line of research probed dual tasking, or our limited capacity to carry out two tasks literally at the same time.[20] By the 1990s, an explosion of research into multitasking had ignited, inspired by the work of Alan Allport, Gordon Logan, David Meyer, Stephen Monsell, and Harold Pashler, among others—and by the demands of life today. It's not a coincidence that such research has blossomed in an era when human work has become increasingly wedded to the rhythms of the most complex, intelligent machines ever to appear on earth. (In part, Meyer is known for his work with computer scientist and cognitive psychologist David Kieras, using computers to model the brain's cognitive architecture, including the "mechanics" of task switching.)[21] The question of how our brains compare with artificial information processors, and how well they can keep up, underlies much of our fascination with multitasking. We're all air traffic controllers now.

Back in the booth, I tackled a different experiment, this one measuring the speed at which I could alternate between two complex visual activities. Although the first experiment tested my ability to respond to simultaneous stimuli, both effectively measure task switching, for we can do very few things exactly at the same time. Reading e-mail while talking on the phone actually involves reading and *then* chatting, chatting and *then* reading. Cell phoning while driving demands similar cognitive switching. In this second test, when a zero popped up in one of four spaces in a line on the screen, I was to press a corresponding key with my finger. A zero in the first spot meant that I should press my index finger key. A zero in the second place prompted my second finger, and so on. Tap, tap. I got it. Easy. That was the compatible round. Next, I was supposed to hit keys that did not correspond with the zeros in the old lineup. When I saw a zero at the end of the line, I was to strike my index finger key. There was a pattern, but I barely grasped it before I had to begin alternating between compatible and incompatible cues, depending on whether the zeros were green or red. I panicked, blindly hitting any key in the harder, incompatible rounds and was thoroughly relieved when it ended. Yes, William James, there's a whole lot more going on here than just simple inputs and outputs. My brief cerebral tussle in the test lab, in fact, neatly exemplifies the age-old, inescapable tug-of-war we experience each waking minute of our life as we struggle to stay tuned to and yet make sense of our world.

To understand multitasking, first consider the lowly neuron, especially in the three-dozen regions of the brain that deal with vision—arguably the most crucial attentional sense. They lead something of a dog-eat-dog life. Neurons in the retina initially transmit an object's simple, restricted characteristics, such as its color and position, while more lofty neurons in the cortex and other areas code the object's complex or abstract features, such as its meaning. (Is this a face or a toaster, my neighbor or my mother?) This hierarchy of neurons must work in concert, firing up a coordinated "perceptual coherence field" in scientist Steven Yantis's words, to meaningfully represent the object in the brain.[22] But with so much to process and so little time, multiple neuron groups often compete to represent sensory information to the brain for possible subsequent encoding into memory. What is the key to making meaning from this jumble? Attention. Paying attention, whether deliberately or involuntarily, highlights one coherence field and suppresses activity from "losing" neuron groups, forcing our perception of the object they are representing to fade away. Attention is so crucial to how we see the world that people with damage to areas usually in the brain's right parietal lobe—a region key to certain forms of attention—can completely fail to notice objects in their view even though their vision is perfect. Such patients with "visual neglect" will eat only the food on the left side of their plate or dress just the left side of their bodies.[23] They literally have blind spots, no-go zones for their attention. And yet even for those of us with healthy brains, focus itself creates a kind of blindness. When we shine our attentional spotlight on an object, the rest of the scene doesn't go blank, but its suppression is truly dramatic. "The intuition that we open our eyes and see all that is before us has long been known to be an illusion," notes Yantis.[24]

We aren't built, however, to tune out life. Our survival lies in the tricky push and pull between focusing and thus drawing meaning from the world, and staying alert to changes in our environment. This is the real tug-of-war. As much as we try to focus on pursuing our goals, at heart we are biased to remain alert to shifts—especially abrupt ones—in our environment. Babies and children are especially at the mercy of their environments, since it takes many years and much training for them to develop the brain capacity to carry out complex, goal-oriented behaviors, including multitasking. Older toddlers whose mothers constantly direct them—splicing and controlling the focus of their attention—show damaged goal-setting and independence skills a year later.[25] Even as adults, our "top-down" goal-oriented powers of attention constantly grapple with our essentially more powerful "bottom-up," stimulus-driven net-works.[26] Pausing along the trail to consider whether a plant was edible, our ancestors had to tune out their environment long enough to assess the would-be food. But they had to be better wired to almost unthinkingly notice the panther in the tree above—or they would have died out rapidly. We are born to be interrupt-driven, to give in Linda Stone's term "continuous partial attention"[27] to our environment, and we must painstakingly learn and keep striving to retain the ever-difficult art of focus. Otherwise, in a sense, we cede control to the environment, argues physicist Alan Lightman in an essay titled "The World Is Too Much with Me." After realizing that gradually and unconsciously he had subdivided his day "into smaller and smaller units of 'efficient' time use," he realized that he was losing his capacity to dream, imagine, question, explore, and, in effect, nurture an inner self. He was, in, a sense, becoming a "prisoner of the world."[28]

When we multitask, we are like swimmers diving into a state of focus, resurfacing to switch gears or reassess the environment, then diving again to resume focus. This is a speeded-up version of the push and pull we do all day. But no matter how practiced we are at either of the tasks we are undertaking, the back-and-forth produces "switch costs," as the brain takes time to change goals, remember the rules needed for the new task, and block out cogni-tive interference from the previous, still-vivid activity.[29] "Training can help overcome some of the inefficiencies by giving you more optimal strategies for multitasking," says Meyer, "but except in rare circumstances, you can train until you're blue in the face and you'd never be as good as if you just focused on one thing at a time. Period. That's the bottom line." Moreover, the more complex the tasks, the steeper the switch costs. When I had to consider both tones and colors in the first experiment, I began responding almost twice as slowly to the easier color tasks as I also tried to concentrate on getting the hard-to-hear tones right. Perhaps recalling which finger key corresponded to which color word, or in Meyer's words "rule activation," inhibited my performance. Perhaps my brain was slowed by "passive proactive interference"; in other words, it was still tied up with the work of distinguishing the tones, a sticky business for someone whose hearing has been eroded by years of city living. Similar trade-offs occurred during the second experiment. I slowed down in doing the easy compatible work, while trying like mad to speed up my responses to the infuriatingly illogical second round of zeros. Predictably, the accuracy of my responses often suffered. These lab rat exercises and millisecond "costs" may seem abstract. Sure, an instant of inattentional blindness or a delayed reaction in noticing a darting child makes an enormous difference in a car flying down the road. The split-focus moment literally may result in shattered lives. But scale up and out of the lab and ask, how much does this matter off the road or away from the radar screen? Is multitasking as much of a scourge as Meyer believes?

Perhaps the cumulative, fractional "switch costs," the cognitive profit-loss columns of our split-screen life, are not the only problem. These are inefficiencies, surely a danger in some circumstances and a sin in this capitalist society, which we undoubtedly will try to shave away by sharpening our multitasking skills. More important, perhaps in this time-splicing era we're missing something immeasurable, something that nevertheless was very much with me as I struggled to act like a good test monkey in Meyer's lab. How do we switch gears in a complex environment? Talk to a cognitive neuroscientist or an experimental psychologist such as Meyer and chances are, within minutes, he or she will stress the limitations of our highest form of attention—the executive system that directs judgment, planning, and self-control. Executive attention is a precious commodity. Relying on multitasking as a way of life, we chop up our opportunities and abilities to make big-picture sense of the world and pursue our long-term goals. In the name of efficiency, we are diluting some of the essential qualities that make us human. . . .

Now, most of us are information-age workers . . . relentlessly driving ourselves to do more, ever faster. This relentless quest for productivity drives the nascent but rapidly burgeoning field of "interruption science," which involves the study of the pivot point of multitasking. For multitasking is essentially the juggling of interruptions, the moment when we choose to or are driven to switch from one task to another. And so to dissect and map these moments of broken time is to shed light on how we live today. What emerges, in the jargon of leading interruption scientist Gloria Mark, is a portrait of "work fragmentation." We spend a great deal of our days trying to piece our thoughts and our projects back together, and the result is often an accumulation of broken pieces with a raggedy coherence all its own. After studying workers at two West Coast high-tech firms for more than one thousand hours over the course of a year, Mark sifted the data—and was appalled. The fragmentation of work life, she says, was "far worse than I could ever have imagined."[30]

Workers on average spend just eleven minutes on a project before switching to another, and while focusing on a project, typically change tasks every three minutes, Mark's research shows.[31] For example, employees might work on a budget project for eleven minutes but flip between related e-mails, Web surfing, and phone calls during that time. This isn't necessarily all bad. Modern life does demand nimble perception . . . and interruptions often usher in a needed break, a bit of useful information, or a eureka thought. Yet as well as coping with a high number of interruptions, workers have a tough time getting back on track once they are disconnected. Unlike in psychology labs, where test takers are cued to return to a previous task, workers have to retrieve a lost trail of work or thought themselves when interrupted. Once distracted, we take about twenty-five minutes to return to an interrupted task and usually plunge into two other work projects in the interim, Mark found.[32] This is partly because it's difficult to remember cognitive threads in a complex, ever-shifting environment and partly because of the nature of the information we are juggling today. The meaning of a panther's presence is readily apparent in a glance. But a ping or a beep doesn't actually tell much about the nature of the information. "It is difficult to know whether an e-mail message is worth interrupting your work for unless you open and read it—at which point you have, of course, interrupted yourself," notes science writer Clive Thompson. "Our software tools were essentially designed to compete with one another for our attention, like needy toddlers."[33] Even brief interruptions can be as disruptive as lengthy ones, if they involve tasks that are either complex in nature or similar to the original work (thus muddying recall of the main work), Donald Broadbent has found.[34] In total, interruptions take up 2.1 hours of an average knowledge worker's day and cost the U.S. economy $588 billion a year, one research firm estimated.[35] Workers find the constant hunt for the lost thread "very detrimental," Mark reports dryly. . . .

Mary Czerwinski, an energetic Microsoft researcher designs a kind of high-tech "wallpaper" to better our age. Czerwinski is the manager of the Visualization and Interaction Research Group in the company's thought ghetto, Microsoft Research Labs. She originally wrote her dissertation on task switching, spent time helping NASA determine how best to interrupt busy astronauts, and now develops ways for computer users to cure that uncertainty rap—the necessity to unveil an interruption to size up its importance— mainly by bringing our information into the open, so to speak.

Czerwinski and Gary Starkweather, inventor of the laser printer, are developing a forty-two-inch computer screen so that workers can see their project, files, or Web pages all at once. That's three-feet-plus of LCD sensurround, a geek's heaven. Moreover, within this big-screen universe, Czerwinski and her team are figuring out new ways to make interruptions instantly visible. A program called Scalable Fabric offers a peripheral zone where minimized but still visible windows are color-coded and wired to signal shifts in their status. A new e-mail, for example, might glow green in a partly visible in-box. Another project creates a round, radar screen–type window at the side of the screen, where floating dots represent pertinent information.[36] Czerwinski is, in effect, decorating the walls of cyberspace with our thoughts, plans, conversation, and ideas. Can the "pensieve"—the misty fountain that conjures up the stored memories of Harry Potter's sage headmaster, Albus Dumbledore—be far behind?

Working memory is the Achilles' heel of multitasking, and so is the focus of Czerwinski's work. The "lost thread" syndrome that bedevils multitaskers stems from the fact that we have a remarkably limited cerebral storehouse for information used in the daily tasks of life. (Even a wizard, it seems, is a forgetful creature.) "Out of sight, out of mind" is all too true, mainly because, for survival purposes, we need to have only the most pertinent current information on our mind's front burner. Our working memory is a bit like a digital news crawl slithering across Times Square: constantly updated, never more than a snippet, no looking back. Nearly a half-century ago, memory researchers Margaret and Lloyd Peterson found that people forget unrelated letters and words within just a few seconds once they are distracted or pulled away to another task.[37] In his classic 1956 paper "The Magical Number Seven Plus or Minus Two," George Miller hypothesized that people could hold about seven pieces of information, such as a telephone number, in their short-term verbal working memory. The seven bits, however, could also be made up of "chunks" of longer, more complex, related information pieces, noted Miller, a founder of cognitive psychology. Recent evidence, in fact, suggests that Miller was overly optimistic and that people can hold between one and four chunks of information in mind.[38] Moreover, when your working memory is full, you are more likely to be distracted. This is one reason why viewers remember 10 percent fewer facts related to a news story when the screen is cluttered by a crawl.[39]

When I first talked to Czerwinski by telephone, she began the conference call by teasing a PR person on the line for failing to send out an advance reminder of the appointment.[40] "When I don't get a meeting reminder, you might as well hang it up," she said. To Czerwinski, the solution to the "lost thread" syndrome is simple: use technology to augment our memories. Of course, this is not entirely new. The alphabet, Post-it note, PDA, and now Czerwinski's innovations represent a long line of human efforts to bolster our working memories. But while multiple streams of color-coded, blinking, at-a-glance reminders will undoubtedly jog our memories, they run the risk of doing so by snowing us even more, Czerwinski admits. Bigger screens lead to lost cursors, more open windows, time-consuming hunts for the right information, and "more complex multitasking behavior," she observes. I would add that simultaneous data streams flatten content, making prioritization all the harder. The crawl, for instance, effectively puts a grade-B headline on a par with a top news story read by the anchor. Thirty shifting color-coded screen windows vying for our attention make trivia bleed into top-priority work. "Better task management mechanisms become a necessity" is Cerwinski's crisp conclusion. In other words, we need computers that sense when we are busy and then decide when and how to interrupt us. The digital gatekeeper will provide the fix.

And that's exactly the vein of research being mined by bevies of scientists around the country. "It's ridiculous that my own computer can't figure out whether I'm in front of it, but a public toilet can," says Roel Vertegaal of Queen's University in Ontario, referring to automatic flushers. Vertegaal is developing a desktop gadget—shaped like a black cat with bulging eyes—that puts through calls if a worker makes eye contact with it. Ignored, the "eyePROXY" channels the interruption to voice mail. An MIT prototype mouse pad heats up to catch your attention, a ploy we might grow to loathe on a hot summer day. IBM software is up to 87 percent accurate in tracking conversations, keystrokes, and other computer activity to assess a person's interruptability.[41] The king of the mind-reading computer ware, however, is Czerwinski's colleague and close collaborator, Eric Horvitz. For nearly a decade, he's been building artificial intelligence platforms that study you—your e-mail or telephone habits, how much time you spend in silence, even the urgency of your messages. "If we could just give our computers and phones some understanding of the limits of human attention and memory, it would make them seem a lot more thoughtful and courteous," says Horvitz of his latest prototype, aptly named "Busy-Body."[42] Artificial intelligence pioneer John McCarthy has another adjective to describe such programming: annoying. "I feel that [an attentive interface] would end up training me," says McCarthy, a professor emeritus at Stanford.[43] Long before "attentive-user interfaces" were born, French philosopher Paul Virilio had similar qualms about the unacknowledged power of the personal computer itself, which he dubbed a "vision machine" because, he said, it paves the way for the "automation of perception."[44] Recall David Byrne's impish observation that PowerPoint "tells you how to think."

Is hitching ourselves to the machine the answer? Will increasingly intelligent computers allow us to overcome our limitations of memory and attention and enable us to multitask better and faster in a Taylor-inspired hunt for ever-greater heights of efficiency? "Maybe it's our human nature to squeeze this extra bit of productivity out of ourselves, or perhaps it's our curious nature, 'can we do

more?'" asks Czerwinski. Or are we turning over "the whole responsibility of the details of our daily lives to machines and their drivers," as Morris feared, and beginning to outsource our capacity for
sense-making to the computer? To value a split-focus life aug-
mented by the machine is above all to squeeze out potential time
and space for reflection, which is the real sword in the stone needed
to thrive in a complex, ever-shifting new world. To breed children
for a world of split focus is to raise generations who will have ceded
cognitive control of their days. Children today, asserts educator
Jane Healy, need to learn to respond to the pace of the world but
also to reason and problem-solve within this new era. "Perhaps
most importantly, they need to learn what it feels like to be in
charge of one's own brain, actively pursuing a mental or physical
trail, inhibiting responses to the lure of distractions," writes
Healy.[45]

Ironically, multitasking researcher Arthur Jersild foresaw this
dilemma generations ago. Inspired by Taylor's and other time management and piecework theories, Jersild quietly published his pioneering dissertation on task switching. Then he went on to become
a developmental psychologist known for urging schools to foster
self-awareness in children. His views were unusual. At the time,
educators didn't consider children self-perceptive and, in any case,
they felt that emotional issues were the purview of the family. In a
1967 oral history given upon his retirement from Columbia, Jersild
argued that children must be taught to "see themselves as capable,
if they are; to be aware of their strengths; to try themselves out if
they seem hesitant; . . . to prove to themselves that they have certain powers."[46] Jersild, the sixth of ten children of a strict Midwestern Danish immigrant minister, was kindly, sensitive, and doggedly
self-sufficient himself. At age fourteen, while boarding as a farm-
hand in South Dakota in 1916, he stood in the cornfield he was
weeding, raised a fist to the sky, and vowed, "I am getting out of
here!" By the end of his career, he had come full circle from his early

concerns about how fast workers could do piecework to worrying that the education system placed too high a premium on speed and not enough on reflection. "It is essential for conceptual thought that a person give himself time to size up a situation, check the immediate impulse to act, and take in what's there," said Jersild. "Listening is part of it, but contemplation and reflection would go deeper." The apt name of his dissertation was "Mental Set and Shift."

Depending too heavily on multitasking to navigate a complex environment and on technology as our guide carries a final risk: the derailing of the painstaking work of adding to our storehouses of knowledge. That's because anything that we want to learn must be entered into our long-term memory stores, cognitive work that can take days and even months to accomplish. Attention helps us to understand and make sense of the world and is crucial as a first step to creating memory. But more than simply attending is necessary. "We must also process it at an abstract, schematic, conceptual level," note researchers Scott Brown and Fergus Craik. This involves both rote repetition and "elaborative rehearsal," or meaningfully relating it to other information, preferably not too quickly.[47] To build memory is to construct a treasure trove of experience, wisdom, and pertinent information. If attention makes us human, then long-term memory makes each of us an individual. Without it, we are faceless, hence our morbid fascination with amnesia of all kinds. Building these stores of memory takes time and will. When we divide our attention while trying to encode or retrieve memories, we do so about as well as if we were drunk or sleep deprived. In the opening scene of Alan Lightman's chilling novel *The Diagnosis*, successful executive Bill Chalmers loses his memory while taking the subway to work.[48] Rapidly, he disintegrates into a lost soul who recalls only his company's motto: "The Maximum Information in the Minimum Time." He regains his memory only to contract a mysterious, numbing illness that ultimately reveals the emptiness of his life. Like the alienated protagonists of film and literature from *The Matrix* to *The Magic Mountain*, Chalmers is a prisoner of the modern world. A culture of divided attention fuels more than perpetual searching for lost threads and loose ends. It stokes a culture of forgetting, the marker of a dark age. It fuels a mental shift of which we are not even aware. That's what we're unwittingly teaching baby Molly as her budding gaze meets the world.

Meyer's voice rose. He was hollering. We were back in his university office, and he was attacking the "myth" that we can operate at top speeds on multiple tasks as well as if we were doing one at a time. "That's ridiculous," he practically shouted. "That's ludicrous!" Like William Morris, Meyer often multitasks, reading *The New York Times*, chatting with his granddaughter, watching television all at once. Indeed, as we talked on the telephone one weekend morning, he interrupted me once or twice to read me the Wimbledon scores off the TV. But that's for fun, he insisted. "I'm getting little bits and pieces of information as a result of engaging in each of these tasks, but the depth of what I'm getting, the quality of my understanding is nowhere as good as if I was just concentrating on one thing," he said. "That's the bottom line." Once during our many conversations, he sadly confided the reason why he first began to be willing to speak up about multitasking: his seventeen-year-old son, Timothy, was broadsided and killed by a distracted driver who ran a red light one night in 1995. Spreading the word about the inefficiencies of multitasking is a little bit of "payback" for Tim's death. But that's only part of the story. Now Meyer speaks out about the costs of multitasking because he's convinced that it exemplifies a head-down, tunnel vision way of life that values materialism over happiness, productivity over insight and compassion. He's optimistic, taking a Darwinian view that people eventually will realize that multitasking's larger costs outweigh its benefits. But first Meyer believes that the few in the know will have to do a whole lot of hollering before we recognize the magnitude of the problem and begin to change. So he's raising his voice, as much as he can.

notes

This chapter has been published in an abridged version.
Any notes corresponding to the omitted text have been
deleted.

1. Interview with Daniel Anderson, May 2006.
2. Daniel Anderson and Heather Kirkorian, "Attention and Television," in *The Psychology of Entertainment*, ed. J. Bryant and P. Vorderer (Lawrence Erlbaum, 2006), pp. 35–54.
3. John E. Richards and Daniel Anderson, "Attentional Inertia in Children's Extended Looking at Television," *Advances in Child Development and Behavior*, ed. R. V. Kail (Academic Press, 2004), p. 168.
4. Daniel Anderson and Tiffany Pempek, "Television and Very Young Children," *American Behavioral Scientist* 48, no. 5 (January 2005), p. 508.
5. Marie Schmidt et al., "The Effects of Background Television on the Toy Play of Very Young Children," *Child Development*, in press.
6. Heather Kirkorian et al., "The Impact of Background Television on Parent-Child Interaction," poster presented at the biannual meeting of the Society for Research in Child Development, Atlanta, April 2005.
7. Victoria Rideout and Donald Roberts, *Generation M: Media in the Lives of Eight- to Eighteen-Year-Olds* (Henry J. Kaiser Family Foundation, March 2005), p. 9.
8. Marshall McLuhan, *Understanding Media: Lectures and Inter-*

views, ed. Stephanie McLuhan and David Staines (MIT Press, 2003), p. 129.

9. Barbara Schneider and N. Broege, "Why Working Families Avoid Flexibility: The Costs of Over Working," paper presented at the Alfred P. Sloan International Conference "Why Workplace Flexibility Matters," Chicago, May 17, 2006.

10. Eulynn Shiu and Amanda Lenhart, "How Americans Use Instant Messaging" (Pew Internet & American Life Project, 2004), http://www.pewinternet.org/PPF/r/133/report display.asp.

11. Bonka Boneva et al., "Teenage Communication in the Instant Messaging Era," in *Computers, Phones and the Internet: Domesticating Information Technology*, ed. Robert Kraut, Malcolm Bryin, and Sara Kiesler (Oxford University Press, 2006), pp. 201–18.

12. Lisa Guernsey, "In the Lecture Hall, A Geek Chorus," *New York Times*, July 24, 2003.

13. Ibid.

14. Caryn James, "Splitting. Screens. For Minds. Divided," *New York Times*, January 9, 2004.

15. August Fuhrmann, *Das Kaiserpanorama und das Welt-Archivpolychromer Stereo-Urkunden auf Glas* (1905), p. 8. Reprinted in Stephan Oettermann, *The Panorama: History of a Mass Medium*, trans. Deborah Lucas Schneider (Zone Books, 1997), p. 230.

16. Interview with David Meyer, May 2006.

17. Jonathan Crary, *Suspensions of Perception: Attention, Spectacle and Modern Culture* (MIT Press, 1999), p. 29.

18. Ibid., pp. 11–12 and 27.

19. Arthur Jersild, "Mental Set and Shift," *Archives of Psychology* 29 (1927).

20. Interviews with Steven Yantis and David Meyer, May, June, and July 2006.

21. David E. Meyer, *Professional Biography Published on the Occasion of His Distinguished Scientific Contribution Award* (American Psychological Association, 2002), http://www.umich.edu/-bcalab/Meyer_Biography.html.

22. John Serences and Steven Yantis, "Selective Visual Attention and Perceptual Coherence," *Trends in Cognitive Sciences* 10, no. 1 (2006), pp. 38–45. Also Steven Yantis, "How Visual Salience Wins the Battle for Awareness," *Nature Neuroscience* 8, no. 8 (2005), pp. 975–77.

23. Serences and Yantis, "Selective Visual Attention," p. 43.

24. Yantis, "How Visual Salience Wins," p. 975.

25. Susan Landry et al., "Early Maternal and Child Influences on Children's Later Independent Cognitive and Social Functioning," *Child Development* 71, no. 2 (2000), p. 370.

26. Charles O'Connor, Howard Egeth, and Steven Yantis, "Visual Attention: Bottom-Up versus Top-Down," *Current Biology* 14, no. 19 (2004), pp. R850–52.

27. "Linda Stone's Thoughts on Attention," http://continuouspartial attention.jot.com/WikiHome.

28. Alan Lightman, "The World Is Too Much with Me," in *Living with the Genie: Essays on Technology and the Quest for Human Mastery,* ed. Alan Lightman, Daniel Sarewitz, and Christine Dresser (Island Press, 2003), pp. 287 and 292.

29. Joshua Rubenstein, David Meyer, and Jeffrey Evans, "Executive Control of Cognitive Processes in Task-Switching," *Journal of Experimental Psychology, Human Perception and Performance* 27, no. 4 (2001), pp. 763–97.

30. Clive Thompson, "Meet the Life Hackers," *New York Times Magazine*, October 16, 2005, pp. 40–45.

31. Gloria Mark, Victor Gonzalez, and Justin Harris, "No Task Left Behind? Examining the Nature of Fragmented Work," proceedings of the Conference on Human Factors in Computer Systems (Portland, Oregon, 2005), pp. 321–30. Also interview with Gloria Mark, July 2006.

32. Ibid.

33. Thompson, "Meet the Life Hackers," p. 42.

34. Tony Gillie and Donald Broadbent, "What Makes Interruptions

Disruptive? A Study of Length, Similarity and Complexity," *Psychological Research* 50 (1989), pp. 243–50.

35. Jonathan Spira and Joshua Feintuch, *The Cost of Not Paying Attention: How Interruptions Impact Knowledge Worker Productivity* (Basex, 2005), pp. 2 and 10.

36. Suzanne Ross, "Two Screens Are Better Than One," *Microsoft Research News and Highlights*, http://research.microsoft.com/displayArticle.aspx?id=433&0sr=a. Also Tara Matthews et al., "Clipping Lists and Change Borders: Improving Multitasking Efficiency with Peripheral Information Design," *Proceedings of the Conference on Human Factors in Computer Systems* (April 2006), pp. 989–98.

37. Scott Brown and Fergus I. M. Craik, "Encoding and Retrieval of Information," *Oxford Handbook of Memory*, ed. Endel Tulving and Fergus I. M. Craik (Oxford University Press, 2000), p. 79.

38. Ibid. See also Sadie Dingfelder, "A Workout for Working Memory," *Monitor on Psychology* 36, no. 8 (2005), http://www.apa.orgmonitor/sep05/ workout.html, and Jan de Fockert et al., "The Role of Working Memory in Visual Selective Attention," *Science* 291, no. 5509 (2001), pp. 1803–1804.

39. Lori Bergen, Tom Grimes, and Deborah Potter, "How Attention Partitions Itself During Simultaneous Message Presentations," *Human Communication Research* 31, no. 3 (2005), pp. 311–36.

40. Interview with Mary Czerwinski, July 2006.

41. W. Wayt Gibbs, "Considerate Computing," *Scientific American* (January 2005), pp. 55–61. See also Peter Weiss, "Minding Your Business," *Science News* 163, no. 18 (2006), p. 279.

42. Horwitz quoted in Gibbs, "Considerate Computing."

43. Searle quoted in Weiss, "Minding Your Business."

44. Paul Virilio, *The Vision Machine* (Indiana University Press, 1994), p. 59.

45. Jane Healy, *Endangered Minds: Why Our Children Don't Think* (Simon & Schuster, 1990), p. 153.

46. Arthur T. Jersild, "Reminiscences of Arthur Thomas Jersild: Oral History 1967," interviewer T. Hogan (Columbia University, 1972), pp. 2, 20, 40–41, 79, and 246.
47. Brown and Craik, *Oxford Handbook of Memory*, pp. 93–97. See also John T. Wixted, "A Theory About Why We Forget What We Once Knew," *Current Directions in Psychological Science* 14, no. 1 (2005), pp. 6–9.
48. Alan Lightman, *The Diagnosis* (Pantheon Books, 2000), pp. 3–20.

<Lee Siegel>

a dream come true

Excerpted from *Against the Machine* (pp. 125–37).

LEE SIEGEL is *The Daily Beast's* senior columnist. He publishes widely on culture and politics and is the author of three books: *Falling Upwards: Essays in Defense of the Imagination* (2006), *Not Remotely Controlled: Notes on Television* (2007), and, most recently, *Against the Machine: How the Web Is Reshaping Culture and Commerce—And Why It Matters* (2008). In 2002, he received a National Magazine Award for reviews and criticism.

WEB 2.0" is the Internet's characteristically mechanistic term for the participatory culture that it has now consummated and established as a social reality. In this topsy-turvy galaxy, no person, fact, or event is beyond your grasp.

Web 2.0 is what the Internet calls its philosophy of interactivity. It applies to any online experience that allows the user to help create, edit, or revise the content of a website, interact with other users, share pictures, music, and so on. Amazon.com is a product of 2.0 technology because it allows visitors to write their own reviews of books that Amazon offers for sale, and to sell their own used books as well. eBay is 2.0-based because buyers and sellers interact with each other. Web 2.0 rules the social-networking sites like

MySpace, Facebook, and Friendster, and also the blogosphere, whose essence is the online exchange of opinions, ideas—and spleen.

Although Web 2.0 is the brainchild of businessmen, many of its promoters extol it with the rhetoric of "democracy," that most sacred of American words. But democracy is also the most common and effective American political and social pretext. While the liberal blogosphere thundered with cries of hypocrisy about Bush's claim that he was bringing democracy to Iraq, no one bothered to peek behind the Internet's use of the word "democracy" to see if that was indeed what the Internet was bringing to America.

Here is Lawrence Lessig, the foremost advocate of Internet freedom in the realm of copyright law, on the Internet's capacity for "capturing and sharing" content—in other words, for offering full participation in the culture:

> You could send an e-mail telling someone about a joke you saw on Comedy Central, or you could send the clip. You could write an essay about the inconsistencies in the arguments of the politician you most love to hate, or you could make a short film that puts statement against statement. You could write a poem that expresses your love, or you could weave together a string—a mash-up—of songs from your favorite artists in a collage and make it available on the Net . . . This "capturing and sharing" promises a world of extraordinarily diverse creativity that can be easily and broadly shared. And as that creativity is applied to democracy, it will enable a broad range of citizens to use technology to express and criticize and contribute to the culture all around.

Before you try to figure out what Lessig is saying, you have to get through the Internetese, this new, strangely robotic, automatic-pilot style of writing: "A poem that expresses your love" . . . for what?

How do you "express . . . the culture all around"? As usual, the Internet's supreme self-confidence results in lazy tautology: "This 'capturing and sharing' . . . can be easily and broadly shared." And never mind that elsewhere, in the same book—*Free Culture: How Big Media Uses Technology and the Law to Lock Down Culture and Control Creativity*—Lessig defines democracy, strangely, as "control through reasoned discourse," which would seem to disqualify Comedy Central from being considered one of the pillars of American democracy.

More telling is Lessig's idea of "democracy," a word that in the American context means government by the people through freely elected representatives. Lessig seems to think it means "creativity," or, as they like to say on the Internet, "self-expression." But even tyrants allow their subjects to write love poems or exchange favorite recordings. The Roman emperor Augustus cherished Ovid for the latter's love poetry—until Ovid's romantic dallying came too close to the emperor's own interests. And only tyrants forbid their subjects to make political criticisms—loving to hate a politician in public is hardly an expansion of democracy. It's the result of democracy. Lessig has confused what makes democracy possible—certain political, not cultural, mechanisms—with what democracy makes possible: free "expression."

Lessig isn't the only one singing 2.0's praises who seems confused about fundamental terms. Jay Rosen, a professor of journalism at New York University, is maybe the most voluble booster of the "citizen journalism" that he believes fulfills the blogosphere's social promise.

Rosen has started a blog-based initiative called Assignment Zero, in which anyone, journalist or not, can file an "investigative" news article. Rosen called this "crowdsourcing" in an interview with *The New York Times*'s David Carr, who reported the story without expressing the slightest skepticism and without presenting an opposing view to Rosen's. And there is an opposing point of view.

In the world of Assignment Zero, if you are someone working for a politician with an ax to grind, you could use Assignment Zero to expose a pesky journalist. Or you could just go on the blog to take down someone who has rubbed you the wrong way. No institutional layers of scrutiny, such as exist at newspapers, would be there to obstruct you.

Yet Rosen celebrates the 2.0-based blogosphere for what he portrays as its anticommercial gifts to democracy.

We're closer to a vision of "producer democracy" than we are to any of the consumerist views that long ago took hold in the mass media, including much of the journalism presented on that platform. We won't know what a producer public looks like from looking at the patterns of the media age, in which broadcasting and its one-to-many economy prevailed.

But we do know what a "producer public" will look like. Alvin Toffler described it thirty years ago. It will look like a totalized "consumerist" society, where everyone's spare moment is on the market and where journalists in the blogosphere will have their every word quantified and evaluated by vigilant advertisers. Where "producers" are simply consumers made more dependent on the marketplace by the illusion of greater participation in the marketplace. On the blog Assignment Zero, the public pays for the stories it wants to see reported. Rosen hasn't escaped the constrictions of commerce. He's made them tighter.

Lessig and Rosen are true believers in the Internet, people who have staked their professional (and economic) futures on its untrammeled success. It's in their interest to confuse American democracy's meaning with what American democracy means to them. *Time* magazine, on the other hand, has no stake in the triumph of the Internet.

Yet like every other "old" media news organization, *Time* is so frightened by the Internet boosters' claims of "old" media's impending irrelevance that for its "Person of the Year" in 2006, it put a picture of a computer screen on the magazine's cover with the single word "You." Then it went on to celebrate Web 2.0 as "the new digital democracy":

> It's a story about community and collaboration on a scale never seen before. It's about the cosmic compendium of knowledge Wikipedia and the million-channel people's network YouTube and the online metropolis MySpace. It's about the many wresting power from the few and helping one another for nothing and how that will not only change the world, but also change the way the world changes. . . . Silicon Valley consultants call it Web 2.0, as if it were a new version of some old software. But it's really a revolution. . . . We're looking at an explosion of productivity and innovation, and it's just getting started, as millions of minds that would otherwise have drowned in obscurity get backhauled into the global intellectual economy.
>
> Who are these people? Seriously, who actually sits down after a long day at work and says, I'm not going to watch *Lost* tonight. I'm going to turn on my computer and make a movie starring my pet iguana? I'm going to mash up 50 Cent's vocals with Queen's instrumentals? I'm going to blog about my state of mind or the state of the nation or the steak-frites at the new bistro down the street? Who has that time and that energy and that passion?
>
> The answer is, you do. And for seizing the reins of the global media, for founding and framing the new digital democracy, for working for nothing and beating the pros at their own game, *Time's* Person of the Year for 2006 is you.

Yes, seriously, who has the time, energy, and passion to make a movie about his pet iguana and broadcast it over the Internet? Who has reached that level of commitment to democracy? Who has the time, energy, and passion to mash up 50 Cent's vocals with Queen's instrumentals, to blog about his state of mind or the state of the nation or steak-frites? *Time*'s encomium to a brave new world reads like a forced confession's rote absurdity.

About one thing, however, *Time* was right. All this so-called play was not play at all. Everyone was getting "backhauled"—whatever that means—into the "global intellectual economy," though by "intellectual" *Time* meant nonmaterial, mental. Deliberately or not, *Time* was adding its voice to the general gulling of Internet boosterism and giving a helpful push to the facile shift of culture to commerce.

Tim O'Reilly is more explicit about this commercial democracy, if not all that comprehensible. O'Reilly is the head of an Internet company called O'Reilly Media, and he is generally considered the originator of 2.0. To begin with, O'Reilly has a somewhat different view of the blogosphere from Rosen:

> The blogosphere is the equivalent of constant mental chatter in the forebrain, the voice we hear in all of our heads. It may not reflect the deep structure of the brain, which is often unconscious, but is instead the equivalent of conscious thought. And as a reflection of conscious thought and attention, the blogosphere has begun to have a powerful effect.

"It may not reflect the deep structure of the brain, which is often unconscious, but is instead the equivalent of conscious thought." If your toaster could write a sentence, it would write one just like that. O'Reilly goes on:

> First, because search engines use link structure to help predict useful pages, bloggers, as the most prolific and timely linkers, have a disproportionate role in shaping search engine results. Second, because the blogging com-

munity is so highly self-referential, bloggers paying attention to other bloggers magnifies their visibility and
power . . . like Wikipedia, blogging harnesses collective
intelligence as a kind of filter . . . much as PageRank produces better results than analysis of any individual document, the collective attention of the blogosphere selects
for value.

PageRank is Google's algorithm—its mathematical formula—
for ranking search results. This is another contribution, according
to its touters, to access to information, and therefore yet another
boon to "democracy." PageRank keeps track of websites that are
the most linked to—that are the most popular. It is, in fact, the
gold standard of popularity in Web culture. What O'Reilly is saying, in plain English, is that the more people blog, and the more
blogs link to each other, the more highly ranked the most popular
blogs will be. When O'Reilly writes in his appliance-like manner
that "the collective attention of the blogosphere selects for value,"
he simply means that where the most bloggers go, people who are
interested in general trends—businessmen and marketing experts,
for instance—will follow. "Value" in O'Reilly's sense is synonymous
with popularity.

In this strange, new upside-down world, words like "democracy"
and "freedom" have lost their meaning. They serve only to repel
criticism of what they have come to mean, even when that criticism
is made in the name of democracy and freedom.

>>> through the looking glass

What would you have said if I had told you, ten years ago, that there
would soon come a time when anyone with something to say, no
matter how vulgar, abusive, or even slanderous, would be able to

transmit it in print to millions of people? Anonymously. And with impunity.

How would you have reacted if I had said that more drastic social and cultural changes were afoot? To wit: Powerful and seasoned newspaper editors cowering at the feet of two obscure and unaccomplished twentysomethings, terrified that this unassuming pair might call them "douchebags" in a new gossip sheet called Gawker. An obscure paralegal in Sacramento, California, who often makes glaring grammatical mistakes on his blog, becoming one of the most feared people in American literary life, on account of his ability to deride and insult literary figures. High school kids called "administrators" editing entries in a public encyclopedia, entries that anyone, using an alias, could change to read in any way he or she wanted. Writers distributing their thoughts to great numbers of people without bothering to care about the truth or accuracy of what they were writing; writers who could go back and change what they wrote if they were challenged—or even delete it, so that no record of their having written it would exist.

You would have laughed at me, I'm sure. Maybe you would have thought that I was purposefully and ludicrously evoking Stalin, who rewrote history, made anonymous accusations, hired and elevated hacks and phonies, ruined reputations at will, and airbrushed suddenly unwanted associates out of documents and photographs. You might have said, What point are you trying to make by saying that our American democracy is moving toward a type of Stalinism? How trite, to compare American democracy to its longtime nemesis using crude inversions. Are you some sort of throwback to the anti-American New Left?

And what if I had, to your great irritation, persisted and told you that anyone who tried to criticize one or another aspect of this situation would immediately be accused of being antidemocratic, elitist, threatened by change, and pathetically behind the times? If I had told you that in fact, because of these risks, few people ever did offer any criticism? The gospel of popularity had reached such an extent in this upside-down world that everyone, even powerful, distinguished people, cringed at the prospect of being publicly disliked.

What I've been describing is the surreal world of Web 2.0, where the rhetoric of democracy, freedom, and access is often a fig leaf for antidemocratic and coercive rhetoric; where commercial ambitions dress up in the sheep's clothing of humanistic values; and where, ironically, technology has turned back the clock from disinterested enjoyment of high and popular art to a primitive culture of crude, grasping self-interest. And yet these drastic transformations are difficult to perceive and make sense of. The Internet is a parallel universe that rarely intersects with other spheres of life outside its defensive parameters.

Here is John Battelle, a co-founder of *Wired* magazine, in his book, *The Search: How Google and Its Rivals Rewrote the Rules of Business and Transformed Our Culture*. Like Toffler and Gladwell, Battelle is all for bringing leisure time into the marketplace:

> On the Internet, it can be argued, all intent is commercial in one way or another, for your very attention is valuable to someone, even if you're simply researching your grandmother's genealogy, or reading up on a rare species of dolphin. Chances are you'll see plenty of advertisements along the way, and those links are the gold from which search companies spin their fabled profits.

Battelle wants to press home the importance of multiple searches to advertisers. He uses the following quotation to make his point:

> Thorstein Veblen, the early-twentieth-century thinker who coined the term "conspicuous consumption," once quipped, "The outcome of any serious research can only

be to make two questions grow where only one grew
before" . . . In fact, Pew research shows that the average
number of searches per visit to an engine [that is, a search
engine, like Google] is nearly five . . . This copious diversity
drives not only the complexity of the search itself, but also
the robustness of the advertising model that supports it.

But Veblen was talking about the humanistic value of research,
not the commercial value of a "search"! He was saying that the
world was ultimately mysterious and unfathomable, and that
therefore the quest for knowledge had no terminus—that the disinterested, endless quest for knowledge was an end in itself. Battelle can only understand Veblen in the context of commerce and
the Web.

Which context is often so unreal, yet so confident in its unreal-
ity, that it has the very real effect of making any criticism of it seem
absurd.

That's what Alice Mathias, a senior at Dartmouth College, discovered. On a blog in the *New York Times* called "The Graduates:
Eight College Seniors Face the Future," Mathias contributed a dry,
witty, yet openhearted column titled "Love in the Digital Age." She
concluded it like this:

> For example, Dartmouth students have recently had to deal
> with the construction of the website boredatbaker.com
> (which has cousins at the other Ivies, the Massachusetts
> Institute of Technology, New York University and Stan-
> ford). Intended as a community tool, this website has
> mutated into a forum for the anonymous publication of very
> personal attacks on students who must try their best not
> to be emotionally affected when people publicly question
> their sexuality, comment on their appearance and speculate
> about their value as humans.

In anonymous Internet attacks, people can say things they would never mention aloud while looking their target in the eye. No one need take any personal responsibility. The victims of these unfortunate manifestations of free speech must suspend their emotions and try to trust that people around them (including love interests) aren't the ones who are writing or consuming this stuff. The safest thing to do in our boredatbaker-shadowed community is to be emotionally isolated from everyone until graduation brings escape.

College students used to be the active arm of society's conscience. The ones, like Mathias, with the most sensitive consciences often protested war, racial bias, inequitable social policies. If an instance of corruption or injustice occurred in the town or city where they went to school, they often took to the streets to demonstrate or to march with the local townspeople or to stand on a picket line. Or maybe they just edited a mordantly honest literary magazine. Now they tremble helplessly before the Internet's Alice-in-Wonderland, truth-eliding, boundary-busting juggernaut.

What can they do? The language of protest college students once used—democracy, freedom, power to the people, revolution—has been taken over by the very forces that are invading and bruising their inner lives. The people who run boredatbaker.com would no doubt respond to criticism of their anonymous character assassinations by echoing Lawrence Lessig, Jay Rosen, and others and crying "free speech" and "democracy" and "don't fight the future." Graduation probably won't bring escape, either. At Gawker.com, a Manhattan-based website that makes random attacks on media figures, a site run by people you've never heard of—who might just as well be anonymous—you even have the opportunity to buy the official Gawker T-shirt, which has the word "Douché," referring to a favorite Gawker insult, printed on the front. Incredibly, the high school stigma of unpopularity has become so great that the accomplished adults of the New York media world live in fear of this adolescent silliness.

In this upside-down new world, student rebellion would have the appearance of reactionary resentment. But then, in this new upsidedown world, politically active students appear in long threads on political blogs as "hits" rather than as real bodies protesting in the streets.

<William Deresiewicz>

the end of solitude

Originally published in *The Chronicle of Higher Education* (January 30, 2009).

WILLIAM DERESIEWICZ is an author, essayist, and book critic. Deresiewicz is a contributing writer for *The Nation* and a contributing editor for *The New Republic*. His work has also appeared in *The New York Times Book Review, Bookforum*, and elsewhere. *A Jane Austen Education: How Six Novels Taught Me About Love, Friendship, and the Things That Really Matter* was published in April. More information at www.billderesiewicz.com.

WHAT DOES THE contemporary self want? The camera has created a culture of celebrity; the computer is creating a culture of connectivity. As the two technologies converge—broadband tipping the Web from text to image, social-networking sites spreading the mesh of interconnection ever wider—the two cultures betray a common impulse. Celebrity and connectivity are both ways of becoming known. This is what the contemporary self wants. It wants to be recognized, wants to be connected. It wants to be visible. If not to the millions, on *Survivor* or *Oprah*, then to the hundreds, on Twitter or Facebook. This is the quality that validates us; this is how we become real to ourselves—

by being seen by others. The great contemporary terror is anonymity. If Lionel Trilling was right, if the property that grounded the
self, in Romanticism, was sincerity, and in modernism it was
authenticity, then in postmodernism it is visibility.

So we live exclusively in relation to others, and what disappears
from our lives is solitude. Technology is taking away our privacy
and our concentration, but it is also taking away our ability to be
alone. Though I shouldn't say taking away. We are doing this to
ourselves; we are discarding these riches as fast as we can. I was
told by one of her older relatives that a teenager I know had sent
three thousand text messages one recent month. That's one hundred a day, or about one every ten waking minutes, morning, noon,
and night, weekdays and weekends, class time, lunch time, homework time, and toothbrushing time. So on average, she's never
alone for more than ten minutes at once. Which means, she's never
alone.

I once asked my students about the place that solitude has in
their lives. One of them admitted that she finds the prospect of
being alone so unsettling that she'll sit with a friend even when she
has a paper to write. Another said, why would anyone want to be
alone?

To that remarkable question, history offers a number of answers.
Man may be a social animal, but solitude has traditionally been a
societal value. In particular, the act of being alone has been understood as an essential dimension of religious experience, albeit one
restricted to a self-selected few. Through the solitude of rare spirits,
the collective renews its relationship with divinity. The prophet and
the hermit, the sadhu and the yogi, pursue their vision quests,
invite their trances, in desert or forest or cave. For the still, small
voice speaks only in silence. Social life is a bustle of petty concerns,
a jostle of quotidian interests, and religious institutions are no
exception. You cannot hear God when people are chattering at you,
and the divine word, their pretensions notwithstanding, demurs at

descending on the monarch and the priest. Communal experience is the human norm, but the solitary encounter with God is the egregious act that refreshes that norm. (Egregious, for no man is a prophet in his own land. Tiresias was reviled before he was vindicated, Teresa interrogated before she was canonized.) Religious solitude is a kind of self-correcting social mechanism, a way of burning out the underbrush of moral habit and spiritual custom. The seer returns with new tablets or new dances, his face bright with the old truth.

Like other religious values, solitude was democratized by the Reformation and secularized by Romanticism. In Marilynne Robinson's interpretation, Calvinism created the modern self by focusing the soul inward, leaving it to encounter God, like a prophet of old, in "profound isolation." To her enumeration of Calvin, Marguerite de Navarre, and Milton as pioneering early-modern selves we can add Montaigne, Hamlet, and even Don Quixote. The last figure alerts us to reading's essential role in this transformation, the printing press serving an analogous function in the sixteenth and subsequent centuries to that of television and the Internet in our own. Reading, as Robinson puts it, "is an act of great inwardness and subjectivity." "The soul encountered itself in response to a text, first Genesis or Matthew and then *Paradise Lost* or *Leaves of Grass*." With Protestantism and printing, the quest for the divine voice became available to, even incumbent upon, everyone.

But it is with Romanticism that solitude achieved its greatest cultural salience, becoming both literal and literary. Protestant solitude is still only figurative. Rousseau and Wordsworth made it physical. The self was now encountered not in God but in Nature, and to encounter Nature one had to go to it. And go to it with a special sensibility: The poet displaced the saint as social seer and cultural model. But because Romanticism also inherited the eighteenth-century idea of social sympathy, Romantic solitude existed in a dialectical relationship with sociability—if less for

Rousseau and still less for Thoreau, the most famous solitary of all, then certainly for Wordsworth, Melville, Whitman, and many others. For Emerson, "the soul environs itself with friends, that it may enter into a grander self-acquaintance or solitude; and it goes alone, for a season, that it may exalt its conversation or society." The Romantic practice of solitude is neatly captured by Trilling's "sincerity": the belief that the self is validated by a congruity of public appearance and private essence, one that stabilizes its relationship with both itself and others. Especially, as Emerson suggests, one beloved other. Hence the famous Romantic friendship pairs: Goethe and Schiller, Wordsworth and Coleridge, Hawthorne and Melville.

Modernism decoupled this dialectic. Its notion of solitude was harsher, more adversarial, more isolating. As a model of the self and its interactions, Hume's social sympathy gave way to Pater's thick wall of personality and Freud's narcissism—the sense that the soul, self-enclosed and inaccessible to others, can't choose but to be alone. With exceptions, like Woolf, the modernists fought shy of friendship. Joyce and Proust disparaged it; D. H. Lawrence was wary of it; the modernist friendship pairs—Conrad and Ford, Eliot and Pound, Hemingway and Fitzgerald—were altogether cooler than their Romantic counterparts. The world was now understood as an assault on the self, and with good reason.

The Romantic ideal of solitude developed in part as a reaction to the emergence of the modern city. In modernism, the city is not only more menacing than ever; it has become inescapable, a labyrinth: Eliot's London, Joyce's Dublin. The mob, the human mass, presses in. Hell is other people. The soul is forced back into itself— hence the development of a more austere, more embattled form of self-validation, Trilling's "authenticity," where the essential relationship is only with oneself. (Just as there are few good friendships in modernism, so are there few good marriages.) Solitude becomes, more than ever, the arena of heroic self-discovery, a voyage through interior realms made vast and terrifying by Nietzschean and

Freudian insights. To achieve authenticity is to look upon these visions without flinching; Trilling's exemplar here is Kurtz. Protestant self-examination becomes Freudian analysis, and the culture hero, once a prophet of God and then a poet of Nature, is now a novelist of self—a Dostoyevsky, a Joyce, a Proust.

But we no longer live in the modernist city, and our great fear is not submersion by the mass but isolation from the herd. Urbanization gave way to suburbanization, and with it the universal threat of loneliness. What technologies of transportation exacerbated—we could live farther and farther apart—technologies of communication redressed—we could bring ourselves closer and closer together. Or at least, so we have imagined. The first of these technologies, the first simulacrum of proximity, was the telephone. "Reach out and touch someone." But through the '70s and '80s, our isolation grew. Suburbs, sprawling ever farther, became exurbs. Families grew smaller or splintered apart, mothers left the home to work. The electronic hearth became the television in every room. Even in childhood, certainly in adolescence, we were each trapped inside our own cocoon. Soaring crime rates, and even more sharply escalating rates of moral panic, pulled children off the streets. The idea that you could go outside and run around the neighborhood with your friends, once unquestionable, has now become unthinkable. The child who grew up between the world wars as part of an extended family within a tight-knit urban community became the grandparent of a kid who sat alone in front of a big television, in a big house, on a big lot. We were lost in space.

Under those circumstances, the Internet arrived as an incalculable blessing. We should never forget that. It has allowed isolated people to communicate with one another and marginalized people to find one another. The busy parent can stay in touch with far-flung friends. The gay teenager no longer has to feel like a freak. But as the Internet's dimensionality has grown, it has quickly become too much of a good thing. Ten years ago we were writing e-mail messages on desktop computers and transmitting them over dial-up connections. Now we are sending text messages on our cell phones, posting pictures on our Facebook pages, and following complete strangers on Twitter. A constant stream of mediated contact, virtual, notional, or simulated, keeps us wired in to the electronic hive—though contact, or at least two-way contact, seems increasingly beside the point. The goal now, it seems, is simply to become known, to turn oneself into a sort of miniature celebrity. How many friends do I have on Facebook? How many people are reading my blog? How many Google hits does my name generate? Visibility secures our self-esteem, becoming a substitute, twice removed, for genuine connection. Not long ago, it was easy to feel lonely. Now, it is impossible to be alone.

As a result, we are losing both sides of the Romantic dialectic. What does friendship mean when you have 532 "friends"? How does it enhance my sense of closeness when my Facebook News Feed tells me that Sally Smith (whom I haven't seen since high school, and wasn't all that friendly with even then) "is making coffee and staring off into space"? My students told me they have little time for intimacy. And, of course, they have no time at all for solitude.

But at least friendship, if not intimacy, is still something they want. As jarring as the new dispensation may be for people in their thirties and forties, the real problem is that it has become completely natural for people in their teens and twenties. Young people today seem to have no desire for solitude, have never heard of it, can't imagine why it would be worth having. In fact, their use of technology—or to be fair, our use of technology—seems to involve a constant effort to stave off the possibility of solitude, a continuous attempt, as we sit alone at our computers, to maintain the imaginative presence of others. As long ago as 1952, Trilling wrote about "the modern fear of being cut off from the social group even for a moment." Now we have equipped ourselves with the means to prevent that fear from ever being realized. Which does not mean that we have put it to rest. Quite the contrary. Remember my student, who couldn't even write a paper by herself. The more we keep aloneness at bay, the less are we able to deal with it and the more terrifying it gets.

There is an analogy, it seems to me, with the previous generation's experience of boredom. The two emotions, loneliness and boredom, are closely allied. They are also both characteristically modern. The *Oxford English Dictionary*'s earliest citations of either word, at least in the contemporary sense, date from the nineteenth century. Suburbanization, by eliminating the stimulation as well as the sociability of urban or traditional village life, exacerbated the tendency to both. But the great age of boredom, I believe, came in with television, precisely because television was designed to palliate that feeling. Boredom is not a necessary consequence of having nothing to do; it is only the negative experience of that state. Television, by obviating the need to learn how to make use of one's lack of occupation, precludes one from ever discovering how to enjoy it. In fact, it renders that condition fearsome, its prospect intolerable. You are terrified of being bored—so you turn on the television.

I speak from experience. I grew up in the '60s and '70s, the age of television. I was trained to be bored; boredom was cultivated within me like a precious crop. (It has been said that consumer society wants to condition us to feel bored, since boredom creates a market for stimulation.) It took me years to discover—and my nervous system will never fully adjust to this idea; I still have to fight against boredom, am permanently damaged in this respect—that having nothing to do doesn't have to be a bad thing. The alternative to boredom is what Whitman called idleness: a passive receptivity to the world.

So it is with the current generation's experience of being alone. That is precisely the recognition implicit in the idea of solitude, which is to loneliness what idleness is to boredom. Loneliness is not the absence of company; it is grief over that absence. The lost sheep is lonely; the shepherd is not lonely. But the Internet is as powerful a machine for the production of loneliness as television is for the manufacture of boredom. If six hours of television a day creates the aptitude for boredom, the inability to sit still, a hundred text messages a day creates the aptitude for loneliness, the inability to be by yourself. Some degree of boredom and loneliness is to be expected, especially among young people, given the way our human environment has been attenuated. But technology amplifies those tendencies. You could call your schoolmates when I was a teenager, but you couldn't call them a hundred times a day. You could get together with your friends when I was in college, but you couldn't always get together with them when you wanted to, for the simple reason that you couldn't always find them. If boredom is the great emotion of the TV generation, loneliness is the great emotion of the Web generation. We lost the ability to be still, our capacity for idleness. They have lost the ability to be alone, their capacity for solitude.

And losing solitude, what have they lost? First, the propensity for introspection, that examination of the self that the Puritans, and the Romantics, and the modernists (and Socrates, for that matter) placed at the center of spiritual life—of wisdom, of conduct. Thoreau called it fishing "in the Walden Pond of [our] own natures," "bait[ing our] hooks with darkness." Lost, too, is the related propensity for sustained reading. The Internet brought text back into a televisual world, but it brought it back on terms dictated by that world—that is, by its remapping of our attention spans. Reading now means skipping and skimming; five minutes on the same Web page is considered an eternity. This is not reading as Marilynne Robinson described it: the encounter with a second self in the silence of mental solitude.

But we no longer believe in the solitary mind. If the Romantics had Hume and the modernists had Freud, the current psychological model—and this should come as no surprise—is that of the networked or social mind. Evolutionary psychology tells us that our brains developed to interpret complex social signals. According to David Brooks, that reliable index of the social-scientific zeitgeist, cognitive scientists tell us that "our decision-making is powerfully influenced by social context"; neuroscientists, that we have "permeable minds" that function in part through a process of "deep imitation"; psychologists, that "we are organized by our attachments"; sociologists, that our behavior is affected by "the power of social networks." The ultimate implication is that there is no mental space that is not social (contemporary social science dovetailing here with postmodern critical theory). One of the most striking things about the way young people relate to one another today is that they no longer seem to believe in the existence of Thoreau's "darkness."

The MySpace page, with its shrieking typography and clamorous imagery, has replaced the journal and the letter as a way of creating and communicating one's sense of self. The suggestion is not only that such communication is to be made to the world at large rather than to oneself or one's intimates, or graphically rather than verbally, or performatively rather than narratively or analytically, but also that it can be made completely. Today's young people seem to feel that they can make themselves fully known to one another. They seem to lack a sense of their own depths, and of the value of keeping them hidden.

If they didn't, they would understand that solitude enables us to secure the integrity of the self as well as to explore it. Few have shown this more beautifully than Woolf. In the middle of *Mrs. Dalloway*, between her navigation of the streets and her orchestration of the party, between the urban jostle and the social bustle, Clarissa goes up, "like a nun withdrawing," to her attic room. Like a nun, she returns to a state that she herself thinks of as a kind of virginity. This does not mean she's a prude. Virginity is classically the outward sign of spiritual inviolability, of a self untouched by the world, a soul that has preserved its integrity by refusing to descend into the chaos and self-division of sexual and social relations. It is the mark of the saint and the monk, of Hippolytus and Antigone and Joan of Arc. Solitude is both the social image of that state and the means by which we can approximate it. And the supreme image in *Mrs. Dalloway* of the dignity of solitude itself is the old woman whom Clarissa catches sight of through her window. "Here was one room," she thinks, "there another." We are not merely social beings. We are each also separate, each solitary, each alone in our own room, each miraculously our unique selves and mysteriously enclosed in that selfhood.

To remember this, to hold oneself apart from society, is to begin to think one's way beyond it. Solitude, Emerson said, "is to genius the stern friend." "He who should inspire and lead his race must be defended from traveling with the souls of other men, from living, breathing, reading, and writing in the daily, time-worn yoke of their opinions." One must protect oneself from the momentum of intellectual and moral consensus—especially, Emerson added, during youth. "God is alone," Thoreau said, "but the Devil, he is far from being alone; he sees a great deal of company; he is legion." The university was to be praised, Emerson believed, if only because it provided its charges with "a separate chamber and fire"—the physical space of solitude. Today, of course, universities do everything they can to keep their students from being alone, lest they perpetrate self-destructive acts, and also, perhaps, unfashionable thoughts. But no real excellence, personal or social, artistic, philosophical, scientific or moral, can arise without solitude. "The saint and poet seek privacy," Emerson said, "to ends the most public and universal." We are back to the seer, seeking signposts for the future in splendid isolation.

Solitude isn't easy, and isn't for everyone. It has undoubtedly never been the province of more than a few. "I believe," Thoreau said, "that men are generally still a little afraid of the dark." Teresa and Tiresias will always be the exceptions, or to speak in more relevant terms, the young people—and they still exist—who prefer to loaf and invite their soul, who step to the beat of a different drummer. But if solitude disappears as a social value and social idea, will even the exceptions remain possible? Still, one is powerless to reverse the drift of the culture. One can only save oneself— and whatever else happens, one can still always do that. But it takes a willingness to be unpopular.

The last thing to say about solitude is that it isn't very polite. Thoreau knew that the "doubleness" that solitude cultivates, the ability to stand back and observe life dispassionately, is apt to make us a little unpleasant to our fellows, to say nothing of the offense implicit in avoiding their company. But then, he didn't worry overmuch about being genial. He didn't even like having to talk to people three times a day, at meals; one can only imagine what he would have made of text messaging. We, however, have made of geniality—the weak smile, the polite interest, the fake invitation—a cardinal virtue. Friendship may be slipping from our grasp, but our friendliness is universal. Not for nothing does "gregarious" mean "part of the herd." But Thoreau understood that securing one's self-possession was worth a few wounded feelings. He may have put his neighbors off, but at least he was sure of himself. Those who would find solitude must not be afraid to stand alone.

<Clay Shirky>

means

Excerpted from *Cognitive Surplus* (pp. 42–64).

CLAY SHIRKY is an adjunct professor in NYU's graduate
Interactive Telecommunications Program (ITP). Prior to his
appointment at NYU, Shirky was a partner at the investment firm The Accelerator Group in 1999–2001. He has had
regular columns in Business 2.0 and FEED, and his writings
have appeared in the *New York Times*, *The Wall Street Journal*,
Harvard Business Review, *Wired*, *Release 1.0*, *Computerworld*,
and *IEEE Computer*. His books include *Here Comes Everybody:
The Power of Organizing Without Organizations* (2008) and
Cognitive Surplus: Creativity and Generosity in a Connected Age
(2010). His website is shirky.com.

>>> gutenberg economics

JOHANNES GUTENBERG, a printer in Mainz, in present-day
Germany, introduced movable type to the world in the middle
of the fifteenth century. Printing presses were already in use,
but they were slow and laborious to operate, because a carving had
to be made of the full text of each page. Gutenberg realized that if

you made carvings of individual letters instead, you could arrange them into any words you liked. These carved letters—type—could be moved around to make new pages, and the type could be set in a fraction of the time that it would take to carve an entire page from scratch.

Movable type introduced something else to the intellectual landscape of Europe: an abundance of books. Prior to Gutenberg, there just weren't that many books. A single scribe, working alone with a quill and ink and a pile of vellum, could make a copy of a book, but the process was agonizingly slow, making output of scribal copying small and the price high. At the end of the fifteenth century, a scribe could produce a single copy of a five-hundred-page book for roughly thirty florins, while Ripoli, a Venetian press, would, for roughly the same price, print more than three hundred copies of the same book. Hence most scribal capacity was given over to producing additional copies of extant works. In the thirteenth century Saint Bonaventure, a Franciscan monk, described four ways a person could make books: copy a work whole, copy from several works at once, copy an existing work with his own additions, or write out some of his own work with additions from elsewhere. Each of these categories had its own name, like scribe or author, but Bonaventure does not seem to have considered—and certainly didn't describe—the possibility of anyone creating a wholly original work. In this period, very few books were in existence and a good number of them were copies of the Bible, so the idea of bookmaking was centered on re-creating and recombining existing words far more than on producing novel ones.

Movable type removed that bottleneck, and the first thing the growing cadre of European printers did was to print more Bibles— lots more Bibles. Printers began publishing Bibles translated into vulgar languages—contemporary languages other than Latin— because priests wanted them, not just as a convenience but as a matter of doctrine. Then they began putting out new editions of works by Aristotle, Galen, Virgil, and others that had survived from antiquity. And still the presses could produce more. The next move by the printers was at once simple and astonishing: print lots of new stuff. Prior to movable type, much of the literature available in Europe had been in Latin and was at least a millennium old. And then in a historical eyeblink, books started appearing in local languages, books whose text was months rather than centuries old, books that were, in aggregate, diverse, contemporary, and vulgar. (Indeed, the word *novel* comes from this period, when newness of content was itself new.)

This radical solution to spare capacity—produce books that no one had ever read before—created new problems, chiefly financial risk. If a printer produced copies of a new book and no one wanted to read it, he'd lose the resources that went into creating it. If he did that enough times, he'd be out of business. Printers reproducing Bibles or the works of Aristotle never had to worry that people might not want their wares, but anyone who wanted to produce a novel book faced this risk. How did printers manage that risk? Their answer was to make the people who bore the risk—the printers—responsible for the quality of the books as well. There's no obvious reason why people who are good at running a printing press should also be good at deciding which books are worth printing. But a printing press is expensive, requiring a professional staff to keep it running, and because the material has to be produced in advance of demand for it, the economics of the printing press put the risk at the site of production. Indeed, shouldering the possibility that a book might be unpopular marks the transition from printers (who made copies of hallowed works) to publishers (who took on the risk of novelty).

A lot of new kinds of media have emerged since Gutenberg: images and sounds were encoded onto objects, from photographic plates to music CDs; electromagnetic waves were harnessed to create radio and TV. All these subsequent revolutions, as different as they were, still had the core of Gutenberg economics: enormous investment costs. It's expensive to own the means of production, whether it is a printing press or a TV tower, which makes novelty a fundamentally high-risk operation. If it's expensive to own and manage the means of production or if it requires a staff, you're in a world of Gutenberg economics. And wherever you have Gutenberg economics, whether you are a Venetian publisher or a Hollywood producer, you're going to have fifteenth-century risk management as well, where the producers have to decide what's good before showing it to the audience. In this world almost all media was produced by "the media," a world we all lived in up until a few years ago.

>>> the button marked "publish"

At the end of every year, the National Book Foundation hands out its medal for Distinguished Contribution to American Letters at its awards dinner. In 2008 it gave the award to Maxine Hong Kingston, author of 1976's *The Woman Warrior*. While Kingston was being recognized for work that was more than thirty years old, her speech included a retelling of something she'd done that year, something that should have made the blood of every publisher in attendance run cold.

Earlier that year, Kingston said, she had written an editorial praising Barack Obama, on the occasion of his visit to her home state of Hawaii. Unfortunately for her, the newspapers she sent the piece to all declined to publish it. And then, to her delight, she realized that this rejection mattered a whole lot less than it used to. She went onto Open.Salon.com, a website for literary conversation, and, as she put it, "All I had to do was type, then click a button marked 'Publish.' Yes, there is such a button. Voilà? I was published."

Yes, there is such a button. Publishing used to be something we had to ask permission to do; the people whose permission we had to ask were publishers. Not anymore. Publishers still perform other functions in selecting, editing, and marketing work (dozens of people besides me have worked to improve this book, for example), but they no longer form the barrier between private and public writing. In Kingston's delight at routing around rejection, we see a truth, always there but long hidden. Even "published authors," as the phrase goes, didn't control their own ability to publish. Consider the cluster of ideas contained in this list: publicity, publicize, publish, publication, publicist, publisher. They are all centered on the act of making something public, which has historically been difficult, complex, and expensive. And now it is none of those things.

Kingston's editorial, it must be said, wasn't any good. It was obsequious to the point of tedium and free of any thought that might be called analytic. The political discourse was not much enriched by its appearance. But an increase in freedom to publish always has this consequence. Before Gutenberg, the average book was a masterpiece. After Gutenberg, people got throwaway erotic novels, dull travelogues, and hagiographies of the landed gentry, of interest to no one today but a handful of historians. The great tension in media has always been that freedom and quality are conflicting goals. There have always been people willing to argue that an increase in freedom to publish isn't worth the decrease in average quality; Martin Luther observed in 1569: "The multitude of books is a great evil. There is no measure of limit to this fever for writing; every one must be an author; some out of vanity, to acquire celebrity and raise up a name; others for the sake of mere gain." Edgar Allan Poe commented in 1845: "The enormous multiplication of books in every branch of knowledge is one of the greatest evils of this age; since it presents one of the most serious obstacles to the acquisition of correct information by throwing in the reader's way piles of lumber in which he must painfully grope for the scraps of useful lumber."

These arguments are absolutely correct. Increasing freedom to publish does diminish average quality—how could it not? Luther and Poe both relied on the printing press, but they wanted the mechanics of publishing, to which they had easy access, not to increase the overall volume of published work: cheaper for me but still inaccessible to thee. Economics doesn't work that way, however. The easier it is for the average person to publish, the more average what gets published becomes. But increasing freedom to participate in the public conversation has compensating values.

The first advantage is an increase of experimentation in form. Even though the spread of movable type created a massive downshift in average quality, that same invention made it possible to have novels, newspapers, and scientific journals. The press allowed the rapid dissemination of both Martin Luther's *Ninety-five Theses* and Copernicus's *On the Revolutions of the Celestial Spheres*, transformative documents that influenced the rise of the Europe we know today. Lowered costs in any realm allow for increased experimentation; lowered costs for communication mean new experimentation in what gets thought and said.

This ability to experiment extends to creators as well, increasing not just their number but also their diversity. Naomi Wolf, in her 1991 book *The Beauty Myth*, both celebrated and lamented the role women's magazines play in women's lives. These magazines, she said, provide a place where a female perspective can be taken for granted, but it is distorted by the advertisers: "Advertisers are the West's courteous censors. They blur the line between editorial freedom and the demands of the marketplace . . . A women's magazine's profit does not come from its cover price, so its contents cannot roam too far from the advertiser's wares." Today, on the other hand, almost twenty years after *The Beauty Myth* appeared, writer Melissa McEwan posted on the blog *Shakesville* a riveting seventeen-hundred-word essay about casual misogyny:

> There are the jokes about women . . . told in my presence
> by men who are meant to care about me, just to get a rise
> out of me, as though I am meant to find funny a reminder
> of my second-class status. I am meant to ignore that this is
> a bullying tactic, that the men telling these jokes derive
> their amusement specifically from knowing they upset
> me, piss me off, hurt me. They tell them and I can laugh,
> and they can thus feel superior, or I can not laugh, and they
> can thus feel superior. Heads they win, tails I lose.

The essay, titled "The Terrible Bargain We Have Regretfully Struck," attracted hundreds of commenters and thousands of readers in an outpouring of reaction whose main theme was *Thank you for saying what I have been thinking.* The essay got out into the world because McEwan only had to click a button marked "Publish." *Shakesville* provides exactly the kind of writing space Wolf imagined, where women can talk without male oversight or advertisers' courteous censorship. The writing is not for everyone—intensely political, guaranteed to anger any number of people—but that's exactly the point. The women's magazines Wolf discussed reached readers who might have had the same reaction as the readers of *Shakesville*, but the magazines simply couldn't afford to reach them at the expense of angering other readers or, more important, their advertisers. McEwan was willing (and able) to risk angering people in order to say what she had to say.

The bargain Wolf described was particularly acute for women's magazines, but it was by no means unique. Nor is the self-publishing model McEwan used unique—people now speak out on issues a million times a day, across countless kinds of communities of interest. The ability for community members to speak to one another, out loud and in public, is a huge shift, and one that has value even in the absence of a way to filter for quality. It has value, indeed, *because* there is no way to filter for quality in advance: the definition of quality becomes more variable, from one community to the next, than when there was broad consensus about mainstream writing (and music, and film, and so on).

Scarcity is easier to deal with than abundance, because when something becomes rare, we simply think it more valuable than it was before, a conceptually easy change. Abundance is different: its advent means we can start treating previously valuable things as if they were cheap enough to waste, which is to say cheap enough to experiment with. Because abundance can remove the trade-offs we're used to, it can be disorienting to the people who've grown up with scarcity. When a resource is scarce, the people who manage it often regard it as valuable in itself, without stopping to consider how much of the value is tied to its scarcity. For years after the price of long-distance phone calls collapsed in the United States, my older relatives would still announce that a call was "long distance." Such calls had previously been special, because they were expensive; it took people years to understand that cheap long-distance calls removed the rationale for regarding them as inherently valuable.

Similarly, when publication—the act of making something public—goes from being hard to being virtually effortless, people used to the old system often regard publishing by amateurs as frivolous, as if publishing was an inherently serious activity. It never was, though. Publishing had to be taken seriously when its cost and effort made people take it seriously—if you made too many mistakes, you were out of business. But if these factors collapse, then the risk collapses too. An activity that once seemed inherently valuable turned out to be only accidentally valuable, as a change in the economics revealed.

Harvey Swados, the American novelist, said of paperbacks, "Whether this revolution in the reading habits of the American public means that we are being inundated by a flood of trash which will debase farther the popular taste, or that we shall now have available cheap editions of an ever-increasing list of classics, is a question of basic importance to our social and cultural development."

He made this observation in 1951, two decades into the spread of paperbacks, and curiously Swados was even then unable to answer his own question. But by 1951 the answer was plain to see. The public had no need to choose between a flood of trash and a growing collection of classics. We could have both (which is what we got).

Not only was "both" the answer to Swados's question; it has always been the answer whenever communications abundance increases, from the printing press on. The printing press was originally used to provide cheap access to Bibles and the writings of Ptolemy, but the entire universe of that old stuff didn't fill a fraction of either the technological capacity or the audience's desire. Even more relevant to today, we can't have "an ever-expanding list of classics" without also trying new forms; if there was an easy formula for writing something that will become prized for decades or centuries, we wouldn't need experimentation, but there isn't, so we do.

The low-quality material that comes with increased freedom accompanies the experimentation that creates the stuff we will end up prizing. That was true of the printing press in the fifteenth century, and it's true of the social media today. In comparison with a previous age's scarcity, abundance brings a rapid fall in average quality, but over time experimentation pays off, diversity expands the range of the possible, and the best work becomes better than what went before. After the printing press, publishing came to matter more because the expansion of literary, cultural, and scientific writing benefited society, even though it was accompanied by a whole lot of junk.

>>> the connective tissue of society

Not that we are witnessing a rerun of the print revolution. All revolutions are different (which is only to say that all surprises are surprising). If a change in society were immediately easy to understand, it wouldn't be a revolution. And today, the revolution is centered on the shock of the inclusion of amateurs as producers, where we no longer need to ask for help or permission from professionals to say things in public. Social media didn't cause the candlelight protests in South Korea; nor did they make users of PickupPal more environmentally conscious. Those effects were created by citizens who wanted to change the way public conversation unfolded and found they had the opportunity to do so.

This ability to speak publicly and to pool our capabilities is so different from what we're used to that we have to rethink the basic concept of media: it's not just something we consume; it's something we use. As a result, many of our previously stable concepts about media are now coming unglued.

Take, as one example, television. Television encodes moving images and sounds for transmission through the air and, latterly, through a cable, for subsequent conversion back to images and sound, using a special decoding device. What is the name of the content so transmitted? Television. And the device that displays the images? It is a television. And the people who make that content and send out the resulting signal—what industry do they work in? Television, of course. The people who work in television make television for your television.

You can buy a television at the store so you can watch television at home, but the television you buy isn't the television you watch, and the television you watch isn't the television you buy. Expressed that way, it seems confusing, but in daily life it isn't confusing at all, because we never have to think too hard about what television is, and we use the word *television* to talk about all the various different parts of the bundle: industry, content, and appliance. Language lets us work at the right level of ambiguity; if we had to think about every detail of every system in our lives all the time, we'd faint from overexposure. This bundling of object and industry, of product and service and business model, isn't unique to television. People who collect and preserve rare first editions of books, and people who buy mass-market romance novels, wreck the spines, and give them away the next week, can all legitimately lay claim to the label *book lover.*

This bundling has been easy because so much of the public media environment has been stable for so long. The last really big revolution in public media was the appearance of television. In the sixty years since TV went mainstream, the kinds of changes we've seen have been quite small—the spread of videocassette tapes, for example, or color TV. Cable television was the most significant change in the media landscape between the late 1940s (when TV started to spread in earnest) and the late 1990s (when digital networks began to be a normal part of public life).

The word *media* itself is a bundle, referring at once to process, product, and output. Media, as we talked about it during those decades, mainly denoted the output of a set of industries, run by a particular professional class and centered, in the English-speaking world, in London, New York, and Los Angeles. The word referred to those industries, to the products they created, and to the effect of those products on society. Referring to "the media" in that way made sense as long as the media environment was relatively stable.

Sometimes, though, we really do have to think about the parts of a system separately, because the various pieces stop working together. If you take five minutes to remind yourself (or conjure up, if you are under thirty) what media for adults was like in the twentieth century, with a handful of TV networks and dominant newspapers and magazines, then media today looks strange and new. In an environment so stable that getting TV over a wire instead of via antennae counted as an upheaval, it's a real shock to see the appearance of a medium that lets anyone in the world make an unlimited number of perfect copies of something they created for free. Equally surprising is the fact that the medium mixes broadcast and conversational patterns so thoroughly that there is no obvious gulf between them. The bundle of concepts tied to the word *media* is unraveling. We need a new conception for the word, one that dispenses with the connotations of "something produced by professionals for consumption by amateurs."

Here's mine: media is the connective tissue of society.

Media is how you know when and where your friend's birthday party is. Media is how you know what's happening in Tehran, who's in charge in Tegucigalpa, or the price of tea in China. Media is how you know what your colleague named her baby. Media is how you know why Kierkegaard disagreed with Hegel. Media is how you know where your next meeting is. Media is how you know about anything more than ten yards away. All these things used to be separated into public media (like visual or print communications made by a small group of professionals) and personal media (like letters and phone calls made by ordinary citizens). Now those two modes have fused.

The Internet is the first public medium to have post-Gutenberg economics. You don't need to understand anything about its plumbing to appreciate how different it is from any form of media in the previous five hundred years. Since all the data is digital (expressed as numbers), there is no such thing as a copy anymore. Every piece of data, whether an e-mailed love letter or a boring corporate presentation, is identical to every other version of the same piece of data.

You can see this reflected in common parlance. No one ever says, *Give me a copy of your phone number.* Your phone number is the same number for everybody, and since data is made of numbers, the data is the same for everybody. Because of this curious property of numbers, the old distinction between copying tools for professionals and those for amateurs—printing presses that make high-quality versions for the pros, copy machines for the rest of us—is over. Everyone has access to a medium that makes versions so identical that the old distinction between originals and copies has given way to an unlimited number of equally perfect versions.

Moreover, the means of digital production are symmetrical. A television station is a hugely expensive and complex site designed to send signals, while a television is a relatively simple device for receiving those signals. When someone buys a TV, the number of consumers goes up by one, but the number of producers stays the same. On the other hand, when someone buys a computer or a mobile phone, the number of consumers and producers both increase by one. Talent remains unequally distributed, but the raw ability to make and to share is now widely distributed and getting wider every year.

Digital networks are increasing the fluidity of all media. The old choice between one-way public media (like books and movies) and two-way private media (like the phone) has now expanded to include a third option: two-way media that operates on a scale from private to public. Conversations among groups can now be carried out in the same media environments as broadcasts. This new option bridges the two older options of broadcast and communications media. All media can now slide from one to the other. A book can stimulate public discussion in a thousand places at once. An e-mail conversation can be published by its participants. An essay intended for public consumption can anchor a private argument, parts of which later become public. We move from public to private and back again in ways that weren't possible in an era when public and private media, like the radio and the telephone, used different devices and different networks.

And finally, the new media involves a change in economics. With the Internet, everyone pays for it, and then everyone gets to use it. Instead of having one company own and operate the whole system, the Internet is just a set of agreements about how to move data between two points. Anyone who abides by these agreements, from an individual working from a mobile phone to a huge company, can be a full-fledged member of the network. The infrastructure isn't owned by the producers of the content: it's accessible to everyone who pays to use the network, regardless of how they use it. This shift to post-Gutenberg economics, with its interchangeably perfect versions and conversational capabilities, with its symmetrical production and low costs, provides the means for much of the generous, social, and creative behavior we're seeing. . . .

>>> the shock of inclusion

I teach in the Interactive Telecommunications Program, an interdisciplinary graduate program at NYU. In the decade I've been there, the average age of my students has stayed roughly the same, while my average age has grown at the alarming rate of one year per year; my students are now fifteen or twenty years younger than I am. Because I try to convey an understanding of the changing media landscape, I now have to teach the times of my own youth as ancient history. Seemingly stable parts of the world I grew up in had vanished before many of my students turned fifteen, while innovations I saw take hold with adult eyes occurred when they were in grade school.

Despite half a century of hand-wringing about media contraction, my students have never known a media landscape of anything less than increasing abundance. They have never known a world with only three television channels, a world where the only choice a viewer had in the early evening was which white man was going to read them the news in English. They can understand the shift from scarcity to abundance, since the process is still going on today. A much harder thing to explain to them is this: if you were a citizen of that world, and you had something you needed to say in public, you couldn't. Period. Media content wasn't produced by consumers; if you had the wherewithal to say something in public, you weren't a consumer anymore, by definition. Movie reviews came from movie reviewers. Public opinions came from opinion columnists. Reporting came from reporters. The conversational space available to mere mortals consisted of the kitchen table, the water cooler, and occasionally letter writing (an act so laborious and rare that many a letter began with "Sorry I haven't written in so long. . . .").

In those days, anyone could produce a photograph, a piece of writing, or a song, but they had no way to make it widely available. Sending messages to the public wasn't for the public to do, and, lacking the ability to easily connect with one another, our motivation to create was subdued. So restricted was access to broadcast and print media that amateurs who tried to produce it were regarded with suspicion or pity. Self-published authors were assumed to be either rich or vain. People who published pamphlets or walked around with signs were assumed to be unhinged. William Safire, the late columnist for the *New York Times*, summed up this division: "For years I used to drive up Massachusetts Avenue past the vice president's house and would notice a lonely, determined guy across the street holding a sign claiming he'd been sodomized by a priest. Must be a nut, I figured—and thereby ignored a clue to the biggest religious scandal of the century."

My students believe me when I tell them about the assumed silence of the average citizen. But while they are perfectly able to make intellectual sense of that world, I can tell they don't feel it. They've never lived in an environment where they weren't able to speak in public, and it's hard for them to imagine how different that environment was, compared with the participatory behaviors they take for granted today.

Nik Gowing, a BBC reporter and author of *"Skyful of Lies" and Black Swans*, about media in crises, offers an illustrative story. In the hours after the London subway and bus bombings of July 7, 2005, the government maintained that the horrific damage and casualties had been caused by some sort of power surge. Even a few years earlier, this explanation would have been the only message available to the public, allowing the government time to investigate the incident more fully before adjusting its story to reflect the truth. But as Gowing notes, "Within the first eighty minutes in the public domain, there were already 1,300 blog posts signaling that explosives were the cause."

The government simply could not stick to the story about a power surge when its falsehood was increasingly apparent to all. Camera phones and sites for sharing photos globally meant that the public could see images of the subway interior and of a double-decker bus whose roof had been blown to pieces—evidence utterly incompatible with the official story. Less than two hours after the bombings, Sir Ian Blair, the Metropolitan Police commissioner, publicly acknowledged that the explosions had been the work of terrorists. He did so even though his grasp of the situation wasn't yet complete, and against the advice of his aides, simply because people were already trying to understand the events without waiting for him to speak. The choice for the police had previously been "Should we tell the public something or nothing?" By 2005, it had become "Do we want to be part of the conversation the public is already having?" Blair decided to speak to the public at that early stage because the older strategies that assumed that the public wasn't already talking among itself were no longer intact.

The people surprised at our new behaviors assume that behavior is a stable category, but it isn't. Human motivations change little over the years, but opportunity can change a little or a lot, depending on the social environment. In a world where opportunity changes little, behavior will change little, but when opportunity changes a lot, behavior will as well, so long as the opportunities appeal to real human motivations.

The harnessing of our cognitive surplus allows people to behave in increasingly generous, public, and social ways, relative to their old status as consumers and couch potatoes. The raw material of this change is the free time available to us, time we can commit to projects that range from the amusing to the culturally transformative. If free time was all that was necessary, however, the current changes would have occurred half a century ago. Now we have the tools at our disposal, and the new opportunities they provide.

Our new tools haven't caused those behaviors, but they have allowed them. Flexible, cheap, and inclusive media now offer us opportunities to do all sorts of things we once didn't do. In the world of "the media," we were like children, sitting quietly at the edge of a circle and consuming whatever the grown-ups in the center of the circle produced. That has given way to a world in which most forms of communication, public and private, are available to everyone in some form. Even accepting that these new behaviors are happening and that new kinds of media are providing the means for them, we still have to explain why. New tools get used only if they help people do things they want to do; what is motivating The People Formerly Known as the Audience to start participating?

credits

index